# Bodies in Motion

# Bodies in Motion

*A Religious History of Sports in America*

ARTHUR REMILLARD

OXFORD
UNIVERSITY PRESS

Oxford University Press is a department of the University of Oxford.
It furthers the University's objective of excellence in research, scholarship,
and education by publishing worldwide. Oxford is a registered trade mark of
Oxford University Press in the UK and certain other countries.

Published in the United States of America by Oxford University Press
198 Madison Avenue, New York, NY 10016, United States of America.



Library of Congress Cataloging-in-Publication Data
Names: Remillard, Arthur, author.
Title: Bodies in motion : a religious history of sports in America / by Arthur Remillard.
Description: New York, NY : Oxford University Press, [2025] |
Includes bibliographical references and index. |
Identifiers: LCCN 2025004925 (print) | LCCN 2025004926 (ebook) |
ISBN 9780197789773 (paperback) | ISBN 9780197789766 (hardback) |
ISBN 9780197789803 | ISBN 9780197789797 (epub)
Subjects: LCSH: Sports—United States—Religious aspects. |
Sports—United States—History.
Classification: LCC GV706.42 .R46 2025 (print) | LCC GV706.42 (ebook) |
DDC 306.4/830973—dc23/eng/20250211
LC record available at https://lccn.loc.gov/2025004925
LC ebook record available at https://lccn.loc.gov/2025004926

DOI: 10.1093/oso/9780197789766.001.0001

Paperback printed by Marquis Book Printing, Canada
Hardback printed by Bridgeport National Bindery, Inc., United States of America

*To my father, Dr. Vincent L. Remillard (1942–2024)*
*"Il faut cultiver notre jardin."*

# Contents

# Acknowledgments

I became serious about finishing this book only once I made writing a consistent habit. Sitting down most days, embracing the stillness, and focusing on this one task became the necessary antidote to the frenetic and often chaotic pace of my professional and personal life. As I grew to delight in the contemplative joys of writing, I became increasingly motivated by the prospect that someday someone would choose to read this book.

So I begin by thanking you, the kind reader, for choosing to engage with my work. I hope it offers you new perspectives on religion and sports, causes you to ponder this topic, and sparks conversations with others. Whatever this book means to you, please know that your invisible presence over the past few years helped make it happen.

My decision to write this book came after I finished a lengthy overview of religion and sports for an encyclopedia edited by John Corrigan. Upon his review, John commended my final product, giving me the nudge I needed to take the next step. John was my graduate school advisor at Florida State in the early 2000s and the person most responsible for introducing me to American religious history. Throughout my career, I have benefited from his generosity, encouragement, and kindness, and I thank him for his lasting influence.

I am also grateful to the network of scholars who have influenced my thinking on religion and sports. One of the highlights of my career was collaborating with Rebecca Alpert on an edited volume. Introduced to Rebecca through her scholarship, I learned even more about publishing and academic life from our various interactions. Similarly, I first met Joe Price at an academic conference when I was still a graduate student. From that day forward, Joe and I remained in regular contact and developed an ongoing conversation on our shared interests.

Rebecca and Joe were instrumental in bringing me into the American Academy of Religion's "Religion, Sports, and Play" group. As co-chair, I was fortunate to connect with several accomplished scholars, Annie Blazer, Eric Bain-Selbo, Jeff Scholes, Carmen Nanko-Fernandez, Scott Strednak Singer, Linda Borish, and Tracy Trothen. Within this circle, I also interacted with Amy Koehlinger, another one of my treasured graduate school advisors. In a random email exchange long before I started this book, Amy suggested that I could indeed write a comprehensive history of religion and sports. At the time, I didn't believe it. But I am grateful now for Amy's encouragement, as it became one more seed that eventually grew into this book.

Professional conferences and organizations have certainly been important in my career development, but so too have various digital spaces. I thank Paul Harvey for graciously inviting me to contribute to his blog, where I often tested my earliest observations on religion and sports. This opened pathways for me to connect with people like Chris Beneke, with whom I co-wrote an opinion piece referenced in this book's opening anecdote. The blog also brought me into contact with Paul Putz, who has been a steady supporter of this book, offering invaluable advice and feedback from the earliest (very rough) drafts onward.

Indeed, throughout the writing and revising of this book, I have come to realize how many of my scholarly interactions—big and small—have contributed to its publication. From 2012 to 2016 I recorded several podcasts for the *Journal of Southern Religion* and the *Marginalia Review of Books*. Engaging with a wide array of scholars and topics helped me find new ways of making connections and articulating ideas in my own work. I am grateful to Mike Pasquier, Luke Harlow, Doug Thompson, Timothy Michael Law, Charles Halton, David Krueger, and Kristian Petersen for these opportunities.

I am also grateful to Malinda Maynor Lowery and Theda Perdue, who invited me to participate in the 2011 NEH Summer Seminar, "The Ethnohistory of Indians in the American South," at UNC–Chapel Hill. The insights and information I gathered during this seminar, along with access to UNC's archives and research resources, later helped me develop the related sections of this book.

Special thanks to Theo Calderara and the team at Oxford University Press for their commitment to this book and their help in keeping me on track. Theo took an early interest in the project, and throughout the revision process he struck just the right balance between patience and encouragement, providing the support I needed without ever making me feel rushed or overwhelmed.

I wish to thank the following editors and presses for giving me space to state my ideas and reuse some of this material in this book:

"Michael Novak's Seriously Catholic Interpretation of Sports," in *The Companion to Christianity and Sport in Europe and North America*, ed. Brian Bolt et al. (Belgium: Brepols, forthcoming).

"Ted Corbitt: The Once Forgotten and Now Remembered Pioneer of American Distance Running," in *Religion and Sport in North America: Critical Essays for the 21st Century*, ed. Jeffrey Scholes and Randall Balmer (New York: Routledge, 2022), 201–15.

"Religion and Sports in America," in *Oxford Research Encyclopedia*, ed. John Corrigan, online, March 2016.

"Steelers Nation and the Seriously Religious Side of Football," *Marginalia Review of Books*, August 28, 2013.

"Between Faith and Fistic Battles: Moralists, Enthusiasts, and the Idea of Jack Johnson in the New South," *Perspectives on Religious Studies* 39, no. 3 (2012): 219–33.

Thank you to my work home, Saint Francis University, and to all the people who make it a special place, especially my "writing circle" colleagues, Kirk Weixel, Denise Damico, Brennan Thomas, Tim Bintrim, Irene Wolf, Jessica Cammarata, Lance Mekeel, Lori Woods, and Mark Gentry. Ani Bose and Grant Julin were stalwart members of our writing group who passed away unexpectedly and far too soon. We continue our scholarly pursuits in their memory.

My wife Kate, son Abe, and daughter Ruth deserve special mention and thanks for their ongoing love and patience. Our dinnertime conversations, walks in the woods, and assorted other adventures inspire me every day.

Finally, I dedicate this book to my father, Dr. Vincent Remillard, who passed away in February 2024. My dad was a professor of French literature and always championed my life and career. He loved big ideas and illuminated them for others, always eager to foster a sense of meaning, purpose, and direction. I am grateful for his presence in my life and miss him very much.

# Introduction

## The "Something" of Sports

In play the beauty of the human body in motion reaches its zenith.

—Johan Huizinga

My eyes instinctively rolled when I read the headline from the *Washington Post* on Super Bowl Sunday, "Is Religion Losing Ground to Sports?" I might have even groaned too, since it echoed that one recurring question that I encounter when I reveal to people that I study religion and sports. "Is sports a religion?" they ask with eagerness, while simultaneously formulating their own affirmative answer. The glimmer of excitement in their eyes quickly vanishes when I declare unequivocally that no, I do not understand sports to be "a religion." Instead, I have come to resolve that throughout time sports have assumed sacred meaning through the interpretive acts of those who watch and play them. Or, to put it more simply, where there is sports talk, religion talk is almost certain to be present. The distinction, to me, is significant. But I'm not sure that my conversation partners always hear me in the moment. Consequently, this question persists, almost haunting me, spurred on by headlines such as this—a headline, I should note, featuring my name as one of the co-authors.[1]

To be clear, I *did not* choose this headline. That was the work of the editors, who are far more adept at attracting attention than I. Their skilled wordsmithing worked. The article was shared widely on social media, as several other newspapers reprinted it. My email inbox was crowded with commentaries and criticisms, some quite astute and some so completely random that I couldn't hit delete fast enough. A radio program in New Orleans contacted us to discuss the article in detail. And Albert Mohler, president of the Southwest Baptist Theological Seminary, cited our opinion piece

*Bodies in Motion*. Arthur Remillard, Oxford University Press. © Oxford University Press 2025.
DOI: 10.1093/oso/9780197789766.003.0001

to lament that "big-time sports represent America's new civic religion, and football is its central sacrament."[2]

We did not intend to say anything along these lines. Our point was far more mundane. After noting the decline in institutional religious attachment in the United States, we cited evidence to show that sports in this same time had been trending in the opposite direction. We stopped well short of equating religion and sports or saying that the latter was overtaking the former. But as our words became consumed by more people, this was precisely what readers saw. I get it, I really do. After all, in sports we see the ritual activities of players and fans, the elevation of athletes to heroes, and the mythic accounts of victories and losses. All of this is happening as we are told that America's traditional religious structures are in a state of physical and institutional decay, losing more attendees and influence with each passing day.

I've seen it all from my perch in central Pennsylvania, where so many churches struggle to keep their doors open while at the same time the Pittsburgh Steelers attract attention like metal to a magnet. To measure the significance of this team one need only count the innumerable "Terrible Towels" in and around the region's public and private spaces. Originating in 1975 as a gimmick to rally the Steelers in the playoffs, the Terrible Towel has since taken on elevated meaning. When I introduce the idea of sacred objects to my students, I ask them to imagine walking into a bar in this area carrying a Terrible Towel, which you promptly blow your nose into and throw to the floor—perhaps stomping it for good measure. "What would happen?" I ask. The thought alone makes some students visibly flinch. Others chuckle with an uncomfortable familiarity, knowing that the ambulance and police probably wouldn't make it in time. The Terrible Towel is deeply meaningful for "Steelers Nation," a fact that is further evidenced by its uses beyond the football field. People wrap their newborn infants in one, wave them at their weddings, and rest them atop coffins of the departed Steelers faithful.

So, yes, I understand how someone can see all of this and want to proclaim that football is "a religion." But I remain wary. Part of this is due to fatigue on my part. Over twenty years ago, I started studying religion and sports precisely because I too believed that I could prove that sports had become the new American religion. My first scholarly article was about the Seminole mascot debate at Florida State University, where I earned my doctorate. I took to calling this debate over the university's symbol a "holy war" between loyal FSU fans and those who sought to protect the identity and culture of Indigenous people. I certainly would not write this article the same way today, but it remains among my most cited academic pieces of work.[3] It also served as a gateway for me to enter a vigorous and exciting scholarly discussion on religion and sports. At conference after conference and in book after book, I have seen and contributed to what has become the academic equivalent of a sporting event, with team Sports Is a Religion facing off against team Sports Isn't a Religion. After picking sides, advancing the ball, and losing ground, I found that the novelty wore thin. Ultimately, I struggled to understand what we gained or lost by having this debate.

I also struggled with the normative claims of this enterprise. My studies in American religious history have revealed no shortage of people in power using "religion" to classify people and cultures to make unfavorable moral and social distinctions about their subjects. In more recent times, we continue to see "religion" weaponized, often in political debates. "Why Wokeism Is a Religion" makes for a catchy headline, but the ensuing analysis makes clear that this framing is designed to denigrate and disclaim the author's political target—depicting them as mindless and intolerant followers of a presumably misguided ideology. As readers will see, I certainly do my share of identifying and naming religious activities in sports. But my intention is to describe human behavior that orients toward transcendence rather than to impose something on a population of people who would not themselves make such a claim.[4]

Relatedly, I detect in the "religion of sports" trope what scholars call the "secular-religious binary," or an assumption of the inherent separateness of these categories. From my understanding of the academic conversation on secularism, this classification is not so much about religiously neutral activities and spaces but more about how those in power have wielded it to control and restrict the religious expression of marginalized groups. I do not intend to engage with this conversation, other than to say that I have found that such a tidy distinction between "religion" and "the secular" breaks down when examining the history of words, beliefs, and behaviors associated with both religion and sports. While people might engage less with traditional religious structures now, they still have the means for expressing their deepest concerns, for showing what matters most to them.[5]

Therefore, I want to reiterate emphatically that I will not assert in this book that sports constitute "a religion." Instead, my objective is to explore *how* people throughout America's history have employed religious language, imagery, and assorted other references to make sense of the realm of sports.[6] Consider how journalists dubbed the baseball player Sandy Koufax "the Left Arm of God." Certainly Koufax, who was Jewish, was a unique story for his institutional religious allegiance. However, the nickname, undoubtedly influenced by his Jewish background, was an endeavor to encapsulate the athlete's extraordinary prowess in throwing a baseball.[7]

While baseball is regarded by some as "just a game," it holds a significance beyond mere entertainment for its enthusiasts. As the Dutch cultural historian Johan Huizinga has explained, "In play there is something 'at play' which transcends the immediate needs of life and imparts meaning to the action." It is this "something" that is the focal point of this book—that subtle, invisible, elusive force that interpreters recognize as special in the context of sports. Notably, this distinctive quality of sports doesn't spontaneously emerge from nothing. The sociologist Émile Durkheim explained that it is the collective actions and shared consensus of people within societies that give rise to and sustain "sacred things" through ritual behavior.[8] As summarized by Mary Douglas, "the sacred" in Durkheim's perspective are those elements of a society that are "deeply cherished and violently defended." The objects, events, and athletes of sports have been cherished and defended, underscoring the clear power of their *somethingness*.[9]

Thus the following chapters bring into view various "sacred things"—*somethings*—of sports that people have generated over time in American history.[10] Guiding my attention are those people, places, and moments in sports where there exists what David Chidester calls the "traces of transcendence, the sacred, and the ultimate."[11] To identify these "traces," I focus on interpreters—those telling the stories of sports who chose to make these events something more, something special. My aim is to demonstrate that the raw material of sports is nothing more than bodies in motion, bodies that strive, struggle, and sweat. From here, *people*, as both individuals and groups, do the work of interpreting the significance of these motions. They produce stories, venerate images, and generate objects that express what is, and is not, special in these movements.

To advance this claim, I have made ample use of published accounts, newspapers, books, and magazines. In making decisions about what to use and not use, I generally avoided source material showing wherein traditional religious structures (e.g., churches) and leaders (e.g., ministers) have used sports to serve their own (e.g., evangelistic) ends. Instead, I have focused on sources wherein an observer breaks from reciting finishing places and results and uses instead the language of metaphor, of myth, of transcendence. What I have found is that this language has often been entangled with an array of other social forces. For example, Black prizefighters traveling abroad in the early nineteenth century became proxies for an emerging American nation, as stories about their accomplishments were also stories about American slavery. And decades later, as a sport like baseball professionalized, its heroes and heroic moments also became marketing opportunities for businesses seeking to find new revenue opportunities both on and off the field. Sports and the sacred matters that surround them do not happen in a vacuum. Instead, the character of every era and place become woven into these stories.[12]

In structuring the upcoming chapters, I have chosen to highlight three interconnected themes that I've observed across various places, times, and contexts, where people have bestowed a sacred dimension on sports. The first theme revolves around heroes. Rooted in the Homeric tradition, heroes were born from the unions of humans and immortals, existing as demigods in the uneasy space between eternity and the finite. They were both relatable and remote, imminent and transcendent, commendable and flawed. Their inherent paradoxes rendered them even more compelling, as admirers perceived heroes as a bridge connecting eternal truths to the limited understanding of humankind. And heroes were also venerated, both during their life and after. Arrhichion of Phigalia was a legend of the pankration, which was an especially brutal mix of brawling and wrestling. During the 564 BCE Olympics, he found himself in a chokehold and near death. But Arrhichion managed to conjure whatever strength he had remaining to dislocate his opponent's ankle and claim the prize. Alas, in the process Arrhichion died. But his lifeless body was still crowned with the Olympic wreath, and a statue was later erected to celebrate his victory. In the contemporary age, we find the residue of this ancient formulation applied to sports heroes, who similarly have their likenesses represented in statues, their deeds remembered and revered through sacred stories—mythologies—in their lifetime and after. In other words, boxers, swimmers, runners, and baseball players might only punch, stroke, stride, and hit on the field of play. But for their interpreters, these motions become the material for making heroes.[13]

Quite often the "somethingness" of heroes is translated through the realm of *emotion*, which is this book's second theme. Specifically, the emotion of passion is often associated with sports, bringing to the surface the contours of a long-standing disagreement between those who think about the human condition. Immanuel Kant, for example, took a decidedly dim view of passion, calling it a "disease of the soul." He preferred the supposedly stolid and reliable power of reason, suspicious that passion might only open people up to the worst tendencies of their nature. On the other hand, the romantic philosopher G. W. F. Hegel understood passion as being the very thing that ignited the human spirit and guided it toward liberation. Hegel insisted that no great act in history came about without passion. Kant and Hegel offer two ways of interpreting this emotion that contemporary psychologists call "obsessive" and "harmonious" passion. In both categories, people demonstrate love and attachment to an activity. But the former connotes an absence of balance or control, while the latter connects with experiences of fulfillment, satisfaction, and achievement. Thus in sports through the ages, we will see on the one hand suspicious "moralists" who insist that games distract from important things and that emotionally unhinged athletes and crowds give in to behaviors like drinking, gambling, cheating, and rowdiness. On the other hand, the defenders of sports often point to the ways in which a spirited contest is purposeful, with goal-directed behavior adding value to society and giving greater meaning to life.[14]

The defenders also often argue that the emotion of games ultimately creates a sense of belonging, of *community*—this book's third theme. The scenes of major sporting events often resonate ever so closely with what Durkheim called "collective effervescence." For Durkheim, the very foundation of religion rests in these ecstatic moments, when individuals feel "swept up into a world entirely different from the one they have before their eyes." That collective experience can then serve as a foundation for community to form and be sustained. In sports, we see collective identities taking local, regional, and national forms, marked by team names, colors, and other assorted artifacts and activities. If we turn to the international stage, we find sports bearing a certain civil religious quality, the ideals and values of America being projected onto the athletes as their actions become symbolic of broader geopolitical contests with other nations. People also coalesce in sports settings around other shared features of their identity, to include race, gender, and institutional faith. The baseball player Hank Greenberg, for example, became the face of Detroit in the 1930s, while he was also a "pioneer" for American Judaism in a time and place when antisemitism was particularly virulent.[15]

Heroes, emotion, and community are themes that run through the following chapters, which progress chronologically through the age of European contact to the present. Along the way, I present fragments from sports history, arranged to show how different people in different times, places, and social contexts have inscribed an array of sacred meaning onto physical activity.[16] This book does not follow a singular golden thread demonstrating how religion and sports "made America." Others have adeptly done this.[17] Instead, I bring to the surface selected dispatches from the past that reveal the nearly inevitable presence of sacred matters in the interpretation of sports. This is why I don't just begin in the nineteenth century with the "muscular Christian" movement. While I do discuss muscular Christianity, my account situates it as one story among many. But the more scholarly points like these are left to the notes or omitted outright. My first goal is to tell a good story, one that my students and parents and friends might enjoy reading.

It is for this reason that I try to balance the familiar with the unfamiliar, and the high-profile with the relatively obscure. While the "holy trinity" of American sports (baseball, basketball, and football) take up plenty of space in the forthcoming pages, so too do lesser-known sports like tip cat, pedestrianism, and "gander pulling." My intention is not to force novelty into the story but rather to demonstrate how sports of all sizes and significance can take on religious meaning. A crowd of thousands might tell us about the broader appeal of a given contest. But we also find interpreters examining athletes who labor away in obscurity, who play with purpose and intensity simply for the love of the game.

Irrespective of the sport under consideration, readers will find that tension characterizes the framing of each forthcoming chapter, with an emphasis on the push and pull between competing forces. In this way, the structure of the book deliberately plays off Newton's laws of motion, which seek to describe the motion of objects and the forces acting upon them. The following pages therefore examine the polarities between heroes and villains, innovation and anxiety, and so on because as individuals and communities generate sacred matters, they do so in contrast and competition with others.[18] Or to reference Newton once more, for every action there is an equal and opposite reaction. By centering on these tensions, we witness people making decisions about what it means to be human, to live in community, and to live a moral life.

As a final note, what follows is intentionally titled *a* history and not *the* history.[19] In my years of studying the interplay of religion and sports, I have been building a vocabulary and knowledge base for explaining what I think is happening. Along the way, I have allowed my eyes to follow those items that I have found to be interesting, unique, and noteworthy. It is my hope that you will find this material to be equally interesting, unique, and noteworthy. I also hope to offer this story as an invitation to readers to think along with me about the *somethingness* of sports in American history. Perhaps from here we could imagine a better future for sports and ourselves.

# 1

# A Whole New Ball Game

In 1493, while on his second voyage to the Caribbean, Christopher Columbus and his crew witnessed a ball game played by the Taíno that fundamentally changed their understanding of how an object could travel through the air. European eyes were accustomed to the lazy flight patterns of air- and feather-filled balls in folk games like *pallone* or tennis for the privileged class. But the ball at the center of the Taíno game moved, jumped, leaped, and sped across the court with an unfamiliar pace and in unpredictable directions. This was due to the fact that the balls were composed of rubber, a substance unknown in Europe at the time. Additionally, the very physical property of elasticity was a mystery to Columbus and his like. When Columbus returned to Spain with these rubber balls among his collection of items taken during his voyage, observers stood likewise befuddled by what they saw, both fearful and fascinated by the ball and those who used it in their games.[1]

The ball played in this game was but one artifact of an entirely new population for the European gaze to interpret, understand, and colonize. As more Europeans crossed the ocean, many of them commented on Indigenous games in ways that were far from neutral. Instead, Indigenous games became a template for producing a contrast between "civilization" and the "primitive." As one scholar articulated, the term "primitive" depicted Indigenous populations as "a negative structure of concreteness," positioning Europeans as superior conquerors.[2] Thus for European interpreters, Indigenous games and the material associated with them were a means for producing difference and of establishing a hierarchy of humanity. Significantly, Indigenous people themselves had little say in the shaping of their stories in the accounts shared in the forthcoming paragraphs. Instead, we see Europeans doing the work of organizing and stratifying Indigenous society and culture as a way of expressing their own ideological agendas.

*Bodies in Motion*. Arthur Remillard, Oxford University Press. © Oxford University Press 2025.
DOI: 10.1093/oso/9780197789766.003.0002

## "A Thing to Marvel At"

Archaeological evidence indicates that the game Columbus observed, known as *batey*, arrived in the Caribbean around 600 CE, having originated among the Mayans two thousand years prior. The term "batey" encompassed both the game itself and the ceremonial plazas where trade, civic activities, and communal rituals took place. These plazas likely served to demarcate the boundaries between chiefdoms. Consequently, the competitions held in these locations played a crucial role in differentiating local identities and establishing a sense of status based on victories and defeats. Regarding the game, it revolved around a hefty rubber ball that teams volleyed back and forth on a rectangular court. Players could use all parts of their body except for their hands and feet to hit the ball, earning points when the opposing team failed to return it. Both male and female players wore stone and wood collars or yokes around their midsection to strike the ball and protect themselves from injury. On the court's periphery, crowds gathered to watch, cheer, and engage in gambling. For the elite, gambling served to showcase their status within the community, while for others, it was a means of expressing support and seeking divine favor.[3]

The movements, material, and lore of *batey* also connected to the sacred universe of a community, one populated by a complex assortment of gods, ancestors, and the land that they occupied. Stones served as the boundary markers for the courts, and they came engraved with swirls and figures of animals, humans, and players in action. Local mythologies told of gods and humans playing and, in one account, mortals defeating the gods of the underworld, who in turn granted humans their civilization. In its totality, the game was an entangled amalgam of political, social, economic, and spiritual forces.[4]

In time, explorers, missionaries, and assorted other Europeans would attempt to develop an understanding of the game and the material associated with it. Among these voices was the Spanish missionary and eventual "defender of the Indians" Bartolomé de Las Casas. Calling *batey* "a joyous sight to see," Las Casas wrote detailed descriptions of the courts, the players, and the objects. He described one game as having twenty or thirty players on the court who routinely returned the ball with a speed that was "like lightning." Las Casas was not alone in noting the rapid tempo of the game. The Spanish chronicler Gonzalo Fernández de Oviedo, for example, detailed the rhythm of *batey*, calling it "a thing to marvel at." Commending the "skill and dexterity" of the individual players, he described the methods used to keep the ball airborne by striking it with the head, hips, and elbows. Oviedo also took note of the gender dynamics of *batey*, and the role of clothing—or lack thereof. Remaining somewhat unbiased, he explained how in games that matched men and virgin women, the competitors played nude, while married women wore a shawl or petticoat.[5]

In terms of their moral assessment, both Las Casas and Oviedo remained rather positive about the game and its players, thus fitting them in with their overall enterprise of making a case among Europeans for the humanity and consequent convertibility of the Taíno. But there were instances of deep skepticism of the game. Oviedo was wary of *batey*'s perceived incitement of communal violence. The author cited an instance in the buildup to the Taíno Rebellion of 1511, when villagers reportedly played a game of *batey* to determine who would earn the right to execute a high-ranking Spanish official. Other accounts would tell similar stories, which aimed to portray Indigenous people as deeply cruel and uncivilized. For example, a companion of Columbus's claimed that while in Jamaica waiting for the waters to calm so that he could depart in his canoe, a group of Indigenous people gathered and played a game as a wager to see who would kill him and take his canoe.[6]

As missionaries extended their efforts into Mexico and beyond, their depictions of the ball games mirrored those of their predecessors. They sought to strike a balance between portraying the Indigenous populations as primitive while recognizing the potential for their conversion. Jesuit Andrés Pérez de Ribas, active in northwest Mexico among the Ahome, Zuaque, and Yaqui for fifteen years in the early seventeenth century, published an account of his experiences in 1645 titled *History of the Triumphs of Our Holy Faith amongst the Most Barbarous and Fierce Peoples of the New World.* The title alone served to underscore European civilization's assumed superiority over what were considered less advanced cultural patterns in the New World. However, the book's purpose extended beyond mere description; it aimed to educate incoming missionaries and garner support for missions from church officials. Pérez de Ribas vehemently condemned what he saw as the "superstitious idolatry" of these communities, emphasizing that the "devil" worked through the objects they held sacred. Despite this, the missionary also acknowledged the "naturally good" behaviors of the population, highlighting their aversion to thievery and avoidance of "lustful" behaviors. Instead, they were described as favoring a "peaceable" lifestyle as married couples.[7]

As for their games, Pérez de Ribas listed *batey* as one of their "innocuous customs," having witnessed contests at their "clean and very orderly" plazas. He offered limited commentary on the practice of gambling, revealing how colonization had deeply changed this activity. In the mines, Spanish-speaking Indigenous laborers were often appointed as bar drivers, taking a bar and breaking the veins of ore. At the end of each workday, they were rewarded with a basket of ore. These miners would then amble through public spaces "beautifully dressed and adorned." When it came time for gambling, they used their riches to raise the stakes. Material that had once been part of the landscape—uninteresting and unimportant—was now valuable for wagering. And everyone was involved in gambling. Pérez de Ribas alleged that women celebrated the game and its players by cheering, singing, and wagering what they could to show support. When they had nothing material, they would pluck their eyelashes. "Sometimes some of them wept when this happened and others laughed and were entertained."[8]

For Pérez de Ribas, the game and the emotional fervor surrounding it were an entertaining curiosity rather than a threat. Consequently, he allowed baptized Christians to continue playing *batey*. However, *batey* evolved into a means for this missionary, as well as for subsequent Europeans, to emphasize a sense of distinction. The games played by Indigenous people in what would later become the United States likely served a similar purpose, even though missionaries and other travelers to that region probably did not encounter *batey*. Nevertheless, ball courts reminiscent of those found in Mesoamerica surfaced among the Hohokam in present-day Arizona. Figurines depicting padded players, rubber and stone balls, and stone engravings of players suggest that the game held significant cultural importance in this society. By the thirteenth century the game had gradually faded into obscurity, and by the mid-fifteenth century the Hohokam society had collapsed—possibly due to factors such as war, overpopulation, or environmental strain.[9]

From the Caribbean and Mesoamerica northward, *batey* and its variants lost their vitality just as death and depopulation tore through the ranks of those who played them. Left behind were courts surrounded by engraved stones, reminders of a vibrant game that changed and adapted over time. Europeans witnessed a tiny sliver of this history, interpreting the game for an audience across the ocean, creating religious and cultural "others" who lived in this distant land. In time, European audiences would have a new way to learn about Indigenous games, as the written word would soon be accompanied by images of Indigenous bodies in motion.

## "Christians Deserve to Be Trained by These Barbarous Foreign People"

In 1565, Spanish forces invaded a French settlement near the mouth of the St. John's River, massacring approximately 250 of the Huguenot inhabitants. Jacques le Moyne was one of the few who escaped death or capture, accompanying the surviving women and children to safety. An artist, Le Moyne lost nearly all his work in the attack. When he returned to France, he mined his memory to reproduce a series of drawings and watercolors of this unique place and its inhabitants.[10]

Le Moyne's art often reflected the teachings of reformer John Calvin, who proclaimed that "ever since in the creation of the universe [God] brought forth those insignia whereby he shows his glory to us, whenever and wherever we cast our gaze." Accordingly, artists taking Calvin's lead began looking for "sparks of glory" in the everyday world around them. For Le Moyne, this took the shape of his descriptions of creation and the toned bodies of Indigenous people. In one of his accounts, Le Moyne described a crowd of hundreds of men following a Tamaqua king, calling them "handsome, strong, well-made, and active fellows, the best-trained and swiftest of his force." Here and elsewhere, the political and religious conflicts of the time inflected Le Moyne's work, as he showed the New World and its inhabitants to be eminently welcoming of the French Huguenot presence, in contrast to the contested colonial efforts of Spanish Catholics.[11]

Le Moyne soon relocated to London, where he gained favor with notable figures such as Sir Walter Raleigh and John White, which led him to cross paths with the Dutch goldsmith-turned-engraver Theodor de Bry. In the time of Columbus's voyages, Europeans living in their homeland could only use their imaginations as they read accounts trickling in from the New World. The advent of copper engravings marked a revolutionary shift, enabling the production of reproducible and mass-marketed physical images. Recognizing the potential market value in Le Moyne's images, the entrepreneurial De Bry aimed to distribute them through illustrated books utilizing this new technology. However, to De Bry's disappointment, Le Moyne resisted his offers, intending to publish his own account. Le Moyne died before realizing his plan, though, and in 1588 Le Moyne's widow finally sold the images to De Bry, who now had the material to start his new business venture.[12]

De Bry and his sons swiftly embarked on the production and marketing of these images. Keenly attuned to his audience, De Bry crafted images that mirrored events and ideas shaping European identity. For example, Europe in the 1590s grappled with poor harvests and famine, making scarcity a pervasive aspect of daily life. In contrast, De Bry's portrayal of the New World depicted a land of abundance and potential—an untamed paradise inhabited by "savages" who, in his perspective, were constrained by their paganism. One image featured a Timucuan "magician" in a prayer position, presented in such a horrifying manner that, in De Bry's description, "he ceased to resemble a human being" and was "certainly possessed by the devil."[13]

De Bry's enterprise of dehumanizing the Indigenous populations came with concurrent critiques of European decadence. Particularly in his early engravings, De Bry's Indigenous people were stately, composed, and muscular—akin to the ancient Greek gods. Nowhere was this more evident than in his 1591 engraving of young and muscular Timucuan men, running, shooting arrows, and playing a ball game. Admiring of their physique, De Bry exclaimed, "Christians deserve to be trained by these barbarous foreign people, yes even by the ignorant animals, to learn temperance from them."[14] Here the engraver channeled his Calvinist leanings to level criticism against what he perceived as Europe's slide into frivolity and sloth, depicting Indigenous people as physically gifted, as virtuous athletes on a level with the great heroes of the Olympic past.

From De Bry's perspective, the humanity of Indigenous people was simultaneously constrained by "barbarism" and paradoxically held up as an embodied model for European civilization. While De Bry incorporated this ideology into his depictions of the New World, his primary goal was the commercial success of his products. It is noteworthy that many of his engravings portrayed Catholics in the New World as ruthless destroyers and voracious pursuers of profit and people. He strategically targeted these images to markets like Germany, appealing to Protestants. But such depictions were omitted from his Latin volumes, whose primary audience was Catholic. Certainly, De Bry and his sons had settled in Frankfurt largely due to religious persecution, indicating his sensitivity to Reformation politics. This didn't prevent him from entering the markets of his theological adversaries and crafting a message that would resonate with their interests and sensibilities. Ultimately, he operated in a European market that favored the notion of European supremacy and yearned to envision the New World as a realm of limitless possibilities.[15]

## "A Task of Stupid Drudgery"

A ball can be kicked. A ball can spin atop a poll. And in the mid-seventeenth century, the French Jesuit missionary Jean de Brébeuf, who lived among the Huron in Ontario, witnessed balls being flung out from a curiously shaped stick with a basket at one end. As a careful observer of Huron customs and habits, Brébeuf described a stick-and-ball game which he referred to as "lacrosse," inferring that the sticks resembled the crosier carried by bishops in religious processions. Yet this invocation of European religious symbolism was not an endorsement of the game. Instead, he thundered against the "miserable sorcerer" who would prescribe the game as a cure for individual or communal illness, as young men obeyed this call unthinkingly and with unusual fervor. And then there were the crowds of onlookers, perched on the sidelines gambling, cheering, and hexing opponents. For Brébeuf, lacrosse and its assorted customs was nothing more than a collective "wallowing in all sorts of filth," proving to the missionary that demonic forces were at work among the Huron and that only the Catholic Church could save them.[16]

Lacrosse likely originated in the early fifteenth century with the Huron and Iroquois tribes in the St. Lawrence River region. As it spread, the game's rules, rituals, and mythologies adapted to local customs and were folded into tribal identities. Lacrosse was one of many games played by Indigenous populations throughout North America. From relay races to kickball, athletic contests were a ritualized means of pleasing the gods, securing fertility, conjuring rain, prolonging life, expelling demons, and curing illnesses.[17]

For missionaries, however, these games were nothing more than "superstition." Jesuit François Joseph le Mercier echoed Brébeuf as he recounted a "sorcerer" calling for a game of lacrosse to remedy the spread of a persistent illness. Members of the villages responded with haste, as young people flocked to the playing field. When people continued getting sick, though, the villagers confronted the sorcerer, who had nothing to offer in his defense. To Le Mercier, this further discredited the sorcerer's moral authority, while also creating a spiritual opening that the missionary aspired to fill.[18]

French Jesuits telling these stories did so through the vehicle of the *Relations*, a famous collection of commentaries on the New World. While observant of tribal differences and landscapes, the *Relations* became yet another outlet for the making of an Indigenous identity: a "savage" trapped in a heathen world who required God's grace and a committed missionary.

Lacrosse was one point of reference for missionaries seeking to solidify these distinctions. A similar rhetorical project was unfolding in Louisiana, as French colonists made contact with the Choctaw. "They have no religion," exclaimed one anonymous memoir from 1755. "They recognize only the devil, and those among them who invoke him are called jugglers." As evidence of their supposedly demonic impulse, the author cited their gambling practices, claiming that they wagered all their possessions, their wives, and even themselves. To the colonist, the capricious extremes of these practices were evidence enough of the absence of "religion."[19]

These published accounts of Indian games painted a picture of a decidedly different and deranged population. With a slightly less deriding tone, planter Antoine-Simon Le Page du Pratz's history of the Louisiana colony also described the "diversions" of the native inhabitants he reported encountering from 1718 to 1734. His account would be translated into English following the Seven Years' War, when the English took control of the territory, and soon after, Thomas Jefferson featured it on his bookshelf as he engineered the Louisiana Purchase. The preface to the English edition asserted that Le Page's insights would be "of no small consequence and importance to this nation." No doubt, this book had significant authority in the minds of English-speaking readers like Jefferson. In describing Indigenous games, Le Page's account emphasized the drama, allure, and gender dynamics inherent in these activities. Warriors, he detailed, engaged in a game known as "the pole," where two players hurled long poles at a stone target: "The men fatigue themselves much at this game, as they run after their poles at every throw, and some of them are so bewitched by it that they gamble away one piece of furniture after another." Women also participated, albeit discreetly, using smaller cane poles and playing only when unobserved. "They are ashamed to be seen or found playing," Le Page surmised.[20]

A similar interest in the social dimensions of sports marked French explorer Jean-Bernard Bossu's writings. On his first trip to New France in 1751, he traveled along the Mississippi River and was adopted by the Quapaw, who promptly marked him with a leg tattoo, which, they told him, would allow him entry down the Mississippi River. In 1759, Bossu began living among the Choctaw, where he came to witness an intense game of lacrosse. It all started with neighboring villages issuing formal invitations, leading to crowds of men, women, and children dressed elaborately, dancing and singing, as percussion sounds filled the air. Then the game began, itself a demonstration of grace and fair play. Bossu exclaimed, "It is a fine sight to observe the players with their bodies bare." He added that the women played their own match "with much skill," and also naked, "except for the parts which modesty dictates they shall cover."[21]

Bossu's renderings of Indigenous sports were of the "noble savage" variety—differentiated but demanding of attention and even respect. William Bartram's accounts of Indian games followed a similar path, albeit among a different population. From Philadelphia and the son of Quakers, Bartram had unsuccessfully tried his hand at business and art before receiving a commission to collect and document the plants of the Southeast. Starting in 1773, he spent four years filling his notebooks with descriptions of the natural landscape, as well as accounts of Indigenous people. On matters of religion, Bartram endeavored to align Christianity with Indigenous spiritual worldviews. "These Indians are by no means idolaters," he insisted, adding that they "adore the Great Spirit," which he claimed bore a resemblance to the Christian God as a giver of life and death and presider over "the world of spirits." They were, additionally, devout Sabbath observers. An inhabitant reportedly told him that, "it being the white people's beloved day or Sabbath, the Indians kept it religiously sacred to the Great Spirit."[22]

Bartram tended to portray these games as an "exercise and pastime" or "juvenile diversions." The one exception—the "most noble and manly exercise"—was lacrosse, as he marveled at the youth who would invest their "whole substance" into the game: "Here they perform amazing feats of strength and agility." On the evening before a game among the Cherokee, he described a festival of music and dancing that also featured storytelling. According to Bartram, at one point in the evening "an aged chief" delivered an extended oration on the many victories of the past, giving special attention to his own exploits. Accompanying the storytelling was ritualized dancing, women moving with "grace and decency" while men were a dramatization of "masculine strength and activity."[23]

Bartram's book, translated into Dutch, German, and French, drew a wide audience. Romantic writers such as Samuel Taylor Coleridge and William Wordsworth referenced his writings and imagery. As a result, describing Indigenous populations became for Bartram a means for gathering social and monetary currency. Another text that functioned similarly came from James Adair, a deerskin trader and agent in South Carolina from the 1740s through the 1770s. He would go on to call himself the "English Chickasaw," a title that amplified his persona as someone who lived neatly between these two worlds, as depicted in his 1775 book, *The History of the American*

*Indians.* The book gained initial attention, in part, for reviving the claim that the Indians were descendants of the Lost Tribes of Israel.[24]

Ever since 1492, the "Hebraic Indian theory" had become a means for Europeans to situate Indigenous people within a familiar biblical history while also serving political and religious ends. The first significant English-language articulation of the theory came from Puritan minister Thomas Thorowgood, whose books in 1650 and 1660 deployed the theory to encourage the conversion of Indians. In the coming century, this Hebraic Indian theory faded into obscurity, until Adair gave it new life, applying his firsthand experience, rather than just biblical exegesis, to assert the Adamic lineage of Indigenous populations. And part of the project of familiarizing this population to European audiences was his examination of Indigenous games. On the "manly exercise" of lacrosse, he emphasized that the physical strain of this contest would have been suitable even for "the ancient Spartans." Adair witnessed players intensely chasing the ball, seemingly unaware of the physical effort required to maintain a game whose goals reportedly were five hundred yards apart. "It is surprising to see how swiftly they fly," he exclaimed, estimating that the best among them could throw the ball one hundred yards.[25]

Adair also endeavored to highlight what he believed was the spiritual quality of the game. Certain lacrosse balls, he explained, could become "a favorite divine gift." The players' pregame rituals were similarly significant, as they would mortify their bodies, fast, and forsake sleep while crowds of women danced, "chanting religious notes with their shrill voices." At the break of dawn, the men would arrive at the field, painted white and "whooping, as if Pluto's prisoners were all broke loose." The leader then offered an "invocation," and the game would begin. The cumulative force of this spiritual activity led Adair to see a connection between their religious sincerity and their extraordinary physical abilities.[26]

In Adair's assessment of Indigenous "religion," where he acknowledged their perceived "superstition," he bestowed a noble aura upon this population by emphasizing their superhuman strength and endurance. This perspective was notably evident in his depiction of *chungke*, or "running hard labor." In contrast to lacrosse, this game involved only one or two players on each side. The objective was for each player to roll a stone as far as possible and then throw a pole toward the stone, aiming to land it closest to the target. Adair portrayed the contest as a thoroughly exhausting event, conducted under the harsh midday heat, the participants wearing their warrior regalia.

Summing up his observations, he remarked, "All the American Indians are much addicted to this game, which, to us, appears to be a task of stupid drudgery." Yet he acknowledged the game's significance, noting that the rocks used in *chungke* were handled "with the strictest religious care," passed down through generations or sometimes buried with the deceased.[27]

While Adair was unable to feel the creative tension of *chungke*, he avoided dismissing it as being frivolous or demonic. Meanwhile, Bernard Romans expressed a more negative perspective. Romans witnessed Choctaw playing this same game and denounced its violence and the "excess in spirituous liquors." Born in Holland, Romans arrived in Florida in 1768 to work as a surveyor. Like Adair, he wrote a history of the region and its people. Unlike Adair, he resolved that these Indigenous people were "incapable of civilization." It was a problem not of their habits and customs but of their very origin. He wrote, "I am firmly of the opinion that God created an original man and woman in this part of the globe, of different species from any in the other parts."[28]

Romans therefore described this population as being clueless on "religion" and deficient in several more mundane activities, such as not tilling the ground and men and women respectively urinating in a sitting and standing posture. With Indigenous people cast as an entirely separate creation of God, even Romans's complimentary passages on their physical activities contained condemnations. "They are strong, and swift of foot," started one sentence, before then claiming, "They are horridly given to sodomy, committing that crime even on the dead bodies of their enemies, thereby (as they say) degrading them into women." As for lacrosse, Romans fixated on the "amazing violence" of the game, as well as the nakedness of the players. Women participants were an additional signal of disorder, as Romans described with contempt these athletes playing with too much intensity and wagering on the outcome. His description of *chungke* leveled similar critiques, expressing outrage at the fatigue brought about by the game, and repulsed by a story that one gambler took his life after a losing effort.[29]

Romans was Adair's direct foil, offering cynical assessments of what to him was an irredeemable population, captured by the passion of their games. It was a tension that existed from the earliest moments of contact, when a bouncing ball ensorcelled Columbus and his crew with its mysterious elasticity. In subsequent years, chroniclers, missionaries, explorers, and historians meticulously documented the bodies of Indigenous people engaged in play. While descriptions of Indigenous games delved into rules, objects, and physical activities, they simultaneously undertook the task of naming and asserting control over people and places, assigning them positions on hierarchies of humanity. Moreover, interpreters redirected these accounts of Indigenous difference back onto Europe, influencing European patterns of thought and imbuing these games with an additional role in cultural development. A comparable transatlantic exchange unfolded in New England, where Puritans turned their gaze inward, contemplating the perils and possibilities of "legal" and "illegal" sports in their own society.

# 2
# The Alypius Problem

It all began with an offhand remark to his students, as St. Augustine bemoaned those unfortunate souls "held in thrall by the madness" of the circus. The teacher then turned his gaze toward Alypius, silently passing judgment. Despite being certain of the young man's "innate virtue," Augustine was well aware that Alypius had succumbed to "the craze for games." In response, Alypius received his teacher's unspoken rebuke, and with remorse penetrating deep into his being, he committed to forsaking these amusements. However, his conviction proved short-lived. Alypius soon ventured to Rome, where, in Augustine's words, he was once again "bewildered by the bewildering lure of the games." Coaxed by his friends to attend, Alypius at first resisted but eventually gave in. Initially, he attempted to shield his eyes while in the arena to avoid witnessing the spectacle. But as every bloodthirsty sound assailed his ears, Alypius's defenses wore thin. Augustine succinctly summarized the transformation: "No longer the person he was when he entered, he was now entered into the crowd, and one with those who forced him there."[1]

In Augustine's framing, the senses played a central role in the story of Alypius's moral decline. As one historian explained, "It is through his ears that his attention is diverted from within to without: they are a gateway by which the enemy enters the citadel of his eyes and his mind, whence he is taken prisoner."[2] Put another way, the young man relied only on himself, neglecting the Christian tenet espoused by Augustine that only faith in God could break the grip of sin. Importantly, the notoriously gruesome games of Rome served as the backdrop for this story. Over time the Christian inheritors of Augustine's theological legacy would continue looking negatively at the circuses of their specific contexts, worried that such amusements would overwhelm the senses and cast one into a godless pit of passion.

This was precisely John Bunyan's dilemma. Arguably best known for his 1678 Christian allegory, *The Pilgrim's Progress*, over a decade earlier the

*Bodies in Motion*. Arthur Remillard, Oxford University Press. © Oxford University Press 2025.
DOI: 10.1093/oso/9780197789766.003.0003

English Puritan and noted preacher had published his spiritual autobiography, *Grace Abounding to the Chief of Sinners*. Written during his imprisonment, Bunyan documented his lengthy conversion, emphasizing his ongoing struggle with sin, which at one point took the form of a popular game. As Bunyan described it, he lived an aimless youth characterized by fishing and boating as well as "cursing, swearing, lying, and blaspheming the holy name of God." His turnaround began when he married, urged along by his "pious" father-in-law. Bunyan thereafter slowly crept closer to the light, particularly one Sunday morning after hearing a powerful sermon on Sabbath desecration. However, as he strolled from the church grounds with the echo of the sermon in his ears, Bunyan witnessed a game of tip-cat, a popular bat-and-ball game, a precursor to baseball. Participants endeavored to hit a wooden "cat" beyond the reach of opposing players. Much like Alypius at the circus, Bunyan's attention turned entirely to the game, the sight and sound of tip-cat displacing morality and righteousness.[3]

As he played, however, a voice thundered in his conscious: "Wilt thou leave thy sins and go to heaven, or have thy sins and go to hell?" Bunyan's body was seized in terror. Alas, the moment elapsed, and traumatized but not moved, Bunyan continued playing. The promise of heaven, he calculated, had passed him by forever. It wasn't until he happened upon poor women speaking with humility about the joys of "new birth" that he reconsidered his life. Far away from the tip-cat field, their simple and abiding faith in God's love lifted him from ignorance.[4]

Certainly, tip-cat differed significantly from the Roman gladiatorial contests of Augustine's era. Yet both Augustine and Bunyan framed amusements as a moral vortex—a realm where sin could infiltrate through the senses, extinguishing any hope for salvation. Puritans in New England subsequently embraced this assumption about sports, inscribing their distrust for sensory experiences into legal provisions designed to uphold their conception of public order and private godliness. At the same time, they carved out space for specific physical activities considered to possess practical value and a life-affirming quality. A similar tension characterized the legal frameworks of colonial Pennsylvania and Virginia, albeit influenced by a different set of cultural resources. A common pattern across these settings was the tendency for those with power and privilege to make distinctions between sports considered beneficial for the well-being of individuals and the community and those deemed irredeemably sinful due to their potential to arouse passions.

## Puritans at Play

"In New England," exclaimed one journalist in 1907, "the stern Puritan blood frowned upon nearly every kind of diversion." Sports, of course, were one such "diversion," vigorously avoided by Puritans, who were the ultimate killjoys—or at least that's the stereotype as articulated by the likes of H. L. Mencken, who quipped, "Puritanism is the haunting fear that someone, somewhere, may be happy." Despite its prevalence, this image of the "stern" Puritan detached from all of life's pleasures scarcely aligns with the historical record. Worldly things had a place in the Puritan theological formulation, but always subordinated to the glory of God. Consider the example of John Winthrop, the first governor of the Massachusetts Bay Colony, who confessed that a life spent only working with no space for play left him "very melancholic and uncomfortable." Aware of the problem of elevating "earthly delights" to idolatrous levels, Winthrop resolved that "some outward recreation" and "moderate exercise" could add value to life.[5]

The challenge of Puritan leaders like Winthrop was in drawing a line between "lawful" and "unlawful" sports, between those activities that would build up individuals physically and spiritually and those deemed hazardous to public and private morality. Games fitting into the latter category tended to align with the preferences of the lower classes. For example, activities involving the kicking of a ball—generally referred to as "football"—drew scorn from the moralizers. Puritan Thomas Shepard vehemently declared, "Satan now appears with the ball at his foot," intending only "to kick and carry God's precious Sabbaths out of the world with him." Worries of Sabbath desecration frequently accompanied condemnations of football, adding weight to the perceived moral depravity of not only the game but the people playing it. It was a ministerial perspective that had a legacy. Speaking over a century after Shepard, Unitarian minister William Bentley announced, "The bruising of shins has rendered [football] rather disgraceful to those of better education." He then added that refined people preferred handball, or something that was not "unfriendly to clothes, as well as safety."[6]

For Puritans in places of authority, class distinction played a significant role in determining the acceptability of certain sports. This process had historical echoes in the Reformation. Martin Luther advocated archery, fencing, and wrestling as means for preparing young men for battle. No mere pragmatist on the matter, Luther also saw a higher purpose in sports. He labeled dancing an "honorable and useful" exercise, while famously conjecturing that the sound of a bowling ball striking the pins echoed God's command to knock down the devil. For Luther, sports played a role in developing a fit body, mind, and spirit—so long as players guarded against excessive violence and "sinful" behavior like gambling. Similarly, John Calvin enjoyed an occasional game of quoits, and he was known to take leisurely walks. Still, his prohibitions on sports were quite strict in comparison to Luther's. Geneva had a reputation for rowdy festivals and a libertine culture, making the imposition of a theocratic order the principal ambition of Calvin and his followers. They criminalized everything from cards to wedding dances, pillorying offenders in public settings. At the same time, Calvin understood the inevitable appeal of sports and games, lamenting, "As I see that we cannot forbid men all diversions, I confine myself to those that are really bad."[7]

During the Reformation in England, navigating the tumultuous landscape of sports, politics, and theological disputes proved challenging. In 1617, King James I attempted to bring clarity by issuing the *Declaration on Lawful Sports*, permitting "harmless recreation" following Sunday services. However, after the English Civil War in the mid-seventeenth century, victorious Puritans sought to overturn James's declaration. Military officials enforced prohibitions on festivals and folk games, though these measures had only a temporary impact, as games resumed after the Restoration. In colonial New England, the tensions surrounding Sunday play persisted. Puritans carried with them a theological and social contest against the Anglican power structure, reflected in various laws prohibiting specific games, such as shuffleboard, bowling, and horse racing. These regulations emerged from collective worries about the perceived "sinful" activities associated with such activities, including gambling, drinking, and Sabbath breaking.[8]

Another common thread in these laws was a concern about the use of time, whether expressed by public officials or noted in private diaries. Puritans aimed to make every moment meaningful in the context of God's time. Sabbath hours were specifically designated for rest, when engaging in work, play, or unnecessary travel was seen as a violation of this norm. The relentless focus on "improving the time" led to the classification of anything perceived as time-wasting as a criminal offense. Additionally, the physical location of time spent held significance. According to Boston Congregationalist minister Thomas Foxcroft, taverns were not merely places for consuming spirits but were centers of "dreadful consumption of precious time." Despite Foxcroft's acknowledging that certain games aligned with a "pursuit of religion," he asserted that these activities should not take place in a tavern. Consequently, the minister advocated for a legal categorization of diversions to establish a clear distinction.[9]

A similar focus on improving the time applied to holidays such as Christmas, which Puritans associated with the Catholic tradition. The Puritan calendar accordingly had no space for liturgical seasons. However, festivals were part of the culture, carrying a subtle liturgical residue as they aligned with seasonal rhythms. Thanksgiving, for instance, sought to enhance the image of the Puritan founding during autumn. Other festivals included those for Election Day and Commencement Day, held in April and July, respectively. These events were marked by sermons, cakes, and even spirituous beverages, adding a celebratory dimension to the Puritan approach to marking time.[10]

And then there were training days. Held in early spring and late summer, these ritualized communal festivals intended to sharpen and display martial skill; hence the featured contests were foot races, wrestling matches, and shooting. The linkage of games and military readiness has deep roots in Europe, as the unwieldy melees of the twelfth and thirteenth centuries gave way to more orderly affairs like jousting tournaments. Puritan training days became another chapter in this story, interpreted in a way that reflected the values of this population—values such as communal flourishing and orderliness. John Winthrop reported that in 1639, one thousand men gathered for a May training day. That autumn the number rose to twelve hundred. Held on the Boston Common—itself a sacred site, wherein Puritan community took form—Winthrop boasted that the event was a portrait of order and honor, free from drunkenness and quarreling. Adding to the sacred quality, the events were thoroughly imbued with Christian symbolism, opening with prayer and psalm singing. One nineteenth-century chronicler exclaimed, "The all-powerful Church Militant held sway over these gatherings of New England warriors."[11]

Over time, training days became more raucous, due in part to changing social conditions. In 1676, King Philip's War came to an end, and collective worries eased over the threat of an outside attack. Consequently, training days became more celebratory and less aimed toward a specific purpose. In 1704, Sarah Kemble Knight, a teacher by trade, witnessed a military training day on her travels and commented on the significance of these events in New England society. Thick with satire, she also described how rowdy crowds gathered to watch the contests and celebrate the "winners of the Olympic games."[12]

By this time New England had cultivated a thriving sports culture despite legal prohibitions. Across the region, merchants sold packs of cards, gardeners maintained bowling greens, and innkeepers organized contests in shuffleboard, wrestling, horse races, and even cockfighting. When the Puritan leadership disapproved of certain games, their objections were based on interpreting the actions of those engaged in them. In essence, the actions of gamblers, fighters, and Sabbath breakers were seen as signaling social and spiritual disorder, facilitated by the senses that channeled the sin of unbridled passion into the bodies of participants. Conversely, archers, runners, and wrestlers embodied a joyful pursuit of physical improvement and the refinement of martial skill. The moral significance of "lawful sports," therefore, arose from the relationship between the players and the spectators, each with their own concept of time well spent.

## At Play in Pennsylvania

In September 1687, Richard Crosby found himself before a Chester, Pennsylvania, judge for the second time that year. The first instance was for public drunkenness, and this time he faced the same charge along with an additional allegation that he had challenged some men to a "cudgels" match. Cudgels was a frontier game involving two men beating each other over the head with a club until one collapsed. For these offenses, Crosby was found guilty and fined five shillings. A few years earlier, Crosby, a farmer, had emigrated from England with his wife and son, settling along the banks of the Delaware River. Apart from scattered appearances in court records, little else is known about him. He was, as described by one historian, "an average colonist" who had the misfortune of repeatedly conflicting with Pennsylvania's legal establishment.[13]

Crosby's clashes with the legal system reflected broader elements of Pennsylvania's legal structure, which took form through the Great Law of 1682—a series of statutes developed and implemented by the first legislature. The preamble proclaimed that the duty of government was to preserve "true Christianity" while guarding against "all un-Christian licentious and unjust practices." Among the activities listed in the latter category were "riotous sports" such as bullbaiting, cockfighting, and other such "breakers of the peace." Similarly, colonists were prohibited from playing "vain and evil sports" such as cards, dice, and lotteries.[14]

Much like in New England, recreations associated with violence and gambling earned disapproval from those in authority. Also similar was the fact that certain modes of play earned favor in the colony, especially those approved of by the upper classes. It was William Penn who theorized, "Man was made a noble, rational, grave creature; his pleasure stood in his duty, and his duty in obeying God." The threat to such spiritual balance was the wandering eye, which could fixate on "transitory things," as with Adam and Eve in the Garden of Eden. For Penn, the best form of "recreation" would be serving God and doing good. He did concede that in some instances bodily exercise could help one to develop "gravity, temperance and virtue." But Penn lamented that in his time, the rising generation had become fixed on recreation. "It is a mark of great stupidity," he exclaimed, adding, "Surely, those who are to reckon for every idle word, must not use sports to pass away that time, which they are commanded so diligently to redeem."[15]

Despite this spiritual lament, Penn was known to have played "athletic sports" with the Indigenous populations of Pennsylvania, one of several tactics he used to ingratiate himself with these communities. Additionally, Penn and his fellow social elites would frequently race their horses through the streets of Philadelphia—particularly along Sassafras Street, a route that would eventually be renamed Race Street.[16] Horse racing, a defining example of elite sports culture, was also part of Philadelphia's physical and moral geography. By the era of the American Revolution, the city's sporting landscape, which had been deeply influenced by a Quaker past, began to assume Enlightenment contours as well.

One significant influence in this development was the physician Benjamin Rush, a leading thinker in the American Enlightenment. Part of his project was oriented toward improving physical health. In 1771 and 1772, Rush published three sermons on this topic, the final one addressing exercise specifically. For Rush, physical movement was at the core of humankind's origin story. "Man was formed to be active," he attested. "The vigor of his mind, and the health of his body can be fully preserved by no other means than by labor of some sort." Rush developed his argument from scripture, asserting that since "the fall" humans have had to labor in order to survive. It was a punishment that revealed "the goodness of the Supreme Being." A toiling humanity would remain strong and vital into the future.[17]

Rush perceived a connection between God's design for humankind and exercise, while also recognizing that not all forms of physical movement were created equal. Walking garnered high praise as it "invigorates and strengthens the system." In contrast, he deemed running too violent and excessive, estimating that the "running footmen" of the world had short lives and poor overall health. This was due in part, in Rush's view, to their excessive sweating. The walker, in contrast, simply "perspired," a designation that Rush believed made fluid emission from the skin far more dignified and health giving. The same was true for dancing. To advance this point, Rush drew inspiration from Jewish ritual dancing, seeing it as evidence that ancient civilizations had long recognized the value of this form of physical activity. Similarly, he embraced swimming and sailing, citing Jewish and Muslim cleansing rituals as proof of ancient precedent for the beneficial effects of contact with water. For Rush, all these activities had the common benefit of invigorating the whole person. He asserted, "The PASSIONS as well as our reason should always be exercised as much as possible."[18]

Rush's sermon ended with a parable, set on the island of Ceylon in the Indian Ocean. There a group of physically challenged and chronically ill individuals were gathered around "several venerable figures" who dispensed elixirs and medicines, all made in places like America and Germany. Then thunder rumbled from the sky, and a light shown through, revealing the heavenly figure of Hygiea, goddess of health. She began by announcing, "Ye children of men, listen for a while to the voice of instruction. Ye seek health where it is not to be found." She continued, denouncing the curing claims of manufactured medicines, gesturing instead to nature and, by extension, exercise as the sources of health. Following this divine command, a man with gout cured himself by walking four to five miles each morning. Another, with digestive issues, cleared his condition by gardening for two to three hours a day. The "hysteric patients" benefited from horseback riding, while the melancholy became joyful through dance.[19]

Rush carried his message to the speakers circuit, such as in 1790, when he addressed a Methodist academy where he argued against their assorted prohibitions on play. Starting with the ancient Greeks, Rush noted that games and amusements had been rooted in military ends. This was a connection that he wanted to abolish, particularly when it came to young men. In Rush's mind, the United States had less need for combat and more for business and labor as well as citizenship. He therefore proposed physical activities that would build character and assist young men with their future. "Wars originate in error and vice. Let us eradicate these, by proper modes of education," Rush insisted, certain that any future enemies would be intuitively repelled because "they will 'find nothing in us' congenial to their malignant dispositions."[20]

Rush did not limit his prescription for exercise to young men. In a 1787 address to the Young Ladies' Academy in Philadelphia, he began by charging that a principal duty of women was watching over their husband's property. Therefore, education should aim to impart the skills in women that would help them in their domestic duties. This meant physical exercise, such as one of Rush's favorites, dancing, which, anticipating objections, he assured his audience was "an agreeable substitute for the ignoble pleasures of drinking, and gaming."[21] Just as he had used play to argue for a peaceful yet strengthened American male, he was likewise envisioning physical activity as being necessary for the homebound protectress.

Rush's enlightened and almost utopian view of sports came at the same time that the new American nation was reading British publisher John Newbery's *Little Pretty Pocket-Book.* First published in 1744, this groundbreaking book—the first of its kind created specifically for children—combined rhymes, moral lessons, and a collection of sports and games for British youth. While pirated copies came to America in the early 1760s, the first major printing was done in 1787 by Isaiah Thomas in Worcester, Massachusetts. Thus, in addition to seeing the first printed mention of "baseball," American children received an education on the supposed character-building value of sports. Through "amusements," Newbery believed, young people could learn about themselves and the world—an insight drawn and developed from the philosopher John Locke. In *Some Thoughts concerning Education,* Locke stressed the crucial role of health in the pursuit of "business and happiness," affirming specifically the importance of recreation as being "as necessary as labor or food."[22]

With Locke as his philosophical guide, Newbery aimed to develop a text for enlightened character-building that would produce children who were "strong, hardy, healthy, virtuous, wise, and happy." An impediment to such development, according to Newbery, was found in those "indulgent people" who shielded their children from hardship and challenge. He passionately urged mothers, in particular, to permit their children to play freely outdoors, asserting that "it is this that gives life and spirits, circulates the blood, strengthens the sinews, and keeps the whole machinery in order." The book also detailed various games, each accompanied by a "moral" or "rule of life." In his commentary on baseball, for instance, the author depicted a game that channeled passions in a virtuous direction, serving as an antidote to "sinful and unlawful recreations."[23]

For those like Newbery and Rush favoring Enlightenment ideals, their preferred modes of exercise meshed with a desire to build a healthy and moral republic. Democracy could survive only if its people were virtuous, and playful activities could be used to this end. For those living in the southern colonies, a similar dynamic was in play insofar as certain sports favored by the elites became how community took shape. But unlike their northern contemporaries who had ambivalent feelings about horse racing, the passion for this sport in the South was an unquestioned feature of their way of life.

## Planters at Play

In 1774, the Continental Congress pledged to "discourage every species of extravagance and dissipation," citing an assortment of blood sports and rough games, as well as "horse-racing." With war on the horizon, the intention was to place limits around how people used their time and resources. And for a New Englander in particular, these activities tended to fall outside of their moral zone of acceptability. Further south in the colonies, however, the restriction on horse racing would have hardly registered. As historian George Bancroft explained, for Virginia planters in the colonial era horses had become "an object of pride." He continued, "Speed was especially valued; and 'the planter's pace' became a proverb."[24]

Interpreters of horse racing in Virginia like Bancroft have repeatedly cited this "proverb." Writing shortly after Bancroft, one historian described "the planter's pace" by depicting riders who "made the forests echo to the clatter of flying hoofs, as well as to the sound of joyous laughter." As folklorist Wolfgang Mieder has explained, "Proverbs fulfill the human need to summarize experiences and observations into nuggets of wisdom that provide ready-made comments on personal relationships and social affairs." Some proverbs flow out of religious and cultural traditions, are inscribed into sacred texts, or are reproduced through ritual. Others, such as "the planter's pace," have emerged spontaneously through common observation and consent.[25]

In colonial Virginia, this specific proverb denoted the desired characteristics of the planter—a man of refinement who eagerly embraced the thrill of speed atop his horse. Planters were not, however, prone to exert themselves physically in any other manner. According to the Anglican minister Hugh Jones, the "common planters" mostly avoided "manly exercise." And yet they were "lovers of riding." Jones explained, "I have known some spend the morning in ranging several miles in the woods to find and catch their horses to ride only two or three miles to the church, to the courthouse or to a horserace." Horses were, therefore, an integral part of how planters did their business and conducted their lives.[26]

Jones's optimistic portrayal reflected the dominance of a planter class that had consolidated power across the colony and asserted its influence. Bacon's Rebellion of 1676 marked a high point of tension among planters, indentured servants, and surrounding Indigenous populations in the colony. Faced with instability, planters shifted to utilizing enslaved Africans for labor, as British immigration slowed and poorer White people either acquiesced to their societal position or departed. As the seventeenth century progressed, Virginia's White population coalesced around a shared identity rooted in their whiteness, which they deemed superior to both Indigenous peoples and enslaved Africans. Simultaneously, the ritual of horse racing became a symbolic expression of racial identity, occasionally intersecting with Anglicanism. In 1691, for instance, Governor Sir Francis Nicholson declared St. George's Day a time for martial games and horse races. In earlier European periods, the tale of St. George vanquishing a dragon served as a versatile metaphor for Christians contesting everything from paganism to Islam. In seventeenth-century Virginia, this allegory took a racial turn, with whiteness being celebrated through the symbolic figure of the horse and rider.[27]

When observers spoke of horse racing among the planter elites, they were not framing the sport in terms of novel competition, drunken revelry, and honor-driven gambling. Instead, they emphasized a ritual activity that expressed, asserted, and reconfirmed the values and beliefs associated with the planter class. The boundaries of this way of life took shape not only through local customs but also through the courts. In 1674, a court in York County, Virginia, fined James Bullock one hundred pounds of tobacco for arranging a horse race with one Matthew Slader. The criminal act was not the race itself. Rather, the court found fault with Bullock's social status—he was a tailor. Horse racing, the court asserted, was "a sport only for gentlemen." But the punishment did not end with Bullock. Slader was found guilty of cheating during the race, an offense that sent him to the stocks for one hour.[28]

Horse racing in Virginia was an elite White person's sport, with rules governing not only the matches themselves but also those who engaged in it.

Planters would race only their social peers, and high-stakes gambling likewise made for an atmosphere of exclusivity, as well as a representation of the risk inherent in the lives of the elite. Tobacco growers faced various challenges, including falling prices, illnesses among the laboring class and enslaved population, sunken cargo ships, and droughts—all of which could diminish profits. Horse racing, in this context, served as a ritualized representation of the daily experiences of risk endured by these individuals.[29]

Throughout this period, planters sought increased wealth and status, showcasing their prosperity through their horses. The norm for horse racing involved quarter-mile competitions on straight dirt tracks, influenced in part by the available horse breeds. In 1609, when settlers arrived in Jamestown, they brought horses, mainly Irish Hobbies and Scottish Galloways. By the century's end, a new breed called Chickasaws, originating from Spain and named after the Indigenous people who bred them, had made their way to the colony. Narragansett Pacers from Rhode Island also became part of the mix. During this phase of the sport's history, planters took pride in their riding skills and actively participated as riders on their racehorses. The absence of a designated starter was common, with competitors selecting lanes and signaling mutually to commence the race. Ideally, the start would be fair, both participants reaching the start line simultaneously. Interference during the race was strongly discouraged, though complaints about fairness had become ingrained in the sport. Planters frequently voiced grievances in public and even in courts, addressing issues ranging from false starts to unexpected obstacles like dogs on the course. In a notable 1690 case, William Soane brought Robert Napier to court for failing to participate in a race they had agreed upon. James Blair, an Anglican clergyman who later founded and became president of the College of William & Mary, served as a key witness. Blair leveraged his priestly status to add moral credibility to Soane's case, and ultimately Soane emerged victorious. The court viewed an agreement to race as a sacred compact, emphasizing the seriousness with which such agreements were treated.[30]

With such interest and intensity surrounding the sport, it was only a matter of time before mythologies—sacred stories of origin, in particular—began to emerge. In histories of horse racing, 1730 would become a break in time, a moment when the entire world of horse racing fundamentally changed. At the center of this mythology was a breeding horse known as Bulle Rock—"boon companion"—who arrived in Virginia that year from England. In the words of one twentieth-century history, "Some authorities insist that Bulle Rock . . . was the Christopher Columbus of the equine tribe." As the legend goes, Samuel Gist arranged to import the horse from England by way of a three-month-long boat trip across the Atlantic. At twenty-one years old, the thoroughbred was far past his racing prime, but he could still sire a generation of horses in Virginia. The ensuing success of Bulle Rock's offspring sparked a trend, leading to an influx of English thoroughbreds being brought to the American colonies in the following decades. With larger and stronger horses resulting from this breeding experiment, racetracks lengthened and became oval shaped. Also, jockey clubs formed throughout Virginia, in Petersburg, Fredericksburg, Portsmouth, Dumfries, and elsewhere. Meanwhile, interpreters of horse racing would write Bulle Rock into Virginia's racing myth of origin. "We know Bulle Rock only as a name," wrote Charles Trevathan. "He is to us now only the first race horse to come."[31]

The empty space in Bulle Rock's history opened room for imaginations to fill the gaps. A nineteenth-century account reminisced about a quarter-mile race in Brunswick, Virginia, held roughly a century earlier, where two competing racehorse owners—one from Virginia and the other from North Carolina—recognized that Bulle Rock was on the verge of fundamentally transforming the horse racing landscape. With spectators lining the entire distance, the riders mounted, and after three passes the horses took off "with the velocity of lightning." The crowd was transfixed, the only noise the galloping of the horses. The Virginia planter came away victorious, but not without complaints of an unfair start. The event became part of a bittersweet drama that would live on, even though quarter-mile races would not.[32]

As the years passed, turf enthusiasts marveled at every feature of the horses they wagered on, watched, and cheered. In the pre-revolutionary years, the English import Filmnap became a major attraction in the southern colonies. Commenting on the horse in 1773, Josiah Quincy observed Filmnap standing alongside "a file collection of excellent, though high-priced, horses." Just the sight of the horse, wrote Quincy, was an experience of "the singular art and mystery of the turf." Outsiders couldn't help but take notice of the fervor around horse racing. In 1773, Philip Fithian came to Virginia to tutor the sons of Robert Carter III. He was astounded by the "loud disputes" that would erupt between and within families over horses and horse racing. Fithian would try in these instances to shift the conversation away from the sport. He exclaimed, "I was seldom heard," unless they wanted him to adjudicate a dispute, which would always disappoint his questioners. Fithian concluded, "How different the manners of the people! I try to be as cheerful as I can, and yet I am blamed for being stupid as a Nun."[33]

Englishman John F. D. Smyth had similar observations. He toured the colonies in the early 1770s, before publishing an account that he admitted would be "descending to the minutia" of daily life among those he encountered. Critics charged Smyth with taking liberties with the truth, for making his account intentionally fanciful. He wrote, for example, of a snake "charming" a bird into its mouth, relaying a folk story as if it were fact. Still, the traveler's descriptions of horse racing did convey a sense that this sport had shaped a unique culture in the region. He announced, "The Virginians, of all ranks and denominations are excessively fond of horses, and especially those of the race breed." From gentlemen to "the most indigent person," all possess and treasure their horses. Put simply, "their horses are their pleasure, and their pride."[34]

Smyth was one of many observers of Virginia who understood horse racing as being central to the region's identity. After the war, with jockey clubs springing up throughout the southern states, the idea of horse racing as a way of life extended beyond Virginia's borders. In 1791, the South Carolina Jockey Club formed just as races resumed on the Newmarket Course in Charleston. This was the era, according to Charles Trevathan, when South Carolina experienced a "golden age of racing." For the historian, race week in Charleston was a communal celebration marked by a "universal interest pervading all classes." The author depicted the event as a truly liminal affair, wherein the cares of daily life gave way to "the care of the horses" and there was a "total disregard of the value of time, except by the competitors in the races." Additionally, he saw in race week a distinct "moral influence" insofar as the scene at the track was one of "good morals," "order," "sobriety," and "good fellowship." What gambling existed was secondary to a love of horses and horse racing, all of which made race week "the carnival of the state."[35]

From North to South during the colonial and revolutionary eras, sports gave people a means for considering what kind of society they wanted to create. The egalitarian portrait of race week painted by Trevathan depicted the pure joy of the races as embodying democratic ideals. His account, though, contained a notable omission: a population that did not enjoy the freedoms of America. But as slavery grew and developed in the southern states, so too did the role of enslaved people in the sport of horse racing. Specifically, planters stepped away from the saddle, and Black jockeys took their place. In

North Carolina, planter Willie Jones turned to his enslaved servant Austin Curtis to jockey and train horses. Curtis made his name in the quarter-mile event, sometimes gaming opponents to gain an edge. By all reports, Jones and Curtis were inseparable when they traveled. In 1791, Jones petitioned the North Carolina General Assembly to free Curtis, emphasizing that Curtis had remained loyal to America even though England pledged emancipation to enslaved people who joined their cause. The request was granted, but this one case would not necessarily set a precedent. Enslaved people would become co-laborers on the track in one respect, but never truly equals. In this way, the sport reinforced the institution of slavery as it contributed to shaping the concept of racial identity in America.[36] This dynamic would also unfold in another popular sport of the era: prizefighting.

# 3
# American Heroes

"Oh Washington! Thou Hero, Patriot, Sage," proclaimed a Boston newspaper announcing the death of George Washington in 1799. For a relatively new nation, the idea of Washington had powerful symbolic currency. He was called the "Father of Our Country" even before he died; people named their children after him; and it was common to see Washington's name near biblical figures like Moses and Joshua. In time, this mythology took visual form. In 1832, Congress commissioned a sculpture from Horatio Greenough that, once finished in 1840, showed a bare-chested Washington, with his right hand pointing heavenward in a clear hearkening to the god Zeus. Then there was Constantino Brumidi's 1865 fresco on the dome of the rotunda of the U.S. Capitol known as *The Apotheosis of Washington*. Here the godlike figure of Washington gazes down from the heavens, flanked by Roman deities.[1]

To his admirers, Washington embodied both America's inaugural president and its first hero, his story crafted as a blend of courage and virtue, fostering a sense of unity in the diverse American nation. However, amid the grandeur of marble sculptures and lofty proclamations, the lives and labor of the enslaved people who contributed to the nation's construction often went unnoticed.

While it may be tempting to view Washington's narrative as emblematic of *the* American myth of origin, such a perspective risks sidelining alternative voices shaping heroes and sacred stories. In the early years of America, as narratives around Washington and his counterparts evolved, Black boxers and their interpreters constructed a distinct vision of what America was and could be. In bouts primarily hosted in England, this mythology placed Black Americans at the forefront, elevating them as a unique form of hero. Consequently, Black boxers engaged in overseas fights symbolized an America where the White majority refused to acknowledge the full humanity of these athletes.

*Bodies in Motion*. Arthur Remillard, Oxford University Press. © Oxford University Press 2025.
DOI: 10.1093/oso/9780197789766.003.0004

## "The Hero of the Black World"

Writing in and around London in the early nineteenth century, Pierce Egan pioneered a novel form of journalism, one that lifted sports into the literary limelight. His task was to go beyond merely documenting events, opting to describe the athletes, crowds, and happenings as elements of epic contests with meaningful consequences. Among his favorite sports was prizefighting, which was at once illegal in London and at the same time wildly popular. In previous generations, prizefighting lingered in the margins of acceptability. But by the mid-eighteenth century it had gained a measure of mainstream appeal, particularly when the "Father of Boxing," Jack Broughton, implemented the sport's first set of rules in 1743, which limited wrestling, declared that a round would continue until one person was knocked down, allowed thirty seconds for a downed fighter to arise and "square off" against his opponent, and banned hitting a grounded opponent. While there were no similar written instructions for audiences, there were several unwritten rules, mostly related to gambling. Fixed fights were common, as were unscrupulous referees who would make calls favoring one fighter or another, sometimes based on which side's share of the crowd seemed rowdier and more threatening.[2]

The colorful and unpredictable world of bare-knuckle prizefighting was equal parts control and chaos, refined and brutish, and elegant and awkward. Egan, who called this sport "the sweet science," was keen on finding outliers among the outliers—people like Bill Richmond, who Egan called "the Hero of the Black World." Born into slavery on Staten Island, New York, in 1763, Richmond was enslaved by a local divine, Reverend Charlton. According to legend, when Richmond pummeled some British soldiers in a bar, he caught the attention of Brigadier General Hugh Percy, who persuaded Charlton to release Richmond. Percy then took Richmond on as a servant and later set him free in London to learn the trade of cabinetmaking. Richmond didn't start boxing until he was in his forties, and despite his age and relatively diminutive size (he was estimated to weigh between 140 and 147 pounds), he defeated numerous men larger than he. For followers of prizefighting, Richmond became "the Black Terror."[3]

Eagan delighted in promoting a suitably terrifying, yet also gentlemanly, image of Richmond. Recounting a fight in 1814, Egan described the opening scene, with Richmond's opponent refusing to shake hands, attempting to gain a mental advantage. Richmond, however, was only empowered by the snub. Eagan warned, "Impetuous men must not fight Richmond, as in his hands they become victim to their own temerity." The fight found Richmond dominating the entire thirteen rounds, ending with an especially powerful punch that rendered his opponent unconscious. Richmond celebrated by effortlessly leaping over the five-foot-high rope, a physical feat that would become the boxer's trademark exit in future fights.[4]

In Egan's portrayal, Richmond emerged not only as an effective fighter and representative of America but also as a groundbreaking hero who stood up against English racial prejudice. In the aftermath of one of Richmond's more decisive victories, Egan noted that some of the locals remained unimpressed with the Black American. One evening a blacksmith hurled "opprobrious epithets" at Richmond in the street and proceeded to violently kick him on the thigh. In response, Richmond challenged the blacksmith to a match the next morning, but the blacksmith declined, acknowledging Richmond's superior fighting skills. Another challenge to Richmond's honor occurred when an agitator labeled him a "black devil" while he walked down a London street with a White woman, who was the recipient of additional insults. Richmond promptly challenged the agitator to a match the next morning. The news spread rapidly, and a large crowd gathered at the contest site the following morning. While Richmond was prepared to fight, his opponent was nowhere to be found. Undeterred, Richmond and the crowd tracked down the man, who had sought refuge in a brothel. He was coaxed into the ring, where Richmond proceeded to give him a thorough pummeling.[5]

Richmond, arguably at the peak of his prizefighting career, saw his ascent come to a sharp halt on October 8, 1805, when he faced England's top fighter, Tom Cribb. Outsized and outmatched, Richmond lost in what Egan concluded "could scarcely be called a fight."[6] Few details remain, but both fighters were counterpunchers, which likely meant that the match was reduced to a series of tentative engagements. Regardless, even though Richmond's career was in its later stages, he continued fighting after the Cribb match, remaining, in Egan's words, among the "first-rate heroes of the milling art." When Richmond finally did retire, according to Egan, the "taunts and insults" continued to follow the fighter, who in the face of it remained "good-tempered and placid" as well as "intelligent, communicative, and well-behaved."[7]

In Egan's view, Richmond was an American hero even though he never fought in America and barely received notice in his homeland. Still, Egan's printed words created the idea of this American, whose intelligence, industriousness, and physical gifts gained him popular notice. In 1821, Richmond was one of eighteen ushers at the coronation of King George IV, all of them pugilists. Richmond was fifty-seven at the time, still in superb physical condition, and the lone Black man of the group. For a king attempting to capitalize on the image of manhood and strength associated with prizefighting, Richmond served a useful function of embodying this message. When Richmond died, several eulogists sang his praises, including Cribb, who, while unable to attend the funeral, penned a glowing oration for his former rival and eventual friend.[8]

The funeral demonstrated that Richmond had gained considerable celebrity in England, something that was unimaginable in America at the time. He was also instrumental in building up another Black hero, one who arguably gained even more notoriety in England, even though a controversial loss punctuated his story.

## "Forbid It, Heaven—Forbid It, Man!"

According to boxing historian Nat Fleischer, Tom Molineaux first made his mark by boxing his way to freedom. The story goes that in 1801, the planter Algeron Molineaux announced to his enslaved population that he would grant freedom to anyone who could defeat a fighter from a neighboring plantation. Tom Molineaux, whose father was also a prizefighter, stepped forward and eagerly accepted the challenge. When the day came, he dispatched his opponent in five quick rounds. For his efforts, Algeron provided the fighter with not only his freedom but also a portion of the earnings from the fight. With his newfound freedom and money in hand, Tom Molineaux left Virginia to find prizefighting glory in New York City.[9]

The accuracy of this story is questionable at best. Plantation prizefights between enslaved people were a common trope in Black and southern White folklore, including William Faulkner's novel *Absalom, Absalom!* Molineaux's specific story as rendered by Fleischer was likely the product of a notoriously embellished history of prizefighting by Fred Henning. But the historical record does confirm that in around 1809, Molineaux arrived in New York as a free Black person. There he worked as a porter and dockworker, while gaining notice as a fighter in the Catherine Market area, a busy port where sailors eagerly watched and gambled on these brutal and often impromptu contests. Molineaux quickly earned the title "Champion of America," before deciding to seek bigger purses and wider fame in England.[10]

Egan enthusiastically sought to shape the narrative of this emerging boxer, writing, "*Distance* created no obstacles, nor did the raging seas pose an impediment to his heroic views." In Egan's rendering, Molineaux arrived in London in 1809 as a figure who was "unknown, unnoticed, unprotected, and uninformed." But he soon began training with Richmond, and together they issued a public challenge to all contenders. During this phase of Richmond's life, he had transitioned from the ring to a role as a trainer and promoter, using his Horse and Dolphin Tavern as a hub of operations. Egan noted that as a prizefighting mentor, Richmond had developed a sophisticated training philosophy focused on the "preservation of bodies," an approach that eschewed brute strength in favor of emphasizing "dexterity and science" in the ring. This philosophy, as asserted by Egan, ultimately contributed to making Molineaux a more effective prizefighter.[11]

Molineaux continued gaining notice and attention when, on August 21, 1810, the fighter took seventeen minutes and eight rounds to defeat the sailor "Tough Tom" Blake. By the fifth round, Blake was bleeding so profusely that, one account reported, "the ground resembled the floor of a slaughter-house." In Blake's corner was Cribb, England's current champion, who had gone into semi-retirement. The fight and Cribb's presence fueled speculation of a match with Molineaux. Cribb was reluctant to return to the ring, but he certainly didn't want an American and a Black man to take the championship. Molineaux, meanwhile, was reportedly reveling in his fame. Decked out in the finest clothes, he was known to amble around London with a pair of women on his arms. All of this was enough to evoke a combination of awe and intrigue among prizefighting enthusiasts in London. In Egan's words, Molineaux's brashness, race, and nationality had led the boxing public to collectively exclaim when imagining him as champion, "Forbid it, heaven—forbid it, man!"[12]

With public momentum building against Molineaux's rise, the prizefighting public agreed that Cribb was the only person who could preserve the title. Thus the two agreed to meet in the ring on December 18, 1810. During the buildup, Cribb had every advantage that a fighter of his time could want: he trained at the secluded estate of his wealthy sponsor, allowing him to focus single-mindedly on the fight. Molineaux, in contrast, traveled and staged sparring exhibitions, building on his celebrity while at the same time drawing taunts from antagonists. Egan surmised that despite Molineaux's public persona, all the public scorn and scrutiny took its toll on the boxer.[13]

On the day that Molineaux and Cribb finally met, the weather would factor into the outdoor contest, as the conditions were a mix of freezing rain, bitter cold, and wind. Still, an estimated ten thousand spectators surrounded the ring, some standing in mud up to their knees. The fight, according to Egan, was a matter of "national concern." What happened next remains the subject of historical debate. The conventional account would claim that Molineaux was near victory, repeatedly pounding Cribb's head, when the crowd broke into the ring. Members of the mob then pried Molineaux's fingers from Cribb's head, breaking the boxer's fingers in the process. Meanwhile, Cribb was on the ground, unconscious and not moving. But the extra time allowed him to recover and resume the fight. A few rounds later, Cribb was again depleted and seemingly unable to continue. To delay, one of Cribb's seconds accused Molineaux of carrying bullets in his fists, leading to an inspection of the boxer's hands and even more time for Cribb to recover. At this point, according to one observer, "[t]he two men were so dreadfully beaten that their sight was altogether lost, and their bodies were in the most emaciated state." Finally, after nearly an hour of fighting, Molineaux hit his head on a post and exclaimed, "I can fight no more."[14]

In the years to come, this account of bloodshed and chicanery would portray Molineaux as the victim of racial and national prejudice. However, while several news reports thoroughly covered the fight, none mentioned the ring disturbance or the fight stoppage. A five-page report printed in the *Sporting Magazine* even concluded that "the strictest fair play was shown to both parties throughout." What's more, when Molineaux wrote to Cribb requesting a rematch, he made no mention of his unfair treatment. Instead, Molineaux listed the weather as contributing to his loss, claiming that the English native Cribb had an environmental advantage since he was accustomed to the cold and rain. It wasn't until the rematch was set that a newspapers near the fight's projected location, drawing on "whispers" from abroad, printed an account of the crowd rushing the ring. Egan also told this version of the story—ten months after the fight.[15]

Cribb and Molineaux did have a rematch on September 28, 1811. According to one report, a "fearful anxiety" animated the crowd of twenty thousand. But after a furious start, Molineaux tired, and by the eighth round Cribb took control and broke his opponent's jaw. The fight lasted a mere nineteen minutes and ten seconds. As one observer summarized, "It has been a matter of surprise to many of the amateurs, that the Moor should have been beat so quick."[16]

While Cribb entered the ring in superb physical condition, Molineaux had let his fitness decline—a decline that would continue after the fight. Molineaux faced three more boxers, each one finding him less effective than the one before. In 1815, he went to Ireland to teach boxing and host exhibitions. By this point, according to Egan, "his personal appearance . . . was little more than a skeleton, compared to his once fine athletic form." Finally, in 1818 at the age of thirty-four, Molineaux died penniless in a storage closet from liver failure. Despite that inglorious end, Egan had little difficulty in remembering Molineaux as an "American hero." In eulogizing the athlete, Egan remembered the fighter first coming to London: "His frame was perfectly Herculean; and his bust, the best judges of anatomical beauty, considered a perfect picture. It was a model for a statuary."[17]

In elevating Molineux to hero status, Egan produced an American mythology that was quite unlike anything in the United States. Molineaux's body was that of the fighter, the model of manliness that used strength and cunning to defeat opponents. But he also was fighting racial and national barriers—his skin color and homeland made him a perpetual outsider, so much so that thousands of people literally refused to let him win. Initially, White audiences in America paid scant attention to the fighter's overseas exploits. The first significant history of prizefighting in America was published in 1949 and made no mention of Molineaux. But the boxer's image and legacy lived on in popular lore. In 1820 just outside Farnham, New York, crowds began arriving at 6:00 a.m. to see the fight between Hampshire's Fred Strong, a blacksmith and accomplished fighter, and "the New Black from Baltimore." Stories of the latter fighter's ability had been circulating, making prizefighting fans curious to see him in the ring, as promoters called him "the rival of the celebrated Molineaux." The fight lasted forty-two minutes, the Baltimorean dropping to the ground after a stiff right hand to the throat.[18]

Despite the loss, this fight demonstrated that the memory of Molineaux had come to represent the very idea of Black boxing—which, depending on the interpreter, could symbolize excellence or social disorder. In 1910, a full one hundred years after Cribb fought Molineaux, the prizefighting world focused its attention on another interracial match between the champion Jack Johnson and the "great white hope" Jim Jeffries. Some White commentators used the occasion to look back at Cribb's fight against Molineaux, rendering

Cribb the ultimate gentleman fighter, known for his unassuming presence and unquestioned dominance. Molineaux, in this telling of the story, was the complete opposite: brash, undisciplined, and uncouth. "The situation was somewhat similar to that now existing between Jeffries and Johnson," resolved one author. "Cribb was called upon to uphold the supremacy of the race in the ring."[19]

For this White observer, Molineaux's memory became a means for heralding racial supremacy, a condition which many in White America believed was a necessity for social order to exist. For scores of Black boxers, however, the idea of Molineaux was one of racial pride and strength. In 1930, John Henry Lewis, the light heavyweight champion, claimed that Molineaux was his great-great-great-uncle, before reciting the standard account of the fighter punching his way to freedom.[20]

Memories of Molineaux the hero and Molineaux the villain fueled a discourse on race and sports in American life from the earliest years of the nation and onward. All the while, there was a sacred dimension to this story that was not unlike the stories told by White audiences about George Washington. Both are remembered as heroic conquerors, who overcame all obstacles along the way. To be sure, Washington wasn't White America's only hero, as sports also became a place for this population to concentrate on the sacred matters of heroism, beauty, and public morality. Nowhere was this more evident than in horse racing, as thousands of mostly urban dwellers clamored to witness the "sport of kings."

## The Heroic Distance

On the evening of August 8, 1824, a crowd of spectators paid the fifty-cent admission to Vauxhall Garden in New York to witness the launching of a balloon. Throughout America's cities, "balloonomania" was all the rage. Originating in France and England, this new fascination with balloons had developed out of a broader collective interest in modernity, science, and innovation. It was also an opportunity to celebrate prosperity, as evidenced by the atmosphere at Vauxhall Garden, which was extravagant, festive, and vibrant, with "splendid rockets" and music giving triumphant sights and sounds to the event. The crowd cheered when the balloon launched, traveling for fifteen minutes and landing approximately ten miles away in Brooklyn. Everything about the event was thoroughly New York in orientation, right down to the balloon itself. Named "Eclipse," the balloon resembled a horse and rider, evoking images of both a mounted ancient Greek hero as well as the more recent thoroughbred named American Eclipse and his jockey Samuel Purdy. One year earlier, this duo won a match race that drew unprecedented attention in New York and beyond. "Eclipse against the world!" became the enduring tagline of this race, repeated at the balloon launch as a way of melding the identity of New York with the sport of horse racing.[21]

This identity took shape, at least in part, through opposition. Eclipse's opponent on that day in 1823 at the Union Course was Sir Henry, who was trained by the Virginian William R. Johnson. The South had a reputation for breeding and racing the top horses in the country, and Johnson was a leader in this enterprise. In New York, Cornelius Van Ranst was the horse racing upstart who brought Eclipse to fame, amassing an undefeated record and routinely humiliating the South's finest horses. But he hadn't beaten Johnson. Doing so would solidify Van Ranst's reputation as a standard-bearer not only for his sport but for his region as well.[22]

Adding to the drama and intrigue of this race was the specific distance of their contest. While short, one-off races had a place in the sport, racing enthusiasts preferred events that featured speed and endurance (or "bottom"), like the "Heroic Distance"—a best-of-three contest, with four-mile heats separated by thirty-minute intervals. The language of heroism permeated every aspect of this race, capturing the attention of racing enthusiasts in the North and South. On race day, approximately twenty thousand southerners traveled north, contributing to a record-breaking crowd of sixty thousand at the track. The sheer number of spectators was unprecedented for the time. Sir Henry easily won the first race convincingly, creating a crisis for the northern audience and Eclipse's handlers. The blame was largely directed at the jockey, who had nearly fallen off the horse during the final mile. Recognizing the need for a change, Eclipse's handlers turned to Samuel Purdy, who was seated in the stands. A veteran jockey and a White man of means with significant status in horse racing circles and New York City, Purdy had originally been Eclipse's rider. However, the trainers had replaced him with a younger jockey, believing youth would give them an edge. After Eclipse's loss in the first race, the team realized their mistake, rushed into the stands, and begged the aggrieved Purdy to remount—not just to secure a victory, but to represent New York and the North. Purdy, who had conveniently attended the event dressed in his racing gear, answered the call and, after mounting Eclipse, went on to secure victories in the final two heats. Describing the final scene, turf historian Hamilton Busbey exclaimed, "[T]he North was exultant, while Southern hearts felt sore, and Southern pride was humbled."[23]

And yet at the time commentators repeatedly emphasized the uniqueness of the event, and specifically the crowd and its good-natured response to both winning and losing. Despite the potential for disorder, one account claimed that there were no major accidents or disturbances. In fact, after the race, many of the southern visitors gathered at a pavilion with the northerners for a "splendid dinner." At the conclusion of the meal, attendees toasted the event and each other, and the southerners departed having accepted the loss in good spirits. "Thus has ended the great match between the North and South—the last of the kind, we hope, we shall ever hear of." Another account made a similar claim: "The losers kept their temper; the winners subdued their expressions of triumph, and all united in admiration of the speed and bottom of the two coursers." And even though the Virginia congressman John Randolph lost $1,000 on the race, he was willing to praise Purdy from the floor of Congress.[24]

The reasoned response to victory and defeat, though, was a privilege of those who had means. Numerous accounts appeared in the press about gamblers losing everything and even committing suicide. Public laments and jeremiads on decadence and wastefulness followed. "Never did a case happen before, perhaps, in which state pride was so much at stake," exclaimed the *Niles' Weekly Register* in Baltimore. "The money expended or lost, and time wasted on the occasion, is not far short in its value of half the cost of cutting the Erie Canal." The *New York Commercial Advertiser* added, "We should regret to see another heat run in this country on which such sums of money depend." And from the *Baltimore Patriot*, one columnist wrote, "Horses may run, and candidates for office may appear on the political turf, but let not the contest be between the men and horses of North, South, East, and West, but between merits and talents."[25]

The emotional, material, and financial resources surrounding this race revealed its deep significance. While more races between northern and southern horses would take place in the coming years, this one would become *the race* that endured in popular memory. In the years after the Civil War, commentators told stories of Eclipse and Sir Henry as a tragic prelude to sectional conflict, connecting the vicarious animosities on the turf to the blood-soaked battlefields of war. Consequently, horse racing played an active role in the making of American regionalism. But there were other sports that did similar work of binding together collections of people through stylized references to heroes and heroism. In the South, one such pastime involved a horse, a rider, and a goose.

## "The Hero of the Country"

"Reader, do you know what a gander-pulling is?" asked the narrator in William Gilmore Simms's 1852 novel, *As Good as a Comedy.* While frequently celebratory of the South and its people, Simms, himself from Charleston, South Carolina, took an unfavorable view of "gander pulling," a contest wherein mounted riders would charge at a live dangling goose in an effort to snatch its head from its body. In Simms's description of one event, the scene was made by gambling, bloodshed, and rural ignorance. And, to his dismay, the eventual human victor of the event became "the hero of the country." But this was a hero who, in the author's mind, represented all that was wrong with those who occupied the countryside. "Man is undoubtedly a beast, unless you contrive some process for making him a gentleman," Simms lamented, calling gander pulling "one of those sports which a cunning devil has contrived to gratify a human beast."[26]

Other descriptions of gander pulling from nineteenth-century observers echoed Simms's conclusions, gawking at this grizzly spectacle and leveling moral judgment on the passions associated with it. In his *Georgia Scenes,* which was first published in 1835, the southern humorist and writer Augustus B. Longstreet imagined a gander pulling event in rural Georgia between the two "rival towns" of Harrisburg and Springfield. Longstreet intentionally framed the contest in terms of competing political ideologies, the former embodying federalist values, while the latter "espoused the State Rights' creed." In the end, none of the high-minded philosophies of the day won out. Instead, the contest exemplified sheer tumult and disarray, illustrated by the presence of a few women "from the most destitute backgrounds" among the unruly crowd of men. The winner was the uncouth "Fat John Fulger," who won through a stroke of luck, riding his horse "Slouch." For the author, the contest's hero was a suitable proxy for that side of society that was guided by ignorance and unvirtuous behavior.[27]

For Longstreet and Simms, both southerners, gander pulling and the ironic "heroes" of the sport were a means for critiquing the social problems that they believed needed attention and correction. Specifically, each located these structural flaws within the lower classes. Others of their class and stature agreed. A review of *Georgia Scenes* in the *Southern Literary Messenger* called gander pulling "a piece of unprincipled barbarity not unfrequently practiced in the South and West." The author punctuated this point by labeling the crowd a "mob of vagabonds," and competitors "ragamuffins," "villains," and "human devils." Their adulation of the "heroes" of gander pulling was only further evidence of their supposed depravity.[28]

Equally disparaging were accounts of southern gander pulling from northern sources. Only here descriptions of headless geese became a vehicle for advancing the broader rivalry between the sections. "Don't start, gentle reader," announced a Vermont newspaper. "We don't mean to offend 'ears polite,' but simply desire to give you an idea of Southern refinement." The author had read about gander pulling in a book published in 1815 but reasoned that this was a mere fable. Then, while traveling through a northern Georgia town on the Fourth of July, he witnessed this show of "Southern character." The crowd of three hundred to four hundred was made up of all corners of society, eagerly anticipating the arrival of "the hero of the day," which was the "large, powerful, well-proportioned gander, that looked as if he had been the monarch of a thousand gooseponds." The contest started, but several riders were unable to win the prize. When one man finally stripped the beleaguered goose of its head, the crowd gave a wild cheer and continued the revelry at a nearby tavern. Meanwhile, the headless gander hung behind on its post, "a frightful monument of human barbarity." Disgusted, the author left the scene, exclaiming, "[S]corned, hated, detested, loathed, was that region of God's earth, which was covered with such unutterable moral darkness!"[29]

In other northern accounts of gander pulling, authors expressly tethered what they saw as a morally disordered sport to the institution of slavery. In delineating "the morals or rather immorals" of the people he met in slaveholding states, one abolitionist claimed that while traveling through Alabama, he met a "Methodist gentleman" who spoke fondly of a gander pulling contest. The southerner was unphased by the fact that two men were killed in the mayhem surrounding the event. Charles Grandison Parsons developed a similar critique of the South and the "amusements" of its people. A physician from Maine, Parsons was a committed abolitionist who traveled through the South from 1852 to 1853. Irony marked his recollection of a particular contest, during which he observed an inebriated crowd engaging in unrestrained gambling, transforming the "victim of the sport" into a "hero." Underlining the perceived cultural backwardness of the region, he pointed out that gambling was considered "an open profession" in the South, with a status "as honorable and as respectable as the profession of law or medicine."[30]

In this northern account, gander pulling depicted a perceived state of southern rural degeneracy at every level of society and not, as southern sources did, just with the lower classes. Speaking before a gathering of New Yorkers, one minister recalled arriving at a rural Georgia village in the 1840s to take up his first post. On his first Sunday in the village, the churches were empty, while townspeople gathered at the grogshop for a gander pulling contest. "It is an amusement peculiar to the South," the minister explained, himself horrified by the gruesome scene, rowdiness, spirituous liquors, and ample gambling. While this was a community gathered in celebration, the minister found their moral norms to be utterly intolerable. Undeterred, he began his ministry, and before too long all the mayhem had given way to "a Christian congregation, which gives great promise of strength and future usefulness." A New York newspaper covering the minister's talk praised his skillful application of "preaching and praying." The author wondered if the minister could do the same in New York, where they had "wire pullers" instead of gander pullers. The term referred to the manipulators of politics, the behind-the-scenes actors who held undue influence on elected officials. Turning this population into "honest citizens" would be a high charge for the accomplished minister.[31]

With gander pulling deconstructing an image of the chivalrous South, the specter of this contest and its "heroes" in the North served as symbols of how a region defined by slaveholding had a rotted moral core. Not all abolitionists took this line, though. William Wells Brown was born into slavery in Kentucky; in 1834 at the age of twenty, he escaped and made his way to Boston, where he became a noted abolitionist. Writing of his former home, he described gander pulling as a festive and unifying event, the crowds comprising the entire community—men and women of all social classes. The viewers also shared a common conversation, one focused on the speed of the rider as well as shared values like fairness. The heroes of the event, in other words, truly did embody a certain virtuous character that was praiseworthy and venerated. And the goose itself was also an object of praise, especially when it demonstrated "far more sagacity than its torturers." As Brown explained, "After having its head caught once or twice, the gander would draw up its head, or dodge out of the way."[32]

Brown's opposition to slavery did not preclude him from finding value in gander pulling. It was, for him, an opportunity to witness excellence and create a sense of communal belonging. Others shared such sentiments. For example, an 1836 description theorized that the contest was "well calculated to exhibit the dexterity and agility of the equestrian." Another described a father having "the happiest day of his life" upon witnessing his son claim victory in a contest, becoming a local hero as a result. Indeed, the language of "honor" aided admirers in elevating the stature of this sporting event. A Richmond, Virginia, newspaper in 1854 proclaimed that while some might define "civilization" as the railroad, steamboat, telegraph, and gas, the tournament was a true measure of civilization, marked by "Knights, Heralds, Queens of Beauty and Maids of Honor." The author took solace that no one left seriously harmed or injured. While the ring and lance portion of the tournaments had a featured place, the author reserved notice for "the ancient and stirring sport of gander-pulling." Here skill, dexterity, and honor were on high display for the entire community to watch and admire.[33]

In the years after the Civil War, gander pulling would become little more than a curious relic of a plantation past, giving way to euphemisms like "a goose hung high" while also evoking moral tensions about the proper place of passion in popular contests. At a fair in Nashville, Tennessee, in 1873, organizers revived the gander pulling contest after a forty-year lull. Staged as an "Old South tournament," knights charged at the goose as a large crowd encouraged them down the runway. Once a victor claimed his "trophy," some cheered vigorously for their new hero, "while others, particularly the ladies, thought it was really cruel."[34]

As a sport in the American South, gander pulling left a mark on the moral, communal, and aesthetic imagination of those who engaged in it as competitors and observers. It also was one unique way that people constructed a sense of place through the heroic (or villainous) deeds of the participants. The idea of "the South" was both a place on a map as well as a dynamic collection of values and beliefs. A similar process was at work on a larger scale with the more popular sports of the era, such as prizefighting and horse racing. For the latter sport, racetracks became increasingly significant as the nineteenth century continued, both humans and horses competing before large gatherings of enchanted spectators. The strides of the heroes of these sports became the material for interpreters to generate colorful mythologies and turn sports passion into profit.

# 4

# On Humans and Horses

In the aftermath of the Panic of 1837, C. S. Browning actively sought unique and profitable ideas for his Hoboken, New Jersey, racetrack known as the Beacon Course. In addition to traditional horse races, Browning annually featured a series of "athletic sports," including walking, running, wrestling, and leaping. Initially these events struggled to generate revenue, but they laid the groundwork for something that would capture widespread attention a few years later. In 1844, Browning orchestrated the inaugural footrace in a series between runners from England and America, tapping into the ongoing sports rivalry between the two nations. Adding to the event's intrigue was one of the American competitors: John Steeprock, a Seneca from Buffalo.[1]

News reports made ample reference to Steeprock as one of the Americans in the race, but more pointedly as a "wild Indian." This part of his identity would be accentuated through commentary on his physical form. "He runs on a lope and as if he was going through under-brush, frequently bouncing sideways as if jumping a fallen tree," described one observer. When the race began, Steeprock took the lead, much to the delight of the young men in the crowd. But as the miles passed, he slipped behind the front pack and ultimately finished in fourth place. Still, news reports gave outsized attention to Steeprock, who would go on to use this moment to gather more fame in the coming years. Along the way, commentaries on his body emphasized his seemingly natural inclination toward distance running. In 1847, Steeprock ran alone on a track in Batavia, Illinois, with the intent of setting a record at the five-mile distance. One news report read, "Throughout the whole race Steeprock, gave not the slightest appearance of fatigue or effort." The account continued, claiming that his appearance remained fresh after the race: "Instead of sitting down and resting himself, as would have been quite natural for 'a white man,' he continued standing, or walking quietly about as he usually does at home."[2]

Steeprock's story as told by White Americans tapped into a long-standing mythology of the Indigenous person as a "natural runner." This recurring narrative, which had resonance with French philosopher Jean-Jacques

*Bodies in Motion*. Arthur Remillard, Oxford University Press. © Oxford University Press 2025.
DOI: 10.1093/oso/9780197789766.003.0005

Rousseau's "noble savage" myth, began with an assumption that Indigenous people who were untouched by civilization had an inborn advantage in activities involving strength and endurance. This trait was often used in a subtle rebuke of Western decadence, portraying Indigenous people as an ideal to be emulated for supposedly avoiding the deteriorating effects of civilization on White bodies. Anthropologist Walter Hough developed such a conclusion, praising the "graceful movements" of the Hopi runner, going on to state, "Divested of civilized garb, and as a winged Mercury flying with messages to the good beings, he is an object to be gazed on with admiration." Hough's reference to Greek mythology further emphasized that, in his view, the extraordinary nature of these athletes' bodies stemmed from their presumed "primitive" origin and lifestyle.[3]

By the nineteenth century, the "natural runner" mythology and its various entanglements with sacred matters settled into figures like Steeprock, who participated in an emerging entertainment-based athletic culture in America and England. Importantly, these Indigenous sports heroes deliberately played into the mythology, presenting themselves in a way that they knew White audiences would find appealing. Indeed, interpreters and participants made the movements on racetracks into something meaningful and profitable. One especially noteworthy runner who fit into this story was another Seneca known simply as Deerfoot.

## "A Fine Specimen of the Forest"

While Lewis Bennett might not have been a familiar name to many American sports enthusiasts, the moniker "Deerfoot" certainly was. His story began in the 1850s, when he started clinching victories in races at fairs held in New York and Massachusetts. Hailing from the Seneca tribe, Deerfoot occasionally claimed that his alias stemmed from outrunning a horse, while at other times he attributed it to chasing down a deer. Regardless, Deerfoot became the star attraction in the summer of 1861, when he entered a New York City race against three of England's top runners. Although he didn't emerge victorious, Deerfoot's performance caught the eye of promoter and trainer George Martin. Martin extended an invitation to Deerfoot to compete in England, and the Seneca runner accepted, departing during the initial year of the Civil War. As a Seneca, Deerfoot wasn't recognized as a U.S. citizen, exempting him from military service in New York State. He departed from a place where significant sporting events were overshadowed by a war that consumed the majority of attention, people, and resources. In stark contrast, upon reaching London, Deerfoot's races drew substantial crowds with sizable purses. This popularity was attributed not only to his exceptional talent but also to the European fascination with all things related to America's Indigenous population.[4]

With Martin serving as Deerfoot's promoter, the duo played directly to this fascination as well as the rivalry between America and England. One of their tactics was to emphasize the stature of the athlete. Most distance runners of the time looked like William Howitt, known as "Jackson, the American Deer," who had a slight build and weighed roughly 100 pounds. Deerfoot, in contrast, stood nearly six feet tall and had a muscular 160-pound frame. In his races, Deerfoot towered above the competition, giving observers a clear foundation for understanding him as a distinct Indigenous American athlete. "A fine specimen of the forest," wrote one journalist witnessing Deerfoot for the first time, adding that "his countenance is definitely Indian, of a deep and copper color, sharp features, straight black hair."[5]

Deerfoot's distinctive presence extended beyond his size. During races, he donned a wolf-skin blanket and a headband adorned with an eagle feather. Instead of the typical racing spikes worn by other runners, Deerfoot opted for moccasins. Bells hung from his side, creating a rhythmic sound with each stride. Although Deerfoot was proficient in English, Martin arranged for an interpreter to enhance the "noble savage" imagery surrounding him. And then there was Deerfoot's infamous "war-whoop." Employed strategically before, during, and after races, this distinctive yell elicited a response from crowds and opponents alike, evoking a mix of measured terror and curious attraction. In one race, a competitor succumbed to exhaustion, prompting a crowd to rush the track, disrupting the race in an attempt to secure their wagers. Undeterred, Deerfoot seized a flagpole from the stands, reportedly wielding it like a tomahawk while emitting a war whoop as he cleared a path toward victory. In another instance, during a tour of Ireland, Deerfoot encountered a "gentleman" on the street who requested a demonstration of his war whoop. Initially hesitant, Deerfoot eventually acquiesced and unleashed a yell so shrill, ear-splitting, and prolonged that it figuratively "cleft all heads," as described in one news report.[6]

The projection of a manufactured Indian identity took center stage with Martin's introduction of the Deerfoot Running Circus soon after the two arrived in England. Blending athletics and entertainment, Deerfoot and company traveled through England, Scotland, and Ireland, drawing massive crowds along the way. In December of 1861, he participated in a ten-mile race, entering the track on a carriage drawn by two horses and wearing his trademark wolf-skin cape. Approximately fifteen thousand attendees watched as Deerfoot set off to victory and cheered as he celebrated with war whoops and dancing.[7]

The traces of religion interwoven into Deerfoot's athletic accomplishments appeared most forthrightly in his mythological persona. The grandeur and showmanship of his events and behavior sought to create a sense of the sacred breaking through the profane, a performance of superhuman ability that pervaded all dimensions of his being. Some of this performance was done to meet the expectations of English audiences, who associated his behavior with what they believed Indigenous culture and spirituality to be. Consequently he became a unique American sports hero in a place far from his home, where ironically he wasn't even recognized as a citizen. Additionally, back in the United States, where war was the dominant discussion, Deerfoot received little attention, and most of it was negative. An article in the *New York Clipper* wondered if his races were fixed, additionally criticizing his "queer costumes, putting rings on his fingers and bells on his toes, and all that sort of thing." The *Clipper* showed little interest in Deerfoot the curated showman, proclaiming, "He dresses up in Indian gear for the benefit of our transatlantic neighbors and gives the war whoop to the great delight of the crowds that follow him."[8]

No doubt, Deerfoot's persona sold well overseas. When he triumphed in yet another race in December 1861, the Prince of Wales watched from the stands in amazement. Within the week, Deerfoot was dining with the prince at Trinity College, an event that drew both approval and condemnation from onlookers. W. J. Beaumont of Trinity arranged the meal and justified his invitation to Deerfoot by arguing that the runner "was presented to me as a religious man" and that extending the invitation to this distinguished athlete was a Christian gesture of hospitality. Additionally, he asserted, "I believe that we should do better if we associated more with persons of a different rank of life whose character is good, and less with those of the same rank, whose character is notoriously bad."[9]

As Deerfoot's fame was peaking, new revelations would call his character into question. In 1862, a runner in Martin's circus sued the promoter for nonpayment of wages. As the trial unfolded, testimony explained how the promoter fixed races for Deerfoot to win. This revelation circulated widely through the press and nearly ruined Deerfoot's reputation. In response, Martin and Deerfoot set forth to collect as many records as they could, a decision aided by the innovation of precision timing. In 1861, Benson's Marking Chronometer came on the market, calculating down to tenths of seconds, not just quarters. *Sporting Life* called it "a watch of such beautiful, and even marvelous perfection."[10] Gone were the disputes over the accuracy of time. This device had created a new standard, meaning that Deerfoot's times would be authoritative, absolute, and unquestioned.

Even with this assurance, by 1863 his performances began to slip—the consequence of a relentless race schedule and his own reported indulging in British nightlife. Public opinion also started to sour. In one race, Deerfoot reportedly chased after a spectator who attempted to run alongside him. "Such a savage ought not to be allowed loose in this country," complained the spectator. Deerfoot knew that it was time to return to his homeland, but not before putting together one last great performance. On April 3, 1863, he toed the line for his final race in England, wherein he proceeded to break records for twelve miles, eleven miles, ten miles, and the one-hour mark. It was a race that, as one British publication put it, "scattered any prejudice to the winds that may have been felt against him; and he is now acknowledged the most extraordinary pedestrian that has ever appeared in England." Remarkably, his distance for one hour would not be surpassed until 1953, when the Englishman Jim Peters ran a mere sixteen yards further.[11]

Deerfoot departed England with approximately £1,000 in earnings after competing in 130 races over a span of eighty-seven weeks. He had created a powerful mythology that combined elements of spectacle with his extraordinary athletic achievements. Back in the United States once the Civil War ended, Deerfoot began traveling to local fairs and putting on exhibitions. But he soon retired at age forty and returned to the Cattaraugus Reservation, where he spent most of his time living in relative obscurity. In 1893, Deerfoot came back into the public eye when he was featured at the Chicago World's Fair. One journalist noted Deerfoot's youthful appearance given his age, while recounting his remarkable records that still stood. The author asked Deerfoot about a controversy at the fair, which involved the showing of nude statues. Deerfoot reportedly disapproved of the statues and expressed a sense of pride that no Indigenous figure was among them. "He has probably treasured this up as another instance of the superiority of the red man over the pale face," the article concluded. Interestingly, while running in England, Deerfoot's bare chest had become a source of controversy. Concerns over offending the Victorian sensibilities of women, English promoters occasionally compelled Deerfoot to cover his body.[12] But time had erased this memory, and now Deerfoot had assumed the image of a dignified elder statesman of American sports.

With Deerfoot's name and mythology returning to notice, the city of Warren, Pennsylvania, invited him to their centennial celebration in 1895. Situated among roughly two hundred representatives of other Indigenous communities, Deerfoot, who was sixty-seven, had come to Warren as a featured guest and reportedly to participate in an exhibition race. Although the race was meant only as a showcase, the local newspaper emphasized Deerfoot's exceptional physical condition, suggesting he looked like a competitor despite his advanced age. "The grand old Indian is still a wonder," the newspaper concluded.[13]

Deerfoot's passing in 1897 prompted nostalgic tributes from both England and America, with subsequent stories continuing to highlight his Indigenous identity in connection with his remarkable talent. In an 1899 account of Deerfoot's final record-breaking race in England, the author vividly described "his native kilt of light cloth ornamented with porcupine quill-work and beads," emphasizing how Deerfoot proudly "shot out into the track with the steady flight of an Indian arrow," a performance reminiscent of "his ancestral racers on a war trail." Deerfoot's mythology also served commercial interests, as advertising posters for Deerfoot Rye in the twentieth century depicted the bare-chested runner effortlessly outpacing his competition.[14]

Despite his posthumous fame, Deerfoot's physical remains were left in an unmarked grave on his Seneca reservation, a fact that Joseph Keppler found profoundly unjust. As a fellow Seneca, Keppler, who was a political cartoonist and wrestler in the New York City area, was well aware of Deerfoot's extraordinary story. Motivated by a desire to rectify this oversight, he embarked on a mission to raise sufficient funds to relocate Deerfoot's body to an elaborate grave at Forest Lawn Cemetery in Buffalo, New York, where it would rest alongside the noted Seneca orator and chief Red Jacket. This site would serve as a place for visitors to pay their respects to a figure who had made racetracks in both America and Europe special for those who enjoyed the novelty of human footraces.[15]

These same racetracks also played host to horse races, and for fans of this sport the location of these contests held a promise of fostering national reunion in the aftermath of the Civil War.

## "Martyrs of the Race Course"

On February 18, 1865, Charleston, South Carolina, lay in ruins as the city's mayor formally surrendered to the Union. By this point, most of the city's White inhabitants had fled, leaving behind a population of formerly enslaved people tasked with repairing the war's damage. One particular concern in their rebuilding efforts was the horse racing track of a former planter. Before the war, this site served as a venue for planters to race their horses and, in the process, showcase their wealth and status to peers and the public. In the war's concluding year, Confederate soldiers transformed the racetrack into a prison where over 250 Union soldiers perished due to disease and exposure.[16]

Upon first encountering the racetrack prison, James Redpath was appalled by the haphazard way in which bodies were disposed. Having just arrived in Charleston from Boston to assume the role of superintendent of schools, Redpath, a journalist and outspoken abolitionist, sought to shape a memory of the past in Charleston that aligned with his aspirations for the future. To realize this vision, he collaborated with two Black groups, Friends of the Martyrs and the Patriotic Association of Colored Men, who established a proper cemetery on the racetrack. A distinctive feature of the site was an archway crowning the entrance with the inscription "Martyrs of the Race Course." On May 1, Redpath and his wife participated in a public ceremony that commenced with a memorial service at a Black church. Subsequently, a procession of approximately ten thousand people marched two miles to the racetrack, singing songs such as "John Brown's Body." Upon reaching the cemetery, they passed through the archway and adorned the graves of the fallen soldiers.[17]

On his tour of the South after the war, journalist Whitelaw Reid of Ohio's *Cincinnati Gazette* took notice of this site, insisting that the cemetery and inscription at the entrance "must bring shame to the cheek of every Southern man who passes." Similar sentiments echoed in northern newspapers, eventually using the event as an origin story for what would become Memorial Day. In 1867, an Ohio newspaper claimed that the practice of decorating graves was originally a "Yankee notion," derived from the mind of Redpath. "This beautiful ceremony has now been adopted by the rebel women, in order to do honor to their lost cause and lost soldiers." In 1905, a Kansas newspaper also mentioned Redpath, crediting him with compelling the Black inhabitants of Charleston to properly memorialize the fallen soldiers.

A comparable tone rang forth in 1921, when Boston journalist William Justin Mann wrote about this precursor to Memorial Day: "None of the horrors of Andersonville surpassed those of this Charleston place of torture." It was redeemed, the author averred, through the "patriotic songs" of parading Charlestonians.[18]

For the formerly enslaved people who participated in this ritual, fresh prewar memories remained of planters gambling on and racing their horses, as well as how this place became a site of imprisonment during a war. Accordingly, they reclaimed, redefined, and remoralized the Charleston racetrack, writing their own story onto the turf. Once White citizens resumed positions of authority in the city, however, this account would be erased and replaced with a new story that celebrated whiteness through the discourse of reunion. In 1866, the local jockey club started planning races, leading one local journalist to proclaim that "love of fine and fast horses has always been a predominant trait of the Southern people." Despite lingering hostilities with the North, the author found it heartening that the city's "gentlemen" would soon begin importing "the finest Northern stock" for the races.[19]

In these tender years of Reconstruction, racetracks were a location for White northerners and southerners to forge a common identity, assisted by an enthusiastic press, capitalist ambition, and a budding national sports culture. At the same time, this new national discourse of reunion for White audiences only worked to further marginalize Black voices.[20]

## "The Greatest Event in the History of the Turf of America"

"Does not this make the mouths of our magnolia lovers of the horseflesh water," asked John Forsyth, as he gazed at the newly constructed horse racing track in New York City. A newspaperman and politician from Mobile, Alabama, Forsyth visited the site in late summer of 1866. He marveled at the beauty of the track, with its figure-eight design and a grandstand situated for eight thousand spectators, predicting that it was "destined to become not only a New York but a national institution."[21]

After years of a bitter and bloody divide, Forsyth viewed the racetrack as a sacred symbol of reunion, attributing its existence to the imagination and financial support of Leonard Jerome. Recognized as "the King of Wall Street," Jerome amassed his wealth through stock speculation and, during the war, ardently supported the Union cause. Forsyth was well aware of

Jerome's allegiance. However, with the rapturous sounds of war fading, he perceived Jerome was someone who shared a broad commitment to peace and prosperity, along with disdain for "the vindictive and cowardly policy of the Radical party."[22]

Forsyth witnessed Jerome's supposed sectional civility firsthand while dining with him and a dozen other guests at the racetrack. One of two southerners at the table, Forsyth reported that everyone greeted him warmly, even commending the "pluck and heroism" of southern soldiers during the war. For his part, Forsyth spoke unapologetically about the South's wartime cause. But still, he looked forward to joining with the North "to preserve the dignity of Americans." Jerome listened attentively before offering a toast to the soldiers of the North and the South, a gesture that capped an evening characterized by shared optimism in the future.[23]

For Forsyth, people like Jerome, with their wealth and vision, helped to relocate sectional rivalries in America from battlefields to racetracks. The inaugural race at Jerome's track promised to feature a much-anticipated meeting of two thoroughbreds, Kentucky and Asteroid. While the horse Kentucky had a connection to his namesake, the circumstances of the war brought the horse northward. Before the war, the state of Kentucky had a reputation for producing great thoroughbreds, a distinction that sagged as the conflict continued. In addition to the all-consuming nature of the war, raids on stables prompted some breeders to relocate their operations northward. When the fighting ceased, enterprising businesspersons in the East retained these horses, Kentucky among them, and featured them in their conspicuous modes of consumption. As journalist Francis Trevelyan observed, "the Sport of Kings" had become "the playground of the wealthy leisure classes," with its pageantry, competition, Old World connections, and opportunities for high-stakes gambling.[24]

John Hunter was among the northern elites who turned his attention to transferring horse racing dominance eastward. The wealthy New Yorker was the owner of the horse Kentucky, which was one of three noteworthy colts sired in 1861 by another famous horse of the era, named Lexington. The other two were Norfolk, who gained fame racing in California, and Asteroid, who raced in and around the state of Kentucky. For Hunter, the northern ascendency of horse racing required more than owning the horse Kentucky—he had to own the state's prestige as well. Accordingly, defeating Asteroid became a top priority, as the horse had an unmatched reputation in racing circles. At an 1863 race in Louisville, Asteroid was matched against another highly touted horse of the region. On the first day, Asteroid's opponent remained close in the early going of the two-mile course. "The sight was beautiful," wrote an onlooker. "In power and grace of action they are both superb." But in the last half-mile, Asteroid pulled away. The next day, the horses met again for a second heat, but this time Asteroid won with little drama.[25]

Fully aware of Asteroid's fame, in the summer of 1865 Hunter issued a challenge to Asteroid's owner, Robert Alexander. The proposed site was Saratoga Springs, New York, a location that had experienced a renaissance after the war, as wealthy New York City dwellers began vacationing there. In 1865, the artist Winslow Homer captured the pomp and circumstance of the races in an image for *Harper's Weekly*, displaying extravagantly dressed women in the foreground and men furiously cheering behind them. Off to the side was a Union soldier, a reminder that the war was a fresh memory. Still, with the focus on a refined, modern, and passionately engaged crowd rather than on the horses, Homer's image projected the sense that Saratoga was where the sport was generating a unified postwar American identity.[26]

Despite the significance of Saratoga Springs, Alexander, who had made his fortune through ironworks in Scotland and Kentucky, turned away Hunter's challenge. In his written response, Alexander voiced his philosophical objection to matches of this magnitude: "In the first place, it partakes more of gambling than I like; in the second place, it not unfrequently creates no little ill feeling between the parties engaged." There were also practical concerns, as Alexander worried about the toll that travel would take on his horse.[27]

Ultimately, Asteroid did not make the journey to Saratoga Springs, resulting in the Saratoga Cup proceeding without him. But this did not reduce enthusiasm for the event. *Turf, Field, and Farm* extensively covered the races, focusing not only on the track but also on the stands, weaving a narrative about the broader significance of the sport in American life. Part of this narrative involved highlighting the substantial presence of "ladies" at the event, the author going so far as to label them "the life and soul of all genuine and gentlemanly amusements." The author communicated to readers that with the deliberate inclusion of women at the track, this event embodied sophistication and cultural refinement, subtly challenging the prevalent association of horse racing with a less savory side of society.[28]

In the main event, the horse Kentucky clinched the Cup with minimal competition, earning acclaim for both the horse and its owner. However, the horse racing public quickly clamored for a match with Asteroid. After extended negotiations between the owners, they ultimately agreed to race on

September 23, 1866, at the opening of Jerome Park in New York. Anticipation reached its peak, only to be shattered when Asteroid suffered a career-ending injury. *Turf, Field, and Farm* captured the collective disappointment, stating, "A bright star has faded from the racing firmament" and ensuring readers that even the strongest men were justified in shedding tears for Asteroid. The article, resembling an obituary for the horse and a lamentation for what might have been, concluded on a somber note: "Farewell, mighty conqueror of the West, prince of royal blood, and son of a noble sire; though you cannot wear the laurels of the East, your brow is crowned with a wreath of deathless fame."[29]

The absence of Asteroid from Jerome Park's racecourse did not prevent *Turf, Field, and Farm* from declaring the inaugural event there "[t]he greatest event in the history of the turf of America." The author expressed certainty that horse racing was poised to become a permanent fixture in the city, akin to the great urban venues of Greece and Rome and throughout Europe. What set Jerome Park apart, the author explained, was that private parties had invested their personal fortunes for the benefit of the entire community. "The nation may well be proud of such children," the author remarked, "and may this example of patriotism live green in the minds of all." Evidence of this "patriotism" was gleaned from the diversity of the crowd, a heartening scene considering recent history. With an estimated twenty thousand attendees at the track, the author announced:

> Every portion of the country was represented, from the tall, powerful Missourian to the dapper, active little Creole of New Orleans—from the smart, calculating astute New Englander, to the stalwart Kentuckian. Good temper and good nature prevailed on every side. . . . Truly, we Americans are a wonderful people; what foreigner would believe, unless he knew, that those who, little more than twelve months since, had fought in antagonistic ranks, with all the determination, valor and hate that civil war could imbue, would now be hob-nobbing, laughing, joking and fraternizing with all the appearance of a friendship that had lasted for years.[30]

For this author, owners, breeders, and racetracks were the building blocks for the creation of a new America, one defined by both diversity and unity, coexisting in relative harmony. Lost in this portrait were the jockeys, most of whom were Black. The omission was telling. Until the early nineteenth century, planters took pride in racing their horses against each other. But as the institution of slavery expanded, planters began appointing enslaved men to ride on their behalf. After emancipation, Black jockeys stayed in the saddle and managed to grab a measure of fame nationwide and internationally.

The jockey Abe Hawkins, often referred to simply as "Old Abe" or "Abe," was among the best-known athletes of the era. The *New York Times* called him "that consummate artist in the saddle." A formerly enslaved person from Louisiana, he rode at Saratoga and at the opening event at Jerome Park. There Hawkins bested a field of White jockeys in front of a massive crowd that included Ulysses S. Grant. Still, when Hawkins rode at Saratoga neither he nor his fellow Black jockeys were permitted to enter the grandstand. Praise for the rider tended to underplay the fact that his success on the turf did not guarantee him an equal place in society. When Hawkins died in 1867, *Turf, Field, and Farm* published an effusive eulogy of "Old Abe." After covering his nearly three decades of racing, the author summarized, "As a rider and jockey he had no equal in this country."[31]

Black riders would remain prominently featured in racing for a brief period in the years to come. In the 1880s, Isaac Murphy likely held the title of the highest-paid athlete in the country, earning an annual income ranging from $15,000 to $20,000—more than the entire team of the Chicago White Stockings. However, a decade later the grip of Jim Crow tightened, resulting in reduced visibility for riders like Murphy. The landscape of sports celebrity underwent a transformation, aligning with the increased financial incentives and amplified attention achievable through the sport. As Murphy and other Black jockeys were gradually erased from horse racing, the new heroes of the turf became White riders like Tod Sloan. Sloan's forward-leaning crouch in the saddle earned him recognition as an innovator, although he had adopted the pose from earlier Black riders such as Hawkins. Despite this appropriation, White audiences appeared oblivious, hailing Sloan as the "Yankee Doodle Dandy."[32]

The concept of unity, as crafted in the White imagination, assumed sacred significance in the years following the war. It played a central role in a civil religious discourse wherein the North and South forged a collective "Us" after having previously perceived each other as "Them" during warfare. At the heart of this narrative were not only the heroes of horse racing but also the prosperous capitalists who constructed the venues for their competitions. By establishing new public gathering spaces in the form of racetracks, these wealthy individuals were actively shaping America's identity. However, this emerging American myth of origin carried an unmistakable racial core of whiteness, often relegating Black voices to the periphery or entirely excluding them. And despite the celebratory language, there were many within White society who departed from the view of horse racing enthusiasts, viewing the sport not as a signal of peace and prosperity, but as indicative of social decline.

## "These Are the Days of Insidious Wickedness"

"Puritanism may grimly smile at the idea of calling men engaged in the unholy amusement of horse-racing public benefactors," wrote one New Orleans journalist. As for "thoughtful men," however, they recognized the broad value to society brought about by competitions on the turf. As New Orleans grew into a sports hub in the South after the war, a moral argument for and against these activities unfolded in public spaces. In the process, sports advocates deployed the stereotype of the Puritan, gesturing toward the mostly ministerial class who failed to see the value in these activities. Elsewhere, the specter of this overbearing and judgmental scold was referred to as "the moralist." "The moralist considers that he is serving his Maker by doing all the good he can and as little harm," a North Carolina newspaper explained in 1865. But in seeking to ban certain amusements, moralists end up mirroring "that style of Puritanism that has governed the nasal-twanging devotee of our land."[33]

While the labels "Puritan" and "moralist" became terms of abuse, evangelicals in the South continued to focus on "immoral amusements." Many of their commentaries listed gambling as evidence of social harm. But defenders of horse racing made the opposite argument. "We believe that it is generally conceded that human nature has naturally a passion for gambling," theorized one New Orleans journalist, commenting on a forthcoming horse race in the city. The author went on to distinguish between the "common gambler" and the "gentleman." The former occupied his "brilliantly gas-lit hell," drenched in whiskey and surrounded by smoke, as he grasped for money using whatever means were at his disposal. The latter, though, intuitively understood that gambling fed into the wonder of the race: "What is more beautiful than the splendid horse uncovered for the race? Look at his kindly, ye glowing eye—the fire of ambition in it, his curved and distended nostrils—his limbs, clean cut, sinewy and springy as steel, and ready to spurn the turf in his flying course. Is not such a sight enough to arouse a man, and make him feel as though his spirit was in the noble steed?"[34] To observe beauty and striving and to feel part of the race was, for the author, the essence of the horse race. Gambling only drew the enthusiast deeper into this connection, fusing together the bodies of horse and human and placing them both on the track.

Implied in this defense of horse racing was the track itself, and its precise location. City racetracks and jockey clubs were signals of the new era of the sport. Races at agricultural fairs, on the other hand, were one place where evangelicals and horse racing aficionados agreed on their moral boundaries. In 1869, a Methodist newspaper in Raleigh, North Carolina, commented favorably on an agricultural fair in Cape Fear, assuring readers that these events would positively serve the community. The only threat was those "lovers of the turf" who would no doubt desecrate the fair with their horse races. Another writer agreed, interpreting the presence of horse races at agricultural fairs as plain evidence of a lack of "the spirit of Christianity." He thundered, "These are the days of insidious wickedness!" The newspaper's campaign against horse racing at fairs continued in an 1871 article, where one author revised the Puritan trope of time misspent, disappointed in the attention and resources given to these races, "which should be spent on more useful things."[35] As for horse racing enthusiasts, Francis Trevelyan called an 1888 horse race at an agricultural fair in Virginia "[a] Babel, indeed!" His description depicted every element of the race as being supremely disordered. The owners raced only for the money; the tracks were sandy patches of ill-measured circles; the audience was a collection of "peddlers and hucksters"; and the Black jockeys wore ill-fitting clothes and were selected based on a popular belief that they were "endowed with a special power of sticking to a horse."[36]

Trevelyan wrote frequently on the topic of horse racing in America, demonstrating a clear fondness for the sport. But his moral sensibilities flared in opposition at the sight of races at southern fairs. The true racetrack for him and others had to be in the right place and operated by the right people because this space was a location for celebrating excellence, making a collective identity, and constructing public morality. As activity and interest swirled around the age-old sport of horse racing in elite White circles, which served a civil religious end of codifying unity in a previously fractured nation, another new sport gained similar attention and controversy after the war, as baseball grew into "America's pastime."

# 5
# Innovation and Anxiety

At length the war cry's hushed and still,
    And peaceful are the signs,
The cannon's roar affrights us not—
    "All quiet on the lines."
No more the fearful charge we brave—
    For raids we look in vain,
But still excitement we must have,
    And we've base-ball on the brain!

. . .

The darkey, he's freedman now,
    And proud as proud can be;
With "bat," and "ball," and "uniform,"
    There's none so gay as he.
To get him to take up a hoe,
    All efforts are in vain
For the fever rages high, you know,
    And he's base-ball on the brain!

. . .

The girls, too, aping lordly man,
    Have taken up the chase,
And with Bloomer pants, and gaiters high,
    They fly from "base" to "base"!
In faith, I think the truth to tell,
    There's none of us quite sane.
But that we all have Poplar Lawn!
    And base-ball on the brain.

Published in several newspapers in 1867, "Baseball on the Brain" presented a whimsical observation of the ways that the popular game of baseball was

*Bodies in Motion*. Arthur Remillard, Oxford University Press. © Oxford University Press 2025.
DOI: 10.1093/oso/9780197789766.003.0006

intersecting with broader social trends. It began by echoing a shared belief of the baseball faithful that in the postwar era, bats and balls would replace guns and cannons, thereby making for healthy rivalries and shared prosperity. The civil rights leader Octavius Catto echoed this point while also asserting that baseball could become part of Black America's journey toward equality. But as the derogatory imagery in this comic verse indicated, White America was not prepared to recognize the work and dignity of the newly emancipated. In the same year that this comic verse appeared, the National Association of Baseball Players, the sport's first governing body, denied membership to Catto's team, the Pythian Base Ball Club of Philadelphia. Meanwhile, as women also took to the game at Vassar and other colleges, the reference to bloomers made use of the symbolism of women's rights, as this lower-body garment had been the preferred dress of feminist leaders in previous generations, such as Elizabeth Cady Stanton and Susan B. Anthony. This clothing item had hence become a point of reference for a new form of womanhood, born from the necessities of war and now partially manifesting in the game of baseball.[1]

As the "national pastime," baseball grew in popularity throughout the United States after the Civil War mostly in the cities, where players required little equipment and only an open field. It was during this time that the game had also become a civil religious ritual, a public display of an industrializing America seeking to heal the wounds of the past, while also creating sacred boundaries around the emerging and changing racial and gender hierarchies.[2] At the same time, a new breed of Puritanical critics came into the picture, worried that the game was untethering the very fabric of America. To have "baseball on the brain" was nothing to celebrate or sing about; rather it was a signal of social illness. Accordingly, the moral debate that followed centered on the passion generated by the sport, and whether these feelings were a portal to unmendable chaos or a pathway for American unity.

## "Base Ball on the Brain"

"Yesterday, Gotham had base ball on the brain," announced the *New York Times* in 1875 while covering a championship game between the Mutual Club of New York and the Atlantic Club of Brooklyn. The author focused on the crowd, particularly delving into the motivation of the estimated twenty thousand attendees. The excitement began the moment the contest was announced, sparking extended conversations throughout the urban landscape. On game day, despite the sweltering August sun, crowds arrived two hours early, a testament to their "self-sacrificing spirit." The author concluded that no other sport's followers could match the enthusiasm of these hearty souls who passionately loved "our national game."[3]

The imagery of this specific game would soon become the literal portrait of American baseball, when Currier & Ives produced a lithograph of the contest titled *The American National Game of Base Ball.* Styling themselves "a democratic firm in a democratic country," Currier & Ives melded baseball and American identity into their mission, as this image quickly became one of their best-selling products. Patriotism and sports, in other words, had become profitable. This was a relatively new direction in sports images, which had started to gain currency in 1869, when the sporting goods store Peck & Snyder produced a small advertising card with an image of the Cincinnati Red Stockings. The "trade cards" that followed would give baseball both amplified exposure and a new means for generating revenue off the field.[4]

While print firms and others had discovered ways to cash in on the game, baseball itself was undergoing a similar economic transformation. The Cincinnati Red Stockings became the first openly professional baseball team in 1869, as the National Association of Base Ball Players relented to allowing professionalism in the game. While it was an open secret that players were receiving pay in the past, the Red Stockings marked a new moment in the sport, punctuated by a barnstorming tour wherein they amassed a 57–0 record. They also made a meager $1.39 in profit, which, combined with dwindling attention once their winning streak ended, led to speculation about the future of professional baseball. But financial backers in Boston saw promise in this innovation and convinced the team to relocate to New England, where they would experience more success on and off the field.[5]

In the Northeast and Midwest, the Red Stockings and professional baseball at large found themselves navigating an era characterized by an ongoing struggle between payroll considerations, profit motives, and the pursuit of victory. This inevitably ignited moral discussions regarding the role of money in baseball, accompanied by concerns about the potential rise in gambling and game-fixing. Moreover, critics expressed apprehension about the increasing blurring of lines between work and play. According to their argument, the essence of a sport like baseball lay in its ability to provide an escape from the demands and measurements of everyday life—a timeless game untouched by the constraints of the industrial era, notably symbolized by the absence of a clock. Detractors contended that with an emphasis on winning and gate receipts, the sport's "true" value would be jeopardized.[6]

Meanwhile, in the southern states, the innovation of baseball and its moral debate took on a form that was unique to the challenges facing that region after the war. In 1867, Columbia, South Carolina, saw its first baseball action when a group of locals calling themselves the Chicora Club played the Phil Sheridan Club, comprised of members of the 5th U.S. Artillery. The Army unit had arrived in Columbia that summer because of the Reconstruction Acts, and in addition to federal authority, the troops brought "the national game" with them. Shortly upon settling into the city, they published a friendly challenge to the "gentlemen" of Columbia to play a game. The home team lost badly, but that didn't detract from interest in the contest. "The game passed off in a very friendly and agreeable manner," one account summarized.[7]

Set against the backdrop of Reconstruction, a game of baseball between these former wartime foes seemed to hint at the possibility of regional cooperation. Henry Chadwick held out a similar hope. Known as the "Father of Baseball," Chadwick briefly served as a wartime correspondent in Richmond, where his wife was originally from. In 1865 he returned to Richmond and witnessed "a great change in the young Southerners in regard to sports." He credited some of this to Confederate soldiers playing baseball during down times. He found that the game "proved to be contagious," as it spread through the region, from Richmond to New Orleans. According to Chadwick, this was entirely because the game of baseball was uniquely suited for the young men of the South. "The late war proved conclusively their powers of physical endurance," he exclaimed. In essence, baseball became the peacetime venue for southern men to define and embody their identity.[8]

Chadwick was firm in his belief that baseball and the passion that it elicited was a moral benefit to individuals that also helped societies flourish. Additionally, he assured readers that baseball teams gave communities a reason to have pride in their corporate identity. In the South, such pride could be seen in the team's names. An 1867 game in Memphis, for example, found the Stonewall Jackson club facing The Pride of the South. In New Orleans, clubs bore names like Robert E. Lee, Lone Star, and The Southerners. In 1869, members of the latter club went on a traveling tour, winning six of seven games and, according to one account, giving "a new impulse to base ball in our city." Upon their return, crowds met the club at Canal Street. They were the first team to travel from New Orleans, and their lone loss, according to the newspaper, was to the professional Cincinnati Red Stockings, a fact that gave the writer license to dismiss the loss and further herald the character of the home team: "Let us ever strive to keep awake in the breasts of our young men a noble emulation, and base ball is ennobling, for it gives strength to the body and imparts vigor to the mind."[9]

As the national pastime was professionalizing in some places and just taking root elsewhere, the sounds of moral panic also accompanied the game. In 1867 at an agricultural fair near Gallipolis, Ohio, young men with "baseball on the brain" played their game, much to the ire of one local resident. Announcing his displeasure in the local newspaper, the disgruntled fairgoer urged his community to take all steps necessary to eradicate "the disease" known as baseball. Similarly, in Minneapolis, a columnist claimed that the "baseball disease" had infected the area's most promising young men. A Kansas writer likewise denounced the "baseball craze," going as far as to invoke readers to pray for the game's end.[10]

Sylvanus Landrum was also calling upon divine favor to thwart the advance of baseball in America. The pastor of Central Baptist Church in Memphis, Landrum saw nothing right in the game. "It breaks the Sunday laws of the country and the law of God," he proclaimed, adding that baseball was "a bad thing for any day" because "it is a great waste of time and strength." While it might build muscle, baseball "corrupts the youth" through its associated culture of debauchery. Landrum concluded, "It is a nuisance, a plague, to be shunned and removed as you would small-pox."[11]

Landrum was far from alone in his moral posture, as in Memphis at this time newspapers frequently debated the value of baseball, particularly as it related to Sunday play. One article deemed arguments supporting Sunday baseball "quite amusing and illogical." In addition to violating a city ordinance, the author charged, the spectators spend the entire game drinking, cursing, and behaving in an unruly manner. The "apologists" who compared this "national game" to that of the ancient Greek Olympics were misguided: "[The] Olympic games were solemn games. . . .They were religious ceremonies, and not conducted for the development of muscle in a picked nine." This game was anything but noble or virtuous, and the author dispensed with "[the] kind of muscular christianity [*sic*] by Sunday base-ball playing."[12]

## Muscular Christianity

In mentioning "muscular Christianity," the author referred to a relatively new movement in the United States, one that found Protestant ministers in particular extolling the supposed character-building features of sports. "Men believe in Muscular Christianity as well as in the development of the brain," announced a Cleveland newspaper in 1864, insisting that physical strength and godliness were necessary components of overall personal and social health. Achieving this required not just a hearty diet and focused outlook but also "good physical training" in the form of baseball, rowing, swimming, and similar sports. Far from being important just for individuals, the author stressed that physical strength was significant for the health of the nation. "The future Republic wants no dwarfed, puling children," he exclaimed. "It wants men and women of fine physical growth."[13]

One significant thread of the muscular Christian discourse connected to an emerging movement that historians refer to as the "sporting republic." Starting in earnest at the end of the nineteenth century and blossoming from the seeds of the international Olympic contests, the idea of the sporting republic took shape through the voices of politicians, educators, intellectuals, and civic leaders who understood sports to be incubators of civic virtue. This too was a point of emphasis for muscular Christians, most of whom were city-dwelling liberal Protestant elites, such as Unitarian minister Thomas Wentworth Higginson. An avid sportsman as well as a vocal social reformer, Higginson's 1858 article, "Saints, and Their Bodies," stressed that physical health was a matter of national importance and that sports was an ideal means for achieving this end. He therefore dismissed what he characterized as the lingering Puritan prohibitions on physical activity and stressed that both republican virtue and personal happiness were byproducts of the toned spirit and body.[14]

Higginson's article gained widespread circulation, but it faced criticism from those who echoed long-standing concerns about sports contributing to a loss of self and soul. One notable critic was Theodore Cuyler of New York's Market Street Dutch Reformed Church. Cuyler drew a sharp distinction between "recreation" and "amusements." He acknowledged the necessity of recreation for a balanced Christian life, recognizing its value for personal and communal well-being. However, he advocated a calm, quiet, and contemplative form of recreation, citing reading as the "first and purest of our recreations." In contrast, Cuyler viewed physical activity as a mere "amusement," an unseemly pursuit undertaken solely to excite the passions and provide a transient thrill to the individual. Expressing his concerns, Cuyler declared, "Everything that stimulates this nervous system of mine, until I become a walking maniac, weakens my conscience, excites impure thoughts, and makes my soul a terrible house of imagery."[15]

At the forefront of Cuyler's moral concern were the mind and soul of human beings, these unseen and immaterial elements of personhood, which could be upended by a passion for sports. This ran counter to the muscular Christian discourse that was increasingly emphasizing the fitness of bodies—and not just the bodies of trained athletes, but of religious leaders as well. "A sound body is now regarded as requisite for a sound theological mind," announced one Cincinnati newspaper. "People have begun to doubt that it is necessary that preachers should be pale and delicate in order to be spiritual." The article concluded that what they want instead were preachers who were unambiguously "muscular Christians."[16]

This line of thought strongly resonated with Moses Coit Tyler, a Congregationalist minister who, in 1862, left his pulpit in Poughkeepsie, New York, due to health issues. After a journey to Boston and then England, Tyler encountered the fundamental principles of muscular Christianity, applying them to his own life. Having regained his health, he wrote extensively on the subject for American audiences, emphasizing that neglecting one's body was not only unhealthy but also sinful. "[Since] every part of our nature is the sacred gift of God," he wrote, "he who neglects his body . . . commits a sin against the Giver of the body. Ordinarily, therefore, disease is a sin. Round shoulders and narrow chests are states of criminality. The dyspepsia is heresy. The headache is infidelity."[17]

A Chicago newspaper article had proclaimed a similar sentiment a few years prior, even singling out "dyspepsia" as a sign of spiritual weakness: "We believe that the minister of muscle will fight a more valiant and stronger battle with the passions and prejudices of men." Supporting this claim was the example of a local pastor who actively engaged in physical activities at the gymnasium, such as lifting dumbbells, running on the track, and climbing ladders—all in service of his vocation. The article also referenced the revivalist Peter Cartwright, alleging that he once halted his sermon "to flog an insulting rowdy."[18]

A dispatch from Kansas conveyed a comparable image, where a camp meeting was disrupted by a drunken "son of Belial." In response, an unnamed minister and true "muscular Christian" initially attempted to subdue the offender with words before resorting to physical force, pummeling the disruptive drunkard. From the muscular minister to the pugilistic preacher, these discussions about the bodies of religious leaders sought to reframe masculine aggression through a Christian lens. However, the distinction between righteous indignation and unbridled anger remained blurry at best, shaped largely by interpreters and their social standing.[19]

## Gentleman Athletes

British author Thomas Hughes was among the first to deploy the term "muscular Christianity" in his adventure novels that featured principled and rugged male Christian heroes. For Hughes, the "muscular Christian" is one who "has hold of the old chivalrous and Christian belief, that a man's body is given him to be trained and brought into subjection, and then used for the protection of the weak, the advancement of all righteous causes, and the subduing of the earth." In contrast to this was the "muscle man," a mindless mound of flesh who lived by "fierce and brutal passions."[20]

In America as in England, there would be an ongoing moral debate over what precisely separated these two figures of the gentleman athlete and the muscle man. A Chicago newspaper in 1867 called this an "unsolved problem" of muscular Christianity. Everything from walking and fencing could both test a person's strength and create a venue for gambling: "How to conserve the good and eliminate the evil in these—that is again the question." Similarly in New York, one journalist admitted that the sport of prizefighting had merit in strengthening bodies, sharpening skill, and unleashing an inward need to fight. But he also asserted that "the moral disadvantages" of this sport "are immensely greater."[21]

By the end of the nineteenth century, boxing had taken on a more polished veneer, making it a suitable place for gentleman athletes. In the place of bareknuckle brawls, the Marquess of Queensberry Rules became standard, requiring gloves, timed rounds, and a ten-second count. More cities legalized "gloved boxing" as clubs and organizations took form. And then there was the Young Men's Christian Association, an institution that originated in London in 1844 before appearing in New York City in 1852. Intended as a haven for young men and an alternative to saloons and brothels, the YMCA did not originally consider physical recreation part of its mission. Yet while there were no YMCA gymnasiums in 1865, there were approximately four hundred by 1890. Theodore Roosevelt called the growing sprawl of YMCA structures "manhood factories," celebrating their fusion of muscles and morals as a pathway toward living out his ideal of the "strenuous life." Boxing was a key station along this pathway and became part of the YMCA's sports offerings.[22]

Meanwhile, champions of the sport also drew a clear line between the emerging era of boxing and the perceived "brutality" of its forebear, prizefighting. Among these advocates was John Boyle O'Reilly, an Irish immigrant and renowned journalist. In his 1888 work, *Ethics of Boxing and*

*Manly Sport*, penned in Boston, O'Reilly emphatically declared, "Prize-fighting is not the aim of boxing." He argued that the former had been unfairly tainted as a result of the unscrupulous actions of too many professional practitioners, such as gamblers and other disreputable figures. O'Reilly asserted that these individuals should not be the ones to determine the fate of the sport. Boxing was, in fact, a "noble exercise" that involved both physical and mental elements. He dismissed the notion that the sport should be solely associated with unsavory characters and insisted that cultivating both the mind and body through boxing would result in the development of healthy and complete individuals. Offering a vivid comparison, he remarked, "[The boxer's] mind is quicker and more watchful than a chess-player's." Regarding the physical aspect, O'Reilly passionately stated, "Fatness and softness are merely sensuous expressions, or symptoms of disease. They are non-conductors of spiritual messages, stopping or deadening the finer currents of enjoyment, as an insulator stops electricity."[23]

O'Reilly, an Irish Catholic man, was called by one reviewer "intellectually if not physically [a] muscular Christian." Catholic people would continue gaining traction as boxers in Protestant America, particularly through figures like John L. Sullivan, nicknamed the "Boston Strong Boy" and "His Fistic Holiness." But Sullivan would also become a symbol of an old form of the sport that was in its final days. In New Orleans in 1892, the aged bareknuckle legend squared off against the younger, fitter Jim Corbett, who was also a Catholic person. While Corbett trounced his opponent, commentators used the victory to announce the coming of a new age in boxing. Gone were the days of illegal matches hastily organized in random fields to avoid legal repercussions. In its place were sanctioned bouts, sponsored by a respectable club and held indoors.[24]

Moreover, Corbett himself represented something new to the sport. Nicknamed "Gentleman Jim," he had reportedly attended college, worked as a bank clerk, and learned his craft in an elite San Francisco boxing club. When Mark Twain met the champion, he remarked, "Corbett has a fine face and is modest and diffident, besides being the most perfectly and beautifully constructed human animal in the world." And then there was Corbett's style in the ring, which he called his "hit-and-get-away system." "The main principle of this style," the fighter explained, "is to do as much damage as possible without receiving any in return." For Corbett, boxing was a sport of "science and quickness," not brute force and damage.[25]

With boxing in a new era and the Irish Catholic pugilist Corbett as the sport's central heroic figure, Protestant Christians likewise found a vocabulary for wrapping their theological prescriptions around a sport that turns no cheeks. "Muscular Christianity, that's what I call it," proclaimed Congregational minister John Scudder, "and it's the only real Christianity." In 1902, Scudder started teaching boxing to the youth of his Jersey City church, proclaiming that the sport was a physical lesson on moral fortitude. A graduate of Yale, where he captained the football team, Scudder insisted, "If I had not devoted myself to sport, I would not be alive to-day. Religion and health go hand in hand." Baptist minister George Cutten had similar reflections: "I believe in football and baseball and in athletics going hand in hand with religion. . . . I believe in muscular Christianity." In 1897, Cutten arrived at Yale from Nova Scotia, and while finishing his degree and playing football, he also preached at Montowese Union Church. This combination of activities led local journalists to draw comparisons between Cutten and Amos Alonzo Stagg, another famous Christian athlete who made his mark on the Yale team.[26]

Skudder, Cutten, and Stagg were sports heroes of the era who fit into the muscular Christian template. Their chosen sports were highly physical, combative, and warlike. At the same time, they presented as gentleman athletes rather than "muscle men." One method for achieving this end was to tout the virtues of amateurism and a corresponding commitment to fair play. "A man must be an amateur in spirit and in act, disdainful of subterfuge and dishonesty and ashamed to sell his athletic skill," exclaimed Stagg in 1927. "He must be a gentleman and a sportsman, unwilling to win by cheating or unfair tactics."[27] The amateur ethos articulated by Stagg and other muscular Christians grew out of a conviction that money had a corrupting influence on games.

And yet this image of the "gentleman amateur" was another innovation of the era, one that was riddled with contradictions. The discourse swirling around amateurism emanated from universities and exclusive clubs, places where the privileged elite looked with scorn upon what they perceived to be the money-hungry masses whose version of sports was disorderly, greedy, and emotionally unbalanced. Sportswriter Caspar Whitney referred to the professional class of athletes as "vermin," who through their greed and corruption "crushed all semblance of honesty" in athletics. Whitney and the other champions of amateurism instead manufactured a memory of the ancient Olympic games, wherein honor-driven athletes competed for the sake of competition. In actual fact, historians have shown that the original Olympians certainly did prosper from their efforts. But the image of the ancient amateur—a word that derived from the Latin word for "lover" (*amator*)—had become an ideal athlete, the one who played only for the love of playing. The sacred aura around amateurism was particularly strong on college campuses, even though sports at these institutions took on an entrepreneurial, rather than educational, character.[28]

Nevertheless, the concept of amateurism originated among those who could afford to pursue the inherent joys of sports with no expectation of monetary gain. Their vision for the passion that was linked with play was highly regulated and done solely for the "love of the game." Outside of America's elite circles, however, the working class continued to enjoy sports on their own terms, while professional athletes similarly sought to make a living through their physical labors. And many of these athletes played whenever and wherever a crowd could gather—including on Sundays.

## "We Have a Right to a Better Sabbath"

In the spring of 1903, the city of Indianapolis plunged into a debate that was, on the surface, about baseball on Sundays. But as arguments volleyed back and forth, this issue connected to larger questions endemic to the era related to the nature of work and leisure. The early twentieth century was characterized by, among other things, urbanization and industrialization, which gave way to a new leisure class that wanted more than ever to play and watch the games on their own time. For the religious establishment, this desire ran contrary to a biblical injunction to maintain one day of rest so that people are not entirely defined by their work. While muscular Christians were extolling the benefits of sports, concerns over who played and when they played still lingered. The Sunday play debate in Indianapolis was a microcosm of the many ways in which institutional religions were pushing and pulling on issues related to the passions associated with sports and the changing nature of American society.

"We have a right to a better Sabbath," proclaimed the Reverend Frank Otis Ballard of Memorial Presbyterian in Indianapolis in the spring of 1903. Acknowledging that the Sabbath was a product of religious tradition, he argued that American civic life had adopted this requirement for weekly quiet and rest. In their own time, the weekly respite was especially important to workers, freeing them from unending toil. But now, Ballard lamented, his city was considering allowing professional baseball on Sundays, a measure that he believed would open the gates to exploitation and unending work.

The preacher concluded by asserting that a work-free Sabbath was a matter of the health of the nation.[29]

Ballard was not alone; a reported sixty ministers gathered to protest the measure. Laypeople voiced similar concerns. One letter writer asserted that the bill was "fraught with evil consequences," both in terms of worship and for the potential exploitation of workers: "Sound morality and Christianity are the sterling and last qualities that exalt a nation." Many advocates of Sunday baseball claimed that it would benefit working people, those who had neither the time nor resources to attend baseball games during the week. Opponents were quick to address this argument. "This talk about the workingman needing recreation on Sunday is all bosh," announced one letter writer who identified as a "workingwoman." "What the workingmen need is rest," as well as one day of "feeding the soul."[30]

Similarly another author proclaimed, "What about the workingman's wife and children on the sizzling Sunday afternoons which the workingman must spend on the bleachers or in the grandstand getting 'recreation'?" Other letters took this concern for family and folded it into worries over a broader sense of social instability: "Next to the open saloon, no other movement in America has done more to ruin the moral principles of our young men and boys, and not a few women, than this unholy and brazen disregard of Sunday." That author went so far as to predict "moral death and national destruction" should Indianapolis permit Sunday baseball. For another writer, this prediction was all too real, as he claimed to have once lived in a town that authorized Sunday baseball. "The Sabbath day was spent in carousals, drinking, and drunkenness was common, fighting was frequent, gambling was a characteristic sport, swearing and vulgarity abounded," he reported. "Sunday baseball means all this, and worse, for Indianapolis."[31]

But the religious voices were not unanimous in opposing Sunday baseball. Father Joseph Chartrand, a Catholic priest, issued full support for the measure. He reasoned, "After a man has done what his religious convictions require him to do on Sunday, I do not see why he should be forbidden to witness a game of ball, certainly an honest and innocent amusement." The priest acknowledged the correlated "evils" of baseball, but he asserted that these existed on any day of the week. Perhaps anticipating objection from his Protestant counterparts, Chartrand concluded his argument by citing the gospel passage, "The Sabbath was made for man, not man for the Sabbath."[32]

The tactic of using explicitly Protestant language, resources, and history in this debate was common for those who agreed with Chartrand. Although identifying as a "non-churchgoer" himself, one letter writer cited Martin Luther: "If any man forbid you to work on the Sabbath, then exercise your Christian liberty by laboring on that day." Another advocate of Sunday baseball asserted that this limitation on the laboring class was an imposition of the ministerial class, and a betrayal of American freedom: "Has the time come that our lawmakers think that they can pass laws to compel people to be religious?"[33]

Reverend Joshua Stansfield was not swayed by any of these arguments. As chair of a legislative committee of Indianapolis ministers, he took direct aim at Father Chartrand, arguing that the priest was channeling his "Latin rather than American training." In English-speaking countries such as Great Britain and Australia, the minister argued, a proper understanding of Sunday rest governed behaviors on this day. In "Latin" countries like Mexico and "southern Europe," however, a habit of "immoral relaxation" followed Sunday religious observations. Scores of other ministers took to their pulpits and added to this argument. "I believe laboring men have as much conscience concerning the Sabbath as any other class of people," announced one preacher, reportedly to the wholehearted approval of his congregation.[34]

The Indianapolis bill did not pass, thus eliminating the possibility of Sunday baseball in that city. Reluctantly, the mayor pledged to enforce the ban: "I believe a man can fulfill his duty to God and to society and witness Sunday games. But the law is there." It was a similar story elsewhere in the United States, with local law enforcement struggling to stop games and place limits on Sunday events. Meanwhile, the moral debate continued, with concerns voiced over laws ancient and modern. Would Sunday baseball open the doors to exploitation? Or did limiting this activity place boundaries on how the working class could spend leisure time? It was a civil religious debate fueled both by intense interest in this sporting innovation as well as anxiety about what this new thing would do to the American character.[35] Many of these debates were also playing out in other sports. While baseball was taking hold in American cities, Edward P. Weston was becoming one of the most popular walkers in the nation. However, in portraying himself as a gentleman athlete who endured as St. Paul did, to "finish the race," Weston obscured the fact that everything he did was a money-making venture.

# 6
# Enduring Faith

In 1910 a Tennessee newspaper declared, "Edward Payson Weston observes the Sabbath." The article went on to narrate the journey of the renowned walker, detailing his transcontinental trek from California to New York with the goal of completing it in 90 days, improving on his previous year's walk that took 104 days. Notably, Weston was seventy years old at the time, a detail that heightened interest in both his walk and his embodiment of health and righteous living. His refusal to walk on the Sabbath, coupled with his advanced age, served as convincing evidence of his muscular Christian credentials for his admirers. "Weston the Pedestrian" was more than a long-distance walker; he was a living example of endurance, showcasing the ability to persevere in the face of adversity and overcome life's obstacles.[1]

It was Thomas Hughes who wrote in 1867, "Endurance is an evidence of genuine conviction, real faith, true attachment, single and high aim, meek patience, and faithful unyielding perseverance, which are all demanded in quality of the service which God requires and accepts." As one of the principal articulators of muscular Christianity, the British author drew from the example of St. Paul, who used metaphors of distance running and other sports to frame Christianity as a struggle that requires temperance and discipline. In essence, those who demonstrated endurance on the fields of play were, in fact, embodying the Christian message.[2]

For his own part, Weston inscribed endurance into his personal mythology, thereby claiming a certain muscular Christian appeal. At the same time, Weston was a professional athlete as well as a showman, qualities often scoffed at by the muscular Christian establishment who favored—at least in principle—amateurism and humility. From gambling winnings and appearance fees to selling souvenir programs to the thousands of people who came out to the city streets to cheer him on, Weston sought to capitalize on every step that he took. His critics, of course, took note of all of this. Money and gambling in the sport of pedestrianism was a source of contention for his moralizing opponents. But so too was the sport itself. For critics, Weston's physical strain was no noble demonstration of endurance, but rather a

*Bodies in Motion*. Arthur Remillard, Oxford University Press. © Oxford University Press 2025.
DOI: 10.1093/oso/9780197789766.003.0007

mindless fatiguing of the body. Indeed, interpretations of virtue and vice accompanied the movements of Weston and other endurance athletes in the era of muscular Christianity.

## "His Example Is Worth a Hundred Sermons"

"Never, perhaps, in the athletic history of the world has such an exhibition of physical endurance been planned by a man so well advanced in years," exclaimed the *New York Times* as Weston started on his walk across America in 1909. Newspapers throughout the nation followed the walker's quest, making sure to note his advanced age and ambitious goals. Writing for the American Press Association, James A. Edgerton used the walk to pen a glowing profile of Weston, which littered Christian allusions throughout the framing of his career. "He is perhaps the first man in the world's history that ever preached a gospel with his feet," exclaimed Edgerton. With a recurring theme of Weston's embodiment of the faith, Edgerton concluded, "His example is worth a hundred sermons."[3]

While the discourse of muscular Christianity ran through Edgerton's story, there was another religious worldview particular to this era lingering in the subtext. Edgerton was a leader in the New Thought movement, which, among other things, prized positive thinking as a means for physical and spiritual health. Without directly making the connection, Edgerton channeled the basic precepts of New Thought through Weston, praising the walker's lifestyle that included avoiding tobacco and alcohol, eating only two meals a day, and moderate sleep. Beyond the particulars was Weston's mental fitness. "His great secret is the power of will, of mind over body," Edgerton resolved. "Edward Payson Weston is a living example of what open air, temperance, exercise and healthy mindedness will do for the human race." Additionally, Edgerton asserted that Weston did not walk "for money or glory" but for the greater purpose of inspiring others to improve their health.[4]

Edgerton's portrayal of Weston closely aligned with the narrative that Weston himself had been emphasizing throughout his career. He championed walking as a method for enhancing an individual's "powers of endurance," emphasizing the importance of physical well-being over financial gain and cutthroat competition. But despite this emphasis on well-being, Weston pursued competitors and distances with the same fervor with which he sought glory and wagers. Gambling played a significant role in pedestrianism, a sport that originated in seventeenth-century England and gained popularity in postwar America. While some sports of the time, particularly those on college campuses, superficially upheld the virtues of amateurism, pedestrianism made no such claims. Consequently, Weston found an ideal fit in this sport. Before his involvement in pedestrianism, he had worked in various occupations, including as a book salesman and a circus worker, providing him with valuable insights into the art of entertaining the masses.[5]

Weston first grabbed headlines in 1860 when he walked from Boston to Washington, D.C., for Lincoln's inauguration. Mythologizers like Edgerton would later tell this story in a way that omitted the principal reason why Weston did this—namely, that he had lost a bet, which was made in a tavern, where he proclaimed that Lincoln would not win the presidency. The rest of the story went that Weston slogged through snow and ice for ten days, only to arrive shortly after the inauguration and thereby failing to meet the criterion of his wager. As a consolation, he was invited to the White House for Lincoln's first levee, where the new president reportedly offered to pay Weston's train ticket back to Boston. But Weston insisted that he still had to meet the conditions of his wager. So he walked home.[6]

During the Civil War, Weston enlisted as a messenger for the Union, and in this role he supposedly sneaked through the Confederate-controlled areas of Baltimore to deliver mail to soldiers in Washington and Annapolis. After the war, he worked as a reporter for the *New York Sun*, a job that helped him to support his family but not his gambling habit. So he was on the hunt for larger paydays when, in 1867, a sponsor backed his wager of $10,000 that he could walk from Portland, Maine, to Chicago in thirty consecutive days, excluding Sundays. As Weston set forth on his trek, he drew cheering crowds all along the 1,200-mile route until finally reaching his destination one day early, where an estimated crowd of fifty thousand came to see him finish.[7]

At the ensuing celebration, Weston addressed the crowd and discussed his journey at length. The morality and spiritual value of his walk were recurring themes. At one point, he told of meeting a minister who objected to the walk because of the wager attached to it. Weston asserted that if the clergyman would have received the same offer, he would most assuredly have taken it and not donated a penny to the American Tract Society. Weston also recited his testimony to the benefit of exercise: "Athletic sports tend to strengthen the youth of any country, not only their bodies but their mind. A sound mind will be all the sounder for dwelling in a sound body." He then qualified that not all sports were created equal. The violence and excessive passion of prizefighting made athletes and fans alike "forget that they are images of the Great Creator."[8]

The event put Weston and the new sport of pedestrianism squarely in the public eye, with a moral gloss that Weston himself helped to shine. But controversy lingered in the background. During his walk to Chicago, he made three attempts at completing one hundred miles in a single day, with the understanding that he would forfeit over half of his earnings if he failed in this endeavor. Weston's best effort was ninety-one miles, which led to rumors that he intentionally stopped short at the behest of his backers, who had made several side bets on his venture. Weston's defenders dismissed the rumors, claiming that fatigue was to blame. As one North Carolina newspaper put it, Weston was always above the fray and focused on the greater good: "[If] Weston's example shall have the effect of directing general attention to the importance and value of bodily out-door exercise and producing a taste for moderate pedestrianism, the present furor will have accomplished a very good purpose."[9]

Admirers separated Weston from controversy by holding him up as a gentleman and a devoted patron of spiritual and physical health. This defense would reemerge in 1876, when Weston made his way to England to compete in several endurance events. As a way of drawing publicity and attention, he invited medical professionals to test his body's response to the stress of walking. This led to an unexpected revelation during his attempt at walking five hundred miles in six days, when one medical specialist observed Weston chewing on coca leaves—the plant from which cocaine derives. An initial report issued by the physician exonerated Weston from wrongdoing, explaining, "There is no reason why Mr. Weston should not take advantage of every aid which his superior knowledge places at his disposal." As this story circulated throughout England and America, though, critics argued that while coca was not a banned substance, using it violated the moral standards of sportsmanship. Forced to respond, Weston admitted to chewing coca leaves but saw nothing wrong with using a substance that came from "nature." He additionally claimed that he used it only on the advice of his doctor.[10]

While Weston's response was sufficient for some, the *New Orleans Democrat* was not impressed with him nor the sport of pedestrianism more generally. With the noted Louisiana journalist Henry J. Hearsey at the helm, the *Democrat* was the official organ of the state's Democratic Party and a leading voice in ending "carpetbag rule." This political orientation likely influenced an editorial on pedestrianism, wherein the *Democrat* called attention to a race in New York which offered a $50,000 purse: "As a money-making enterprise, the spectacle was certainly an extraordinary success," but for an "enlightened, Christian community" the event stood as proof "that civilization has failed to eradicate utterly the old savage instinct of human nature which delighted in the butcheries of the Roman gladiatorial shows centuries ago."[11]

Interestingly, the article concluded by drawing a contrast to "Indian runners" who engaged in similar contests which "are meant to fit them for their savage conditions of life." As we have seen in the examples of Deerfoot and others, the mention of Indigenous people in this context drew on the long-standing mythology of the "natural runner." It was a tactic that sought to diminish and degrade not only Indigenous people but also the sport of pedestrianism. For the detractors, pedestrianism was an unskilled and purposeless activity that did violence to both the individuals participating and all those whose passions were ignited by the sport. The scolding only grew louder once another kind of pedestrian race gained notice in American cities—ones that featured women.

## "Brutal Torture of Women"

In 1879, a newspaper in Painesville, Ohio, announced that while their city had "withstood the base ball fever," they now faced a larger problem in the form of "the rage for pedestrianism." If the problem of mindless men traipsing around in circles for hours on end wasn't enough, the author expressed outrage that Elsa von Blumen had arrived in Painesville aiming to complete one hundred miles in twenty-seven hours.[12] This particular distance had become a signature event for von Blumen. From Rochester, New York, and born Caroline Wilhelmina Kiner, she assumed her stage name after teaming up with her manager, William H. Roosevelt, whose alias was Burt Miller. After serving in the Civil War, Miller settled in Rochester, where he rose to fame managing the likes of Edward Weston. But he also saw a market for women in this sport—referred to as "pedestriennes."

Prior to von Blumen, Miller's first noteworthy project was Margaret Gangross, or, as she was known more popularly, Bertha von Berg. In 1879, von Berg competed in and won the first known six-day race for women, held at Gilmore's Garden in New York City with eighteen women, all wearing full-length dresses. Six-day races for men had become a sporting sensation ever since P. T. Barnum brought Weston to his famed Hippodrome in 1874 to attempt completing five hundred miles. Weston managed only 326 miles, but the event drew enough spectators that Barnum continued hosting these races. While the women's event drew large numbers, critics fumed with moral outrage. An article in *The Nation*, a weekly magazine in New York, called the event "brutal torture of women." Speculating on the sport's newfound popularity, the author referenced a theory that correlated the rise of pedestrianism with the end of enslavement: "[The] negro no longer being available for the gratification of our inhumanity and cruelty, we have developed the new form of pedestrianism to supply us with a sort of public [n******] whose bodily sufferings and anguish we may get the same pleasure from that we used to get from the writhings of the African under the lash." The author promptly dismissed this argument, however, reasoning that the sport had gained its popularity "in the free and enlightened North." Instead pedestrianism had arisen from "an inborn love of cruel amusements," but at a level heretofore unseen. "It is immeasurably below prize-fighting, bull-fighting, and a number of other cruel sports which the police nowadays break up."[13]

A similar critique came from a Philadelphia newspaper. Calling female pedestrianism "the systematic torture of women," the author reported that of the eighteen participants in the race, several had near-death experiences, and one Bostonian "had gone stark crazy from sleeplessness and exhaustion." The author then told a story about a French woman who left the sport because she was "tired [of] making a slave of herself to keep her husband in drink." This was not just a demeaning and monotonous sport; critics drew upon images of human enslavement, male drunkenness, and torture to stoke fears over the dignity and sanctity of White womanhood.[14]

None of this slowed down von Blumen. As her fame grew, she became known as the "White Fawn" of Rochester, a name given to her by Governor Lucius Robinson of New York after he witnessed one of her walks. Her other nickname was "Queen of Pedestriennes," a title featured on the eve of an event in Hillsboro, Ohio. The local newspaper went to great lengths to assure readers that the event would be respectable and that "the best people" in the city should certainly attend. To further emphasize this point, the article added that von Blumen's walk would in no way "offend the most fastidious lady."[15]

The defenders of women pedestrians celebrated von Blumen as others had Weston, as one who possessed "grit and great powers of endurance." In the 1880s, she turned to another emerging sport, one that featured a machine that encompassed the myriad trepidations and allurements of the era: the bicycle. "In presenting myself to the public in my bicycle exercises," she told *Bicycling World* in 1881, "I feel that I am not only offering the most novel and fascinating entertainment now before the people, but am demonstrating the great need on the part of American young ladies, especially, of physical culture and bodily exercise." She attested that fitness was a key to success in life, and that the bicycle was ultimately a means for greater health.[16]

The interpreters of von Blumen found her to be both a model of female endurance and beauty and a symbol of bodily and social destruction. As we will see in a forthcoming chapter, as bicycling gained more acceptance as a leisure activity, questions remained on how to properly interpret the sight of a woman atop this machine. Irrespective of gender, this was a time when questions swirled around the limits of the human body and whether there were divine prescriptions on the boundaries of endurance.

## The Marathon Craze

"It is horrible, and yet fascinating, this struggle between a set purpose and an utterly exhausted frame," wrote Sir Arthur Conan Doyle of the competitors in the 1908 Olympic marathon in London. The famed author was on site for the event, which was the first marathon raced at the now-standard distance of 26.2 miles. Prior to this, marathons varied in distance between 25 and 26 miles. Following this expectation, the organizers of the London Games had the race starting inside Windsor Castle and finishing almost precisely 26 miles away at White City Stadium in Shepherd's Bush. They would then add 385 yards to the race, bringing competitors into the stadium and finishing in front of the royal family, providing a spectacle and emphasizing the connection between the race and British royalty. While this additional bit of distance was random at the time, it would prove exceedingly consequential to the marathon's outcome.[17]

Among the favorites was Dorando Pietri of Italy, who took a relatively casual pace early, and slowly moved up through the ranks until he finally led with two miles to go. The balmy weather and challenging course, however, had taken its toll on the runner. "At last he came," wrote Doyle. "But how different from the exultant victor whom we expected!" Instead, as Pietri stepped into the stadium to the cheers of 100,000 onlookers, his body had been overwhelmed by miles of dehydration and exhaustion, and he stumbled and fell with each step. As the Italian marathoner entered the final stretch, the crowd's enthusiasm turned to panic when the American competitor Johnny Hayes entered the stadium and seemed determined to pass his collapsing competitor. The rivalry between England and America had been palpable throughout the games, and attendees were content with viewing Pietri as a suitable substitute for one of their countrymen. Despite the yells of the crowd and the willpower of the Italian, it seemed almost inevitable that he would lose to an American. But then, aware of the stakes, a handful of course officials interceded and lifted Pietri to his feet, ushering him across the finish line. The crowd was jubilant, while Hayes finished in second place shortly after. Doyle exclaimed, "No Roman of the prime ever bore himself better than Dorando [Pietri] of the Olympic [*sic*] of 1908." Alas, the American team promptly lodged a formal complaint and Pietri was disqualified for illegal assistance. Queen Alexandra was among the disappointed spectators and, as an act of consolation, gave Pietri a silver cup during the closing ceremony.[18]

While British spectators recounted the race in a tone of tragedy, American accounts were joyous. One newspaper described Hayes's victory as "the most thrilling athletic event that has occurred since that Marathon race in ancient Greece." While Hayes's win was often conflated with the myth of Pheidippides, who, the story goes, died after having run to Athens to deliver news of the victory in the battle of Marathon, his Olympic persona merged with a more distinctly American story of the era—the so-called "Horatio Alger myth," referring to Alger's novels which stressed that through hard work and determination, anyone could become successful in America. Accounts noted that Hayes had been a department store clerk making $20 per week and that he stood just over five feet tall. But after the "terrific struggle" at the Olympics, he was "the biggest thing in New York city." Johnny Hayes, in other words, was living out the American story of rags to riches, of achieving success through his own strenuous efforts.[19]

Hayes's Irish Catholic identity added a unique layer to his mythology. The Irish-American Athletic Club in New York hosted a special celebration for the returning hero at Celtic Park. Hayes was a member of the club, comprised mostly of Irish Catholic athletes who took deep pride in his success. So at the event, roughly twenty-five thousand watched as two firemen carried Hayes into the park. While scheduled to run an exhibition race, the

Olympian couldn't even reach the track because of the enthusiastic crowd. He was instead carried around the track as a band played patriotic songs to accompany the frenzy.[20]

Irish Catholicism and American patriotism came into seamless unity through the form of this victorious Olympic champion. This was significant in a time when anti-Catholic sentiment raised questions about the national loyalties of Catholics. For his part, Hayes was unambiguous in expressing his commitment to his American homeland. In an interview after the Olympics, he was asked about his favorite memory from the games: "It was the moment when we came back into New York Harbor and I got a glimpse of the Statue of Liberty. I've always been a good American. But I don't think any man really knows what patriotism means until he goes through something like this Olympic trip to a foreign land."[21]

With Hayes's fame at a peak, admirers were both lauding and imitating him. "The Marathon craze has spread all over the states," exclaimed a newspaper in Paducah, Kentucky, crediting Hayes's victory in London with sparking interest in this curious sport.[22] As newspapers across America covered the many impromptu contests related to the "craze," it was also a topic in the emerging technology of film. In 1909, the Vitagraph film *Marathon Craze* opened by showing a hapless father reading a newspaper, entranced with the idea of running a marathon. Later he and his entire family march to a local track to compete in a race. One by one, the participants drop out, eventually leaving only the grandmother to emerge victorious. The final scene shows the grandmother being carried off on the shoulders of her grandsons. Vitagraph had other films featuring endurance athletics, including *Mr. Physical Culture's Surprise Party*, which featured a character who was so obsessed with training that he neglected his own birthday. *The Marathon Race* put a more positive angle on the phenomenon by depicting a young man heroically winning a marathon so that he could use the earnings to keep his mother's house from foreclosure by the dastardly lender "Mr. Grab."[23]

Through this new form of popular entertainment, audiences experienced dramatic portrayals of the moral conflict between heroic resilience and zealous depletion. This push and pull also played out in the sport itself. In the final days of 1908, fifteen-year-old Harry Percy Schoen, a student at the College of the City of New York, collapsed and died after completing a training run. Some newspapers claimed Schoen as the first "victim" of the marathon craze. One report that made this argument recounted Hayes's Olympic victory and how it ignited "a craze among the youth of this section of the country to excel as long distance runners." The author then claimed that several physicians had warned against extreme distance running.[24]

The death of Schoen triggered something of a moral panic, a widespread and disproportionate response to a perceived social wrong. One newspaper in St. Louis started by recounting the history of the marathon from ancient Greece onward before asking, "Who is fit to run a Marathon?" No one under eighteen, of course, and no one unwilling to commit to a life of training, sleep, healthy eating, and abstinence. "Few people realize the strain on the heart," the author surmised. "The boy who tackles a Marathon today will feel its ill-effects 20 years from now in his heart action."[25]

A paternalistic concern for "the youth" often accompanied condemnations of distance running. One official from the Amateur Athletic Union exclaimed that "the Marathon craze has gone beyond reasonable bounds and that many of the youths who have competed in them have received injuries that will not easily be overcome." The official pointed to a race in Pittsburgh, where a reported four thousand boys entered a ten-mile race; he called it "almost criminal." Similarly, when Mike Murphy, a noted trainer at the University of Pennsylvania, cautioned against young men running the marathon distance, the sporting public took notice and petitioned the AAU to regulate the event. Murphy reasoned that if an athlete like Dorando Pietri collapsed under the strain of the distance, a young person or improperly trained man would certainly not fare better.[26]

While physical limitations created barriers for "young men" to participate in this sport, social barriers relegated Black athletes to the margins of the marathon craze—especially in the segregated South. In 1909, Lewis Tewanima circled the City Park track in New Orleans to eventually win a twenty-two-mile race. A Hopi runner who competed for the Carlisle Indian School, Tewanima was teammates with Johnny Hayes in the 1908 Olympic marathon, where he finished in ninth place. This exposure made Tewanima an attractive draw for races throughout America, including in New Orleans. "Indian Wins Marathon Race," proclaimed the local newspaper after his victory, describing the "grand ovation" Tewanima received upon breaking the tape. "The only unpleasant feature was an attempt of a negro to enter," the article continued. His name was Charles Burden, and when the Union, Louisiana, native presented himself to physicians before the race, scandal erupted, and he was barred entry. Interestingly, one northern newspaper recounted a very different story. Listing similar details about Burden, the *New York Age* claimed that he had won the event, defeating White and

Indigenous runners in the process. In this story, when Burden's number was called, "the promoters almost had fainting spells, and the doctors refused to examine him."[27]

With segregation gaining strength in the South and White supremacy becoming a racial creed nationally, White eyes perceived the presence of Black skin in sporting venues as a supreme transgression, a breaking of social order. Indeed, the story of sports in the early twentieth century was a story of the making of race in America.

# 7

# "The Lost Religion of Masculinity"

Writing in his diary on July 4, 1910, Reverend David Craig, the pastor of Reidsville Presbyterian Church in North Carolina, grudgingly commented on the news of the day, a prizefight in Reno, Nevada. "It is between a white man and a negro—both brutes! And to see how much is made over this thing . . . in all the newspapers, to me is proof of a very degenerate age." Craig's disposition soured even more the next day. "The Negro whipped the white [man]," he wrote, "and the negroes all over the U.S. especially up North are provoking riots and bloodshed by their boasting." Craig did not lay blame entirely on the Black population for the violence, noting that members of his own race had enabled the "vile" prizefight, leading him to conclude, "I am not sorry the negro brute whipped the degraded white."[1]

The unnamed boxers scrutinized by Craig were Jack Johnson and Jim Jeffries, and the minister's naked disdain for the fight was not unique for White evangelicals of his kind. Wary of wanton violence and misspent time and resources, preachers warned congregations to steer clear of "carnal sports." And yet in the South, as throughout the nation, a rising generation of prizefighting enthusiasts held the sport in high esteem. One New Orleans sportswriter speculated on the eve of the fight that the upcoming bout was the "one absorbing topic of interest at the present time all over the United States, and to a greater or less degree all over the English-speaking world." To those who preached against it, the "moralists," the author responded that this fight was between two great athletes, one Black and the other White, both having prepared through "constant exercise and careful self-denial." Soon thousands would watch these "gladiators" face off because "the fact remains that the English-speaking race dearly loves a brutal fight, especially where there is every guarantee of fair play and an exhibition of nerve, skill and physical endurance." The author was rather unconcerned with race, even though he recognized that White people in the South might find a Johnson victory unacceptable. In the prize ring, the author asserted, "a negro is regarded as the equal and even the superior of the white man."[2]

*Bodies in Motion*. Arthur Remillard, Oxford University Press. © Oxford University Press 2025.
DOI: 10.1093/oso/9780197789766.003.0008

The careful elaboration of the transcendent meaning of prizefighting in this article came punctuated with a counterintuitive suspension of racial norms. In the eyes of the author, within the liminal space of the prize ring athletic prowess held the potential to momentarily supersede entrenched racial hierarchies. This prizefighting enthusiast was representative of many others who cherished this pastime in the South, throughout the nation, and internationally. As the writer Joyce Carol Oates has observed, boxing in the modern age has become "[a] celebration of the lost religion of masculinity all the more trenchant for its being lost." A defining feature of this "religion," in Oates's view, is the male body, which had been domesticated in the age of modernity. The boxing ring therefore serves as a portal, taking viewers to a different time and place, where two individuals embodying a recovered form of manhood do fierce battle until a singular victor emerges. Furthermore, this spectacle of blood and brawn has the power to bind together enthusiasts, giving them a sense of belonging and identity through the drama of the competition.[3]

In the early twentieth century, particularly in narratives involving Jack Johnson, the vivid manifestation of the "lost religion of masculinity" was apparent. Race was a pivotal factor in these stories, boxers assuming the role of racial standard-bearers, thereby rendering this sport a compelling physical representation of the intricate and dynamic delineations between Black and White people in America.

## Prizefighting in Black and White

The American South in the late nineteenth century had a curious and uneven relationship with prizefighting. To begin, because of stiff legal prohibitions on boxing in the Northeast, fighters like the "Boston Strong Boy" John L. Sullivan traveled southward for fights, where the law and culture were slightly more amenable to contests. In 1882, Sullivan and Paddy Ryan trained in New Orleans for their forthcoming bareknuckle brawl, and since ordinances prohibited the fight within city limits, promoters staged it at nearby Mississippi City in Mississippi. Reverend J. William Flynn voiced discontent and urged city officials to cancel the match, expressing worry that the presence of an unsavory crowd could negatively impact the moral well-being of young individuals who might be tempted to associate with such a gathering. Flynn's pleas went unheard. Reports claimed that two thousand people flocked to the fight, many of them prominent figures in New Orleans society. After Sullivan dispatched his competitor, one reporter quipped, "No more orderly crowd ever started for a Sunday School picnic." Taking direct aim at the moralizing of Flynn and others, the author concluded, "A conference of clergymen couldn't have been more staid."[4]

Still, the moral influence wielded by evangelicals in the South continued to impact the region's legal framework. In 1889, when Sullivan returned to New Orleans for a bout against Jake Kilrain, Governor Francis Nicholls, upon learning of the match, vowed to intervene. He dispatched national guardsmen to enforce his order, prompting organizers to swiftly relocate the event to Richburg, Mississippi. The midday match in July endured for seventy-five rounds and two and a half hours, concluding with Kilrain's doctor asserting the fighter's near-death condition. Nevertheless, the legal repercussions extended beyond the ring as authorities arrested Sullivan and Kilrain, imposing a $500 fine on each. During Sullivan's sentencing, the Mississippi judge denounced the fight as a "gross affront to the laws of the State," expressing disdain at the notion of northern fighters holding a match in the South. Similarly, a South Carolina newspaper reversed the moral perspective, expressing incredulity that in the North, they would celebrate the "brutalizing tendencies" of this sport. This, the author argued, highlighted the inverted values of the region that turned Sullivan into a "young man's hero." The true hero, according to the author, was the Mississippi judge who imposed fines on the fighters.[5]

Objections to prizefighting frequently assumed the character of the ongoing sectional rivalry between North and South. Still, northern newspapers were no less critical of prizefighting, nor dismissive of southern states for hosting the fights. This started to change when "Gentleman Jim" Corbett, who we discussed earlier, became the face of the sport. But southern moralists remained suspicious. In 1894, rumors spread that promoters might move a prizefight between Corbett and Charlie Mitchell from Jacksonville, Florida, to Waycross, Georgia. Georgia had not enacted anti-prizefighting laws, and Florida legislators were in an uproar over the fight. Clergymen in Georgia cheered their governor, W. J. Northen, when, in response to the rumor, he sent troops to Waycross to prohibit the fight. Southern preachers weren't alone in their praise for Northen, as Reverend Clarence Greeley of Connecticut wrote a letter to the *New York Times* praising the governor.[6]

Despite all these efforts, the attempt to stop the fight from happening in Florida failed. On the day of the match, roughly three hundred reporters mingled among approximately twenty-five hundred fans to follow the action.

Meanwhile in Atlanta, crowds gathered outside the *Atlanta Constitution* headquarters, eagerly awaiting updates; Corbett won with ease.[7] Despite the calls of evangelicals that boxing degraded the moral status of a city and region, prizefighting remained fantastically popular. However, mixed-race contests would become a common source of White anxiety as the sport grew and developed.

At the 1892 New Orleans Prizefighting Festival, most of the attention went to the feature match between Corbett and Sullivan, which the aged Sullivan lost spectacularly to the handsome upstart. But the featherweight bout had its own drama. George "Little Chocolate" Dixon, a celebrated Black boxer, manhandled his White opponent, Jack Skelly. The New Orleans *Daily Picayune* later gave graphic details of the fight and claimed that Black residents in the city celebrated the victory for two days and nights. Upon further analysis, the author speculated, it was "a mistake to bring the races together on any terms of equality, even in the prize ring." Evangelical critics who had long opposed the sport suddenly had leverage, and their petitions to city officials garnered new attention as New Orleans soon banned interracial boxing.[8]

This marked a moment when an evangelical discourse on boxing partnered with the will of White boxing enthusiasts, as both groups worried about the social implications of interracial boxing. Outside of the South there were unwritten rules around this practice, most aimed at protecting certain sacred spaces in the sport. One year prior to Corbett-Sullivan in New Orleans, Gentleman Jim endured sixty-one grueling rounds against Peter Jackson, a Black native of Saint Croix who had become a boxing sensation in Australia. Held in Los Angeles, the match ended in a draw. Despite the result, Corbett emerged from the fight as the next contender for Sullivan's title, while Jackson watched from afar. But even if Jackson had won, it would have made no difference. As champion, Sullivan had refused to fight a Black man, and when Corbett won the title, he adopted this standard. Curiously, the color line did not extend into the lighter-weight divisions. George Dixon was the bantamweight champion from 1890 to 1892, and the featherweight from 1892 to 1900. Joe Walcott was the welterweight champion for five years after winning it in 1901. And Joe Gans was the lightweight champion from 1902 to 1908.[9]

The heavyweight title, though, was sacred ground, an article of faith in what one historian called a "new religion of whiteness" in America and Europe. Scientific racism, social Darwinism, and the "White man's burden" formed an ideological force that elevated White supremacy to transcendent status. Boxing, especially at the heavyweight level, was a physical performance of this ideal, a bodily expression of White domination. Johnson's Black body represented a form of pollution within this worldview, to be purged at all costs.[10]

Born in Galveston, Texas, Jack Johnson left his home state in 1901 and began traveling America fighting mostly against Black boxers. Slowly he gained notice, and in 1902 he won the opportunity to face Jack Jeffries, the brother of the heavyweight champion, Jim Jeffries. A Los Angeles newspaper predicted, "If there is a favorite, the white man is it." Johnson, though, won convincingly and reportedly informed Jim Jeffries that the same fate would befall the champion if the two met. Jim Jeffries refused to fight Johnson, however, retiring undefeated in 1905. Meanwhile, Canadian Tommy Burns eventually took over as champion, boldly stating that he would defend his title against anyone, irrespective of race.[11]

In 1908, Johnson finally had his chance against Burns in a match staged in Australia. Johnson won in fourteen rounds, reportedly taunting the champion and the crowd the entire time. Novelist Jack London covered the fight for the *New York Herald* and lamented, "The fight! There was no fight. No Armenian massacre could compare with the hopeless slaughter that took place in the Sidney Stadium today." Much like in the United States, Protestant clergymen in Australia went on the defensive. The Sydney Anglican Synod denounced the "inherent brutality and dangerous nature" of prizefighting and worried that it would "corrupt the moral tone of the community." After Johnson won, clergymen continued denouncing the "carnival of savagery," while the broader public worried that the victory could trigger a race war. Johnson, clearly aware of the stir, quipped, "As I am a descendant of Ham, I must bear your reproaches because I beat a white man." He also made a point of criticizing the clergy in Australia. Prior to the fight, he offered to play his bass violin for congregants at a White Methodist church. They denied his request. "I am a churchman, belonging to the Methodist Church," Johnson responded, "but they did not seem to have much use for a colored man in the Methodist churches of that 'white Australia.'"[12]

## The Godsend

As news of the fight reached the United States, Johnson quickly became a hero in Black communities. Booker T. Washington was among his supporters.

Speaking to the Negro Men's Business League in New York, Washington cited the pugilist as a point of reference for his self-help ethos. "In the last analysis, success is what counts," he affirmed. "It is a godsend that he did win. It shows to the Negro race what determination will do."[13]

The "godsend" language grated on the racial sensibilities of one editor in Macon, Georgia: "It is natural, and not particularly objectionable, that the negroes should rejoice in the success of Jack Johnson in the pugilistic field; but to canonize him as 'a godsend'—sent of God—'to the negro race,' is to magnify the habiliment of the soul and to put below it the soul itself." Throughout the article, the author insisted that the true measure of a man was his mind, not his fists and muscles: "If Johnson is the godsend of this generation to the negro, then what is Washington?" The author then turned to Jeffries, dismissively claiming that no one would mention his name "in the same breath with the great men of the white race."[14]

And yet for fans of Jeffries—and Jeffries himself—he was the very embodiment of whiteness and manliness. After his retirement, Jeffries moved to California, got married, and attempted to make a living on an alfalfa farm outside of Los Angeles. At first, he boasted that he had enough money for a lifetime and that the wrangle of prizefighting held no lure. By the next year, however, his financial situation had worsened and a return to the ring seemed a good option—on one condition. "God made me a white man," he affirmed, pledging to fight only White men.[15]

In late 1909, however, Jeffries, strapped for cash and besieged by letters urging him to return, agreed to fight Johnson. The former champion had done very little serious training since his departure. But his supporters had little regard for these limitations. They reveled instead in his mythology, comprising stories about the pugilist curing his pneumonia by consuming a case of whiskey, or a doctor declaring him inhuman after the champion whipped an opponent despite having a broken leg. These legends no doubt helped bind fans to Jeffries, but his whiteness and manliness were potent factors in pulling this community together. "I feel obligated to the sporting public," Jeffries explained, "at least to make an effort to reclaim the heavyweight championship for the white race.... I should step into the ring again and demonstrate that a white man is king of them all."[16]

In the segregated South, White enthusiasts of prizefighting easily embraced Jeffries as the symbol of White America. On the morning of July 4th, the scheduled fight day, the front page of the *Daily Picayune* in New

Orleans depicted a fit, slim, and athletic Uncle Sam practicing boxing moves in a ring, with an eagle in the background saying, "Well! I never expected to see the old man come to this." In contrast, Black communities reportedly prayed for Johnson's victory in their churches, where they also planned to gather for fight updates. However, not everyone shared this enthusiasm. According to a news report from Charlotte, North Carolina, a notable Black minister supported Jeffries, fearing that a Johnson victory "would provoke whites to harbor open enmity toward the negro race." The article claimed other ministers held a similar stance, but it reassured readers that these were merely alarmist predictions, and no hostility would arise from the fight.[17]

When the day finally arrived, some went to churches to learn of the fight, while others gathered at newspaper offices and telegraph companies for round-by-round updates. In Macon, Georgia, an acting company hired two boxers, one Black and the other White, to act out the fight as transcripts arrived. In the end, Johnson scored a convincing victory. "Once again has Johnson sent down to defeat the chosen representative of the white race, and this time the greatest of them," Jack London mourned. "The greatest battle of the century was a monologue delivered to twenty thousand spectators by a smiling negro, who was never in doubt and who was never serious for more than a moment at a time." And in New Orleans, the *Daily Picayune* printed another cartoon of Uncle Sam, only this time his face was badly beaten and bandaged. The caption read, "Somewhat disfigured, but still able to be out."[18]

White enthusiasts were somber, searching for answers and interpreting the fight in ways that downplayed race. A crowd around the *Daily Picayune* "figuratively rubbed its eyes and pinched itself," according to one report. "There was no disorder," the author continued, aware that reports were emerging of riots in major cities. "The consensus of opinion here now is that Jeffries rated the negro too lightly and did not train hard enough." Still, the editorial continued, "[o]nly the very narrow-minded looked upon big Jeff's million dollar scrap with Mistah Johnson as a contest for physical supremacy between the white and black races." Then there was Jeffries's father, a Presbyterian minister. "It's the Lord's will," he commented, noting that the loss was a consequence of his son's less-than-ideal lifestyle—late nights, smoking, and drinking—and that God would use these circumstances to guide Jim toward reflection and a realization of the need for positive change.[19]

Meanwhile Virginia's *Richmond Planet*, a Black newspaper, published a poem titled "Jack Johnson," penned by Lucian B. Watkins:

Jack Johnson, we have waited long for you
    To grow our prayers into this single blow.
To-day we place upon your wreath the dew
    Of tears—the wordless gratitude we owe.
We kiss the perspiration from your face
    And give unbounded love in our embrace.[20]

One *Planet* editorial expressed a measured degree of jubilation, replete with qualifications. "Johnson made many friends as a result of his fairness," the author explained. "He showed too that he had many of the characteristics of the Southern colored man by his modesty, when victory was assured." The author gave minimal notice to the stories of riots, certain that the fight might have caused problems in the North, but in the South "it has proven a God-sent blessing in showing that certain traits and characteristics are inherent in us and when fairly and fully developed make us one of the most powerful races of people on the face of the globe."[21]

In contrast, White newspapers in the city aligned with the trend of downplaying race, sometimes in a surprising manner. The July 5th headline in the Richmond *Times Dispatch* exclaimed, "His Courage as White as His Skin Is Black." Elaborating the next day, the author admitted, "The best man won. He happened to be black, on the outside; but there is general agreement that he was altogether white in his conduct on the most momentous occasion of his life." The author then pivoted toward moralizing, denouncing prize-fighting outright as a profession and pastime. As to the riots in the wake of the fight, they happened "in the Northern part of the great Christian country; in Pittsburgh, which Andy Carnegie has blessed with his benefactions, and where he has preached his homilies on the race question, and in New York, where the sainted members of race equality live." In the South, though, there were no disturbances—except in Atlanta: "Atlanta is the heart of the New South, and is more like a Northern town than any other town in these parts."[22]

The editor took Johnson's victory as an opportunity to deploy a distinctly southern civil religious discourse, one that elevated the moral norms of the Old South and Confederacy and saw northern intrusion as corrosive to their way of life. Southern evangelicals participated in developing this narrative, reasoning that a racially ordered society was a godly society. This view, though, was not particular to the former Confederacy. After the Johnson victory, Bostonian William M. Shaw, general secretary of the United Society of

Christian Endeavor, lobbied governors, mayors, and other elected officials to ban screenings of the Johnson-Jeffries fight footage. Eliminating this "distinctly beastly art" was at the heart of his purity crusade. "Race riots and murders in many places followed the announcement of Johnson's victory in the prize fight," Shaw warned the governor of South Carolina, M. F. Ansel. "These results will be multiplied many fold by moving picture exhibitions." Ansel heeded the warning, as did Governor William H. Mann of Virginia. Officials in the city of Richmond took no chances, as council members quickly drafted a resolution to ban the film, which they assumed would lead to disorder and violence. Atlanta, Lexington, Savannah, and many other cities did the same.[23]

In Macon, an editor applauded the response: "A spectacle that is not only demoralizing per se but will breed inter-racial disturbances should be prohibited." In contrast, the Richmond *Times-Dispatch* was flummoxed: "It looks to us as if a very big mountain is being made out of a very little mole hill." The author puzzled over why governors and municipalities were giving so much credit to the northerner Shaw. "The country has been set on fire by the sensationalists of the press and pulpit. . . . We think that the fight was degrading; but we are more confident of our own strength than to believe that there is any danger in pictures of the fight."[24]

## "To Hell with the Constitution"

One southern legislator saw no mole hill in the fight film controversy. In the aftermath of the fight, U.S. Representative Seaborne A. Roddenberry of Thomasville, Georgia, proposed federal legislation that would limit interstate shipment of the fight films. The bill stalled until 1912, when it passed after Johnson defeated "Fireman" Jim Flynn. Roddenberry led the debate, announcing, "No man descendent from the old Saxon race can look upon that kind of contest without abhorrence and disgust." When Johnson married a White woman, Lucille Cameron, Roddenberry continued his campaign against the boxer, proposing a constitutional ban on interracial marriage. "We can do no greater injustice to the negro," he warned, "than to let our statutes permit him to entertain the hope that at some future time he or his offspring may be married with a woman of the white race. . . . The consequences will bring annihilation to that race which we have protected in our land for all these years." Roddenberry would later elaborate on just what these "consequences" would be: "It is destructive to moral supremacy, and ultimately this slavery of white women to black beasts will bring this nation a conflict as fatal and as bloody as ever reddened the soil of Virginia or crimsoned the mountain paths of Pennsylvania."[25]

To Roddenberry, Johnson's athletic ascendency and interracial marriage symbolized an extreme act of transgression, one that the White politician used to mobilize legal opposition. His proposed amendment ended up being little more than a rhetorical stunt, even though many of Roddenberry's southern colleagues wholeheartedly supported the effort. Elsewhere in the South, opposition to Johnson skipped legislative solutions in favor of lawlessness. At a meeting of governors held in Richmond when news of Johnson's marriage emerged, Governor Cole Blease of South Carolina remarked, "In the South we love our women, we hold them higher than all things else, and whenever anything steps between a Southern man and the defense and virtue of the woman of his nation and his states, he will tear down and walk over it in her defense, regardless of what may [be] the consequences." Blease's point was simple: if Johnson came south, he would be lynched, a crime that had become at this time a ritualized form of vigilante justice that did the work of reasserting boundaries and assuaging White fears over perceived unrestricted Black freedom.[26]

Blease's words drew immediate controversy. Fellow governors asked Blease if he would uphold the Constitution and defend Johnson from lynching. "To hell with the Constitution!" Blease thundered. "When the Constitution steps between me and the defense of the virtue of white women of my state," the governor later explained, "I will resign my commission and tear it up and throw it to the breezes." Blease was censured but showed little concern. "Long after you good governors are no longer governors, the white women of South Carolina will pray for me with their arms around their girls, and will arise from their knees to kiss their husbands and beg them to go to the ballot box and vote for Blease to protect them from their daily terror."[27]

Meanwhile, Johnson continued as boxing's heavyweight champion until one steamy April day in Havana, Cuba, when Kansan Jess Willard knocked him out in the twenty-sixth round. After a litany of "White hopes" had come and gone, Willard finally claimed the title, and his victory led White enthusiasts to pull from their Christian lexicon. "Champion Jess Willard's glorious triumph over Jack Johnson several days ago has proved the salvation of the pugilistic game," declared a Miami newspaper. The author did make one certain prediction, that there would never again be a Black champion.

Indeed, the heavyweight belt would not fit around another Black waist until Joe Louis in 1937.[28]

At the time of the Willard-Johnson match, Johnson was living abroad in exile. In 1913, an all-White jury had convicted him of violating the Mann Act, which barred interstate transportation of women "for the purposes of prostitution or debauchery." The prosecution made the case that Johnson's White girlfriend was a prostitute, a charge he adamantly denied.[29] Johnson spent seven years traveling Europe and the Americas before returning to the United States and serving his sentence of one year and one day.

## The Idea of Jack Johnson

After Johnson departed the prize ring, moralists kept the idea of the fighter handy as a reference point for addressing matters of personal morality. At a public address in Fort Worth, Texas, evangelist Mordecai F. Ham—who would later find fame for converting Billy Graham—evoked Johnson in his crusade against the perceived social evil of dancing: "I don't care whether you call it the tango, the turkey trot, the pollywog wiggle, the puppy snuggle, the cabbage clutch, the lemon squeeze or the fox trot. You can call dancing anything you please, but it's all just plain hugging set to music." This seemingly "innocent amusement," was more sinful than drinking and certainly did not qualify as healthy activity, since "even Jack Johnson has more sense than to take exercise between the hours of 9 o'clock at night and 4 o'clock in the morning."[30]

If one did go dancing and stay up late, one might end up smoking too. At a commencement in Kentucky, a judge told graduates that happiness in life comes to those who follow "the laws of God," which he claimed took form in the "laws of health." The judge exclaimed, "When Jim Jeffries climbed into the ring to box Jack Johnson he was whipped before he got within the ropes. Why? Because he had sapped his vitality by dissipation, especially by smoking cigarettes.... [No] cigarette smoker can succeed in athletics."[31]

Johnson was apparently a popular topic for commencement addresses. In 1915, Reverend E. R. Leyburn of the First Presbyterian Church in Durham, North Carolina, spoke to the graduating class of Davidson College. "All of us wish the highest possible success in life," he said, but he warned them that not all paths to success are noble. "Jack Johnson and Jess Willard, if you will pardon the reference, have both no doubt reached the highest goal of their ambition." Yet they did so in the prize ring. "I have a higher regard for the prize-winner in the dog kennels than I have for either of them or any of their class, for the bull dog is true to his nature . . . while the champion prize fighter is aping the dog."[32]

As the years passed, the evangelical tone on sports and prizefighting in the South started to shift in a positive direction. But Johnson remained a moral counterpoint. Reverend John L. White of the First Baptist Church in Miami was a native of North Carolina and a graduate of Wake Forest. But this credentialed Southern Baptist minister took seriously St. Paul, who himself admired athletes for "their spirit of self-mastery and temperance." For White, sports "have a wholesome influence upon morals." However, he insisted that the intemperate life ultimately brought individuals to spiritual and physical ruin. "It was not age that defeated Jack Johnson," White speculated. "It was dissipation." The minister believed that Johnson's supposedly destructive lifestyle served as a valuable lesson for all athletes, emphasizing the importance of approaching their sports with purpose and steering clear of vices simultaneously.[33]

While White ministers in the South had once railed against the entire enterprise of sports, they were now finding a language to communicate with enthusiasts, negotiating a place between their normative ideals of personal morality and the "lost religion of masculinity." The road to this convergence of Christian theology and sports was a bumpy one. In the American South, segregation accompanied the region's entry into modernity, with industrialization and urbanization bringing new ideas southward. As a result, sports became a location where the idea of race was developed, deployed, and defended. In a similar way, the conditions of the era nationwide created space for another debate to emerge over the place of women in society, and to whether female athletes were living their "true" womanhood or denying it.

# 8

# "She Is What God Originally Meant Her to Be"

In 1896, a Buffalo newspaper declared, "Not so very long ago, the ideal woman was the hapless, strengthless creature who must be protected from the faintest breath of air." As the "new woman" emerged, characterized by greater health and a willingness to engage in competitive sports, the author saw this not just as a rise in female fitness but as a restoration of a divine plan: "She is what God originally meant her to be."[1]

The paradigm shift described in the article had as its pivot point the appropriateness of women participating in competitive sports, with conversations of this nature often revolving around the idea of the "athletic girl." As a Philadelphia newspaper reported in 1900, "Today the term 'athletic girl' is synonymous with 'American girl,' for the modern mother and daughter fully appreciate the value of physical training." The author observed the evolving landscape of female sports, focusing specifically on the popularity of basketball in American gyms. Describing it as the favorite among indoor games, the author emphasized the game's excitement and competitiveness, exclaiming, "The athletic girl does not play this with what is called a 'feminine air,' for free, muscular young bodies act with force and vigor in a loose blouse and bloomers."[2]

Notably, soon after James Naismith introduced basketball to the young men of a YMCA in Springfield, Massachusetts, the physical educator Senda Berenson adapted the game for the women at Smith College. While Naismith, a Presbyterian minister and prototypical "muscular Christian," designed the game with his Christian principles of grace and teamwork in mind, Berenson, a Jewish immigrant, worried about the game's "tendency to roughness." Accordingly, she revised the rules, establishing teams of nine in three zones, limiting ball possession and dribbling, and prohibiting aggressive behavior. Berenson would go on to share her version of basketball widely, including among her coreligionists through the Young Women's

*Bodies in Motion*. Arthur Remillard, Oxford University Press. © Oxford University Press 2025.
DOI: 10.1093/oso/9780197789766.003.0009

Hebrew Association. All the while, she emphasized that her version of basketball was specifically created with women in mind. "[Shall] women blindly imitate the athletics of men without reference to their different organizations and purpose in life," she asked, "or shall their athletics be such as shall develop those physical and moral elements that are particularly necessary for them?"[3]

Using basketball as a platform, Berenson and others sought to redefine the function and meaning of the female body, distinguishing it from men's and challenging the traditional image of "small-waisted, small-footed, small-brained damsel[s]." Christine Terhune Herrick advanced a similar line of thinking. Writing in 1902 in the recreation magazine *Outing*, she asserted, "There is no reason why the athletic girl should be unfeminine," adding that "[the] broadening of her physical powers need not convert her into a mannish woman." Instead, competitive sports "would only ingraft into her nature the gifts she lacks."[4]

For proponents of women in sports, bodily strength and beauty were godly outcomes of the "athletic girl" in action. However, these assertions faced resistance from critics who perceived a fundamental contradiction between athletic effort and womanhood. Thus sports became a battleground for debates over the supposed true nature of women, not only on the field but also in society at large.

## "The Devil's Advance Agent"

"Biking breeds wrinkles," blasted an 1897 headline from Tacoma, Washington. The article went on to describe an "athletic girl" who, once the portrait of feminine beauty, saw all her youthfulness disappear on account of riding a bicycle. But she was a New Yorker, the article reasoned, and in the city, women everywhere were wrinkling their face for the sake of social progress. Other critics similarly located the "athletic girl" in northern cities. In 1898, a reporter from Atlanta visited a rural Georgia town that had become a health resort. As northern tourists arrived, native inhabitants were shocked to see "strange women" dressed in bloomers, riding bicycles through the streets, even on Sundays. And writing in a New Orleans newspaper in 1900, advice columnist Dorothy Dix leveled similar objections, relieved that the "bicycle craze" never penetrated the Southland, where women had no time for the "aggressive" and heartless women of the North.[5]

Debates over women bicyclists had been in motion for over a decade by this point, dovetailing with feminism and feminist causes. The "new woman" of the era was often seen and experienced on a bicycle. Such was the case in 1884 when Belva Lockwood announced that she was running for president. By this point, she had gained a reputation as a trailblazer, becoming the first woman to graduate from National University Law School, the first to practice law in federal courts, and the first to argue a case before the U.S. Supreme Court. But she was also the first woman known to ride a bicycle around Washington, D.C., leading newspapers to depict her conducting her presidential run atop this machine. At this point, the bicycle was a relative novelty, especially regarding women riders. In the mid-1880s, there were roughly fifty thousand bicyclists in America. But by 1895 manufactures in the Northeast produced nearly a half-million bicycles. And even though the country was experiencing an economic depression, the bicycle was having its moment, and women were taking notice.[6]

For the author Stephen Crane, the "bicycle craze" had fundamentally changed the scene in New York City. "All mankind is a-wheel apparently, and a person on nothing but legs feels like a strange animal," he observed. "Everything is bicycle." Crane took notice of "wheelwomen," observing their bloomer-clad bodies peddling these new machines and, in the process, becoming moving symbols of female independence and freedom. While men might have objected to their clothing and physical labors, these women had little concern. "We are about to enter an age of bloomers and the bicycle," Crane exclaimed.[7]

Frances Willard was among those contributing to this age of "bloomers and the bicycle." In 1895, she published *A Wheel within a Wheel*, which served as a double reference to a vision from the prophet Ezekiel in the Hebrew Bible and to her adventures in learning to ride a bicycle in her fifties. Known principally as the president of the Woman's Christian Temperance Union, she also took up such causes as women's suffrage, labor reform, prison reform, economic equality, as well as individual health, which led her to the bicycle. "If I am asked to explain why I learned the bicycle I should say I did it as an act of grace, if not of actual religion," she wrote.[8]

Willard had plenty of company in discerning theological significance in this innovation. "The bicycle is a great teacher of morals," proclaimed the Baptist minister William M. Lawrence in 1896. "You have got to keep on it and continue going on it if you don't want to fall." Lawrence continued with the analogy, emphasizing how forward motion on the bicycle and Christian life required cleanliness, effort, and proper maintenance. It was an image that took literal form with the Bicycle Ride for Christ, the brainchild of Arthur Clark of Newark, New Jersey. In 1896, he and other members of the Christian Endeavor Union donned their uniforms and cycled from their hometown to Washington, D.C., for the organization's national meeting. When plans for the ride made it to the newspapers, other chapters followed suit. The Christian Endeavor grew out of the social gospel movement, which focused on Christianizing the structures of society and advancing the common good. Muscular Christianity folded neatly into this movement, with a stress on healthy bodies and a healthy society. Thus the New Jersey Endeavorers had planned for the men *and* women of their group to participate in the bicycle ride. But worries over the excessive "exertions" of women led to their taking the train to Washington, bringing their bicycles with them for the ride home.[9]

For some, the cycling female Christians registered not as a positive social development but rather as a misguided understanding of the faith and of womanhood. A Delaware newspaper commended the youth of the Christian Endeavor for their "refinement and intelligence" as well as their "good work." But the bicycle ride comprised of men and women was "dangerously vulgar if not blasphemous." The reformer Charlotte Smith pushed this critique even further. "'Bicycle runs for Christ' by the so called Christians," she railed, "should be properly termed 'bicycle runs for satan [*sic*],' for the bicycle is the devil's advance agent." Smith was the founder of the Women's Rescue League, which organized around ministering to "fallen women." In response to the Christian Endeavor's ride, she issued a resolution opposing the "great curse" known as the "bicycle craze." The trend was particularly harmful to women, she asserted, because the bicycle caused physical harm and put them in contact with "evil associations." The implication was that young women could pedal outside of the view of their protectors, making them vulnerable to the sexual advances of unscrupulous men. The panicked tone of the resolution, therefore, called on "all true women and clergymen" to denounce women's bicycling.[10]

In response to the resolution, a Baltimore newspaper surveyed a group of women physicians in the city, all of whom disagreed with Smith. "I have been riding a wheel for more than a year and find myself greatly benefited by it," remarked one. She went on to say that moderation was key with bicycling, but that the aid to breathing was "a godsend to the sex." Another female physician and bicycling advocate went further, blaming the Woman's Rescue League for doing more harm than good by dissuading women from trying this health-giving activity.[11]

While the resolution drew national attention, it was not the kind of attention that Smith had hoped for. "People seem to think I am all bicycle," she exclaimed in the fall of 1896. "The mistakes of my life have been many. There have certainly been none to equal this bicycle business." Smith still insisted that a woman riding a bicycle was "indecent and vulgar." But the vehemence of the backlash had convinced her to step aside from the issue.[12]

While Smith had largely been focused on recreational riders, another development in the sport was also causing moral concern: competitive women bicyclists, particularly those who rode in hundred-mile races. In October 1895, Tillie Anderson, an immigrant from Sweden, entered her first race in the United States, a hundred-mile contest from Elgin to Aurora in Illinois. She went on to build a career around endurance races on the roads and tracks, earning between $5,000 and $6,000 per year in prizes and sponsorships. As crowds flocked to watch "Tillie the Terrible Swede" compete and collect records, she became a champion for women participating in the sport, claiming that the bicycle had transformed her body and given her "sinewy strength."[13]

Predictably, there were assorted detractors. In March 1897, Anderson was a featured rider at Cincinnati's sprawling Music Hall, which coincidentally was also hosting Chicago evangelist Dwight Moody. When reporters told Anderson of the scheduling overlap, she replied that when she lived in Chicago, she had attended his Bible classes. Anderson also knew that Moody would not approve of her athletic pursuits, a fact that would soon be confirmed. "I don't know what we are coming to!" announced Moody when asked about the "bicycle craze." While favoring "wholesome exercise," he worried about the possibility of "lasting injury" from excessive riding. The *Cincinnati Enquirer* played up this controversy, publishing a picture of Moody with a scowl of disapproval alongside Anderson on her bicycle.[14]

Moody's objection was rooted in part in concerns over the nature of womanhood, and the role that athletics played in forming or deforming it. But for Anderson and many other wheelwomen, the bicycle was significant in their turnaround as human beings, in helping them to become fully and wholly who they were intended to be. Sports, in other words, were a means not only for fitness but for bodily conversion.

## Million-Dollar Mermaid

"The new and true gospel of a woman's right to remain beautiful will save more marriages than all the anti-divorce sermons ever preached," wrote Annette Kellerman in her 1918 book, *Physical Beauty.* Originally from Australia, Kellerman drew international attention at the age of seventeen for her two failed attempts at swimming the English Channel. In 1910 she arrived in the United States, where she continued to swim and dive competitively, while also gaining notice as an actress and a fitness advocate. When speaking to women, she emphasized the "right to be beautiful," arguing that intellectual and physical beauty were critical to "happiness and success" in life and family, with extra emphasis on the latter. To achieve this end, Kellerman held up swimming as her ideal. As a self-proclaimed "believer" in the sport, Kellerman maintained that swimming had the power to deliver both physical beauty and physical healing to women. She explained that as a young girl she wore leg braces, the result of childhood rickets, and that competitive swimming strengthened her legs and body to the point where she shed the braces and became a world-class athlete.[15]

Kellerman was not speaking from a formal religious institution, nor did she refer to any specific faith tradition. But her swimming autobiography had an unmistakable Protestant form, insofar as it was a conversion narrative that stressed rebirth and aimed to convert others to the sport. To do this, she deployed a before-and-after structure. Her young life was marked by physical limitations until she discovered swimming. After this, she transformed her entire self and became a model of health, fitness, and, most notably, beauty. Beauty would become central to her mythology and magnetism. In 1910 Dudley Sargent, the director of the Hemenway Gymnasium at Harvard, reported that in his survey of ten thousand young women, Kellerman's proportions had equated to the "perfect" female form.[16]

Kellerman's fame grew substantially when she leveraged her athletic achievements to garner attention, initially as a Vaudeville performer and later in the film industry. In 1916 she had a feature role in the landmark movie *Daughter of the Gods.* Filmed in Jamaica at a cost of roughly a million dollars, it set a new standard for the industry, with over twenty thousand cast members, including a sultan, witches, gnomes, and mermaids. It was also the first film to show full frontal nudity, when Kellerman's bare torso, though mostly covered with her hair, appeared in a waterfall scene. One Washington, D.C., reviewer found the film to be entirely uncontroversial: "With it all, the most prurient will find it hard to point to one incident in all the appearances of the undraped star which is indecent, offensive or inartistic." Other reviewers repeated this sentiment, commending Kellerman's charm and beauty and making note of the distinguished figures who saw the film, such as President Woodrow Wilson and his cabinet.[17]

Through her acting and swimming pursuits, Kellerman actively crafted a heroic mythology that seamlessly merged athleticism with beauty. This narrative found expression not only through words and images but also through the infamous "Annette Kellerman suit," a fixture in female beachwear among the stylish and fashionable of her era and beyond. The suit's origins, while possibly rooted in historical reality, were also accompanied by a tale she began sharing in the 1930s. According to the narrative, shortly after arriving in the United States she went to Boston's Revere Beach with the intention of preparing for a thirteen-mile race, only to face arrest for indecent exposure. At the trial, the judge acknowledged the suit's necessity for athletic competition, permitting Kellerman to wear it as long as she remained covered in a robe until reaching the water. While historical evidence supporting this incident is lacking, it became immortalized in the 1953 film *Million Dollar Mermaid*, with Esther Williams portraying Kellerman. Despite the lack of documentary proof, Kellerman perpetuated the story even after the film's release, intertwining it with her commentary on the emerging fashion trends of the time. Specifically, she criticized the bikini bathing suit, declaring it a "mistake" and asserting that only "two women in a million can wear it."[18]

Kellerman's story helped to advance her image as a barrier breaker and as a leading voice in celebrating the female figure in athletic contexts. She was also singularly important in elevating the stature of swimming, both as a means for exercise and for healing. In 1925 she was featured in a news article alongside Franklin D. Roosevelt on the supposed curative qualities of water and swimming, particularly for "hopeless cripples." Also mentioned in the article was a rising star in competitive swimming, Marie Curtis of Los Angeles.[19]

In 1921, Curtis gained public attention by setting a record time of twenty-seven minutes and fourteen seconds in swimming the Golden Gate channel. While she had been a consistent participant in swimming competitions along the Pacific coast and nationally in distance events, her physical appearance garnered more attention than her swimming prowess. In 1922 Chicago artists immortalized her physique in clay for a city art exhibit, and in 1923 she played a role in the notorious film *Flaming Youth*, described by

F. Scott Fitzgerald as a representative example of Jazz Age defiance. In the film, the lead character, played by Colleen Moore, embodied the "flapper" image, pursuing her mother's former lover. Wearing only undergarments, Curtis and other women were featured in a swim scene, evoking Kellerman's influence.[20]

The connection to Kellerman extended beyond the realm of film for Curtis, who had her own aquatic conversion story. Addressing a gathering at a Los Angeles pool, she emphatically stated that swimming not only saved her life but also contributed to her physical beauty. "Before I embraced [swimming], I was a frail individual," she declared. According to Curtis, her early life was marked by challenges; born weighing less than three pounds and enduring diphtheria and various illnesses throughout her youth, she was a "thin and gawky" teenager. However, her life took a turn when she started swimming at the local YMCA, which she credited as the catalyst for her "physical reconstruction." Within a year, her entire body underwent significant strengthening, transforming her into a completely new person who reveled in the "blessing of perfect health." Curtis concluded her narrative by passionately encouraging every young girl and woman to take up swimming, asserting that the sport was unparalleled in its ability to "create beauty and attractiveness."[21]

The words and actions of competitive swimmers such as Curtis and Kellerman infused their physical activity with sacred allusions and frames of reference, centered around themes of healing, fitness, and beauty. Beyond their athletic achievements, their public personas transcended the ordinary, providing a platform to redefine societal expectations regarding women's capabilities on physical, mental, and spiritual levels. However, in the landscape of American sports during this era, notable disparities existed in the narratives surrounding male and female athletes, particularly concerning the perception of strength and endurance in women.

## Real Girls

After the 1936 Olympics, journalist Jack Bell noted that Jesse Owens had become the primary story of the games. In second place was Eleanor Holm Jarrett. "Mrs. Jarrett," Bell explained, "was kicked off the Olympic team because an old busybody chaperone ran into Eleanor, who was just getting down to her stateroom after a talkfest during which, we must presume, the nectar flowed freely." Bell believed that, on its own, this was an unremarkable story, in part because he found her sport of swimming, and specifically her event of the backstroke, to be "a listless competition." But once the account of a "pretty girl" who drank too much reached Avery Brundage, the president of the U.S. Olympic Committee, he made it into an attention-grabbing news story by claiming that his decision to remove her from competition was for "the respectable citizenry of the United States."[22]

Downplayed in Bell's retelling of these events was the fact that Jarrett was among America's top athletes. She won gold in her event at the 1932 Los Angeles Games and was the favorite to repeat in Berlin. Additionally, even though she did not compete in the Games in 1936, the Associated Press listed her as the sixth best female athlete that year. Her career was impressive enough that in 1980 the Women's Sports Foundation inducted her into their inaugural class of the International Women's Sports Hall of Fame. But because of the 1936 Games, her most notable moment as an athlete came out of the water, a fact that she readily acknowledged. "[Brundage] did make me famous," she remarked years later. "I would have been just another female backstroke swimmer without Brundage."[23]

Part of the memory of Jarrett crossed through the territory of gender discrimination. Plenty of men during the Berlin Games engaged in the exact same activities as she did. But Jarrett was a great athlete who confronted and clashed with a male worldview about female behavior carried forth by Brundage. Brundage would again take the stage as an arbiter of femininity at the 1936 Games in the case of sprinter Helen Stephens. Stephens was the Associated Press's top female athlete of 1936 for having won gold in the 100-meter event in Berlin, defeating her chief rival, Stella Walsh of Poland. After Stephens's win, one aggrieved Polish correspondent accused her of being a man masquerading as a woman. In response, Brundage pledged that Stephens would be "examined" to confirm her gender. With an undisclosed testing method performed, he confirmed that she was, indeed, a "real girl." To add credibility to the claim, reporters questioned Stephens's mother, who emphatically affirmed, "Helen is absolutely a girl."[24]

Like Jarrett, Stephens garnered attention for this off-the-track affair more than for her gold medal. Also like Jarrett, Stephens earned a place in the International Women's Sports Hall of Fame. But in her time, Stephens was among a collection of women who were breaking barriers that men sought to reestablish. In track, one tactic for maintaining the status quo was to question the gender identity of female athletes, thereby seeking not only to invalidate their athletic accomplishments but also to raise broader concerns about "real" womanhood. Throughout Stephens's career, newspapers freely applied masculine descriptors, such as calling her the "brawny miss from Missouri." Following two record-setting performances in Toronto, one newspaper called her a "tall, mannish girl" who wore a size 11 track shoe and "looks like a boy and runs that way."[25]

Adding fuel to the questioning of Stephens's femininity were emerging stories of "the man-woman athlete." Shortly before the 1936 Games, British shot putter and javelin thrower Mark (born Mary) Weston and Czechoslovakian runner Zdeněk Koubek (born Zdeňka Koubková) had both transitioned from female to male. Then there was the aforementioned Stella Walsh, the Polish athlete who finished right behind Stephens at the 1936 Games. Walsh lived most of her life in the United States, mainly in Cleveland. While she considered changing citizenship, she ran under the Polish flag and became one of Poland's most accomplished athletes. Throughout her career, reportedly winning over five thousand events, Walsh set twenty world records while also becoming the first woman to break 11 seconds and 12 seconds respectively in the 100-yard and 100-meter dash. But newspapers often looked past her career, focusing instead on her "manly" appearance. A competitive athlete throughout her life, in 1980 Walsh was robbed and murdered in Cleveland. The ensuing autopsy revealed that she had male sex organs, a revelation that rippled through Cleveland and led to the demeaning catchphrase "Stella's a fella."[26]

Despite Walsh's doings on the track and in her community, her physical appearance took center stage in death just as it did in her athletic prime. Part of this had to do with her particular sport. In 1933, a professor in Italy proclaimed that track sports were "too violent for women." He prescribed instead swimming and skating as well as tennis and golf, so long as they didn't become too competitive. This was a common trend among male observers, such as Caspar Whitney, who in 1894 wrote that noncompetitive golf was "best suited to women." In addition to stressing recreation, Whitney had prescriptions for dress, equipment, and even effort. As one male curator of the game would say, women should avoid taking a "full swing," not because it was beyond their capability but because it would run contrary to the female form.[27]

Limits on physical exertion were one way that men prescribed the boundaries of womanhood, preserving a perceived sacred ideal for female beauty. But in the 1930s, golfers like Patty Berg forged a new path by bringing an element of force and competitiveness into a sport deemed "acceptable" by male standards. In addition to helping to advance competitive golf among women in the United States, she won fifteen major titles during her career. Later observers would heap praise on the golfer for opening doors to the sport. But from her earliest days in the spotlight, her swing was translated through a gendered lens. "She does not poise over the tee with the common feminine hesitancy," exclaimed one 1936 account, seeming to compliment the golfer. "Instead she strides to the ball, gauges her distance and drives off with masculine form."[28]

## Wonder Girl

Fellow professional golfer Mildred "Babe" Didrikson received a similar treatment, amplified on account of her media stardom. Didrikson came into public view after winning two gold medals and one silver in the 1932 Los Angeles Olympics. She returned to her Texas hometown, where thousands cheered her as a conquering hero, just as the media would soon count her as one of the era's greatest athletes, with frequent comparisons to the likes of Jim Thorpe. This also made her marketable. One year after her Olympic performance, a Sports Kings chewing gum card showed her jumping over a high hurdle. The collection included other notable athletes, such as Johnny Weissmuller, Red Grange, Max Baer, and Babe Ruth.[29]

And yet, mixed in with the adulation were intentional efforts to downgrade Didrikson's status as an elite athlete and feminine hero. "Of course when you got right down to elementals she didn't do very much," claimed New York journalist Joe Williams. "All the records she made were ordinary," he reasoned, saying that her marks at the time had been eclipsed by high school boys. "[B]y her championships accomplishments she had merely demonstrated that in athletics women didn't belong, and it would be much better if she and her ilk stayed at home, got themselves prettied up and waited for the phone to ring."[30]

While Williams saw deficiencies in Didrikson, noted sportswriter Grantland Rice perceived an opportunity to create a new kind of hero. Shortly after the 1932 Olympics, Didrikson teamed up with Rice in a golf match against a group of sportswriters. In Rice's account, Didrikson was a newcomer to the sport, requiring assistance on how to even hold the clubs that she was borrowing. And yet she immediately excelled at the game. "She is beyond all belief until you see her perform," Rice beamed. "Then you finally understand that you are looking at the most flawless section of muscle harmony, of complete mental and physical co-ordination the world of sport has ever known."[31]

Of course, some of the details were the product of Rice's mythmaking. While her score was reported to be in the low 80s, the actual number was around 95. More significant, Didrikson had played golf as a high school student in Texas, and after she graduated and worked as a stenographer, she reportedly hit a thousand balls a day at a driving range. None of this would figure into Rice's task of building a persona for the woman that he would infamously call "Wonder Girl."[32]

But Rice wasn't the only one generating a mythology for Didrikson. Paul Gallico was among the journalists participating in this match, and he would go on to write a blistering profile of the athlete in the October 1932 issue of *Vanity Fair*. This was, perhaps, an act of revenge. By the final hole of his golf match against Rice and Didrikson, Gallico and his partner were down one stroke. Then, for no apparent reason, the Olympian challenged Gallico to a race down the fairway, which resulted in a decisive victory for Didrikson. As Gallico sprawled out gasping for air on the green, Didrikson taunted the journalist and went on to win the match for good measure. But Gallico would attempt to find his own victory in print. Over a dozen times he deployed the word "boy" to describe Didrikson, positing that her reason for competing with women in sports was that she could not compete with them in "man-snatching." But the label that followed Didrikson from this article was "muscle moll," a derogatory term intended to call into question her sexual identity and align her with social deviancy.[33]

As insults went, this one carried a great deal of cultural weight. In some gyms in Texas, signs hanging in female locker rooms read, "Don't Be a Muscle Moll." And mothers openly wept at the prospect of their daughters playing softball and becoming "like Babe." Women were among Didrikson's boldest critics. Adela Rogers St. Johns was one of the best-known women reporters of the era, and she too labeled Didrikson a "muscle moll." Writing shortly after the Los Angeles Games, St. Johns claimed that a doctor ordered Didrikson to rest in order to avoid a "nervous break-down or a serious heart ailment." This prescription was clear evidence to the author that women were not designed for the Olympics. Beyond the physical toll, St. Johns described the visuals of the events: "They are awkward, ugly to watch, in many cases thoroughly ridiculous. Cavorting around on the same field with the flower of male champions, they make you ashamed and embarrassed for them." The only sports in which St. Johns believed women should be competing were swimming and diving. "There they are beautiful, graceful and can be the equals of men in form and achievement."[34]

For her own part, Didrikson found creative ways to frame her mythology that sidestepped the critics. In response to claims that track made women too "manly," she retorted, "Marriage is just a decathlon. I'm an all-around athlete but there are ten events to do in a day that would wear me out. Namely: dishwashing, scrubbing, washing, cooking, caring for the baby, cleaning the house, going to the grocer, hanging up the ice card, making the beds and darning socks."[35] By collapsing images of traditional womanhood and track and field, Didrikson adapted to an athletic identity that was equal parts deferential and competitive.

At other times, Didrikson directly confronted the insults. "I never wanted to be a 'muscle moll,'" she remarked when reflecting on her life in sports. "I get lots more fun out of a basket-ball game than I do putting the shot and throwing the discus." Deflecting the "muscle moll" label came with another effort of evading speculation about her domestic future: "One question which always gets my goat is: 'Are you going to get married, Babe?'" She assured readers that she was a "normal girl" in all the ways that they would expect her to be. One of seven children in her household, Didrikson exclaimed that she was skilled in housework and even won a prize for a dress that she designed and sewed.[36]

As Didrikson commanded increased attention, she continued to both adapt to and resist conventional expectations around femininity and sports. In 1935, she entered a women's championship golf tournament in Texas, leading many other women in the tournament to protest that her apparent "manliness" gave her an unfair advantage. In response, Didrikson reportedly duffed her drives on purpose, until she faced Peggy Chandler in the finals for a 36-hole contest.[37]

Chandler came from wealth and matched the look and demeanor that many spectators expected from female golfers. This created a contrast to Didrikson that Gallico delighted in exploiting. While Gallico was not present in Texas, he used a transcript of the match to describe the action, setting the stage by listing Didrikson as "muscular Mildred" and a "track and field star," and Chandler as a "golfer, wife and mother." He extended this contrast into his description of the contest, as he imagined Didrikson landing a chip shot on the penultimate hole and then "swaggering down to her ball, saying,

'Reckon Ah'll hayev to sink this-a one.'" It was all part of Babe's "lifetime vendetta against sissy girls," Gallico conjectured, noting that it was enough to leave Chandler so flustered that she missed a short putt on the final hole. "[Babe] has a self-confidence that is so close to arrogance it is frequently mistaken for this annoying trait," the author resolved.[38]

Gallico's passive-aggressive conclusion once again called into question Didrikson's victory and femininity. Meanwhile Didrikson would continue developing strategies to address these charges. She reportedly wore a girdle at one point, leading her to exclaim to friends, "Goddamn! I'm choking to death." So instead she made a joke of it. "When I wanta really blast one, I just loosen my girdle and let 'er fly!" she told reporters. Marriage proved to be the factor that eventually silenced her critics. Despite her efforts to sustain a career as a professional athlete through barnstorming, exhibitions, and novelty acts, she struggled to make a substantial living. However, her fortunes changed when she met and married George Zaharias, a professional wrestler and promoter. Zaharias's financial success in his field alleviated the concerns of those who questioned Didrikson's career choices, as she was now linked with a conventionally "manly" man. After the conclusion of World War II and the resumption of tournament golf, Didrikson emerged as a dominant force in the sport, achieving a remarkable feat of winning seventeen tournaments in a row from 1946 to 1947. As her success in golf soared, media coverage shifted, now focusing on her physical appearance, style of dress, makeup, and overall demeanor. While still recognized for her competitive spirit, observers began to speak positively about her feminine stature.[39]

Didrikson's new status gave her leverage to bring more women into sports. She was instrumental in founding the Ladies Professional Golf Association in 1948. In short order, she became the LPGA's centerpiece. "Our sport grew because of Babe," remarked Patty Berg. "She had so much flair, color and showmanship, we needed her. Her power astonished galleries." It was a fact that Didrikson was reportedly fully aware of. When accounts surfaced of simmering resentment from the tour's other golfers, she held a meeting and told the women, "You know when there's a star like in show business? The star has her name in lights, right? Well, I happen to be the star of this show and all the rest of you are in the chorus."[40]

Babe Didrikson's story began coming to an end when she received a cancer diagnosis in 1953. In the initial stages, she was able to continue competing in golf tournaments, despite having a colostomy. Recalling a performance in a tournament after her diagnosis, one journalist exclaimed, "Her presence on that first tee was an act of heroism that should have been rewarded with the Congressional Medal of Honor." This journalist was none other than Paul Gallico, writing shortly after Didrikson succumbed to cancer on September 27, 1956. The obituary struck a different tone from that of his previous portrayals, making no mention of the "muscle moll" and instead celebrating her as an "exceptional woman" who had become a pillar in sports and society. Indeed, her name would be closely associated with the so-called Golden Age of Sports, an era in athletics when sportswriters like Gallico and his golf partner Rice made it their business to add literary flare to the deeds and doings of athletes of the time.[41]

# 9

# The Golden Age of Sports

In the early twentieth century, prominent leaders in various sectors of society, such as Theodore Roosevelt, Marcus Garvey, and Billy Sunday, used the emerging mass media of the day to connect with wide audiences and enact significant change. Commenters at the time noted their "personal magnetism," a phrase that referred to a certain rhetorical skill of these leaders that helped to forge an emotional bond with their followers. There was a similar dynamic at work in sports. Observing the power of Babe Ruth and Jack Dempsey to command public attention, the sportswriter Grantland Rice pondered the unique "magnetism" of these athletes, as evidenced by their ability to draw record crowds—crowds that paid money to see them. In Ruth's time with the Yankees, the team became as profitable as similar investments in the Dow Jones Industrial Average. Dempsey's 1921 fight with Georges Carpentier became the first million-dollar gate in the sport. Dempsey had three more fights in the decade that eclipsed the million-dollar mark, and then his 1927 contest with Gene Tunney drew $2,658,660 and attracted millions of radio listeners.[1]

One way that historians have contextualized the "magnetism craze" of this era has been to employ the concept of "charisma," emphasizing that leaders gain their authority through a seemingly otherworldly force. It was the sociologist Max Weber who recovered the word from its Greek and early Christian origins and brought charisma into scholarly discourse, defining it as "a certain quality of an individual personality by virtue of which he is set apart from ordinary men and treated as endowed with supernatural, superhuman, or at least specifically exceptional powers or qualities."[2]

So charisma, from its earliest incarnations onward, has carried with it a spiritual sensibility, a trace of transcendence that, while not always located in traditional religious structures, does a unique kind of religious work of binding together people and their leaders. But charisma is also a production of human effort, of interpreters who tell the story of people in their supposedly magnetic rhetoric and activity. In the world of sports, it was journalists like Grantland Rice who made the so-called Golden Age of Sports into the

*Bodies in Motion*. Arthur Remillard, Oxford University Press. © Oxford University Press 2025.
DOI: 10.1093/oso/9780197789766.003.0010

Golden Age of Sports Writing. Put another way, the rise of the charismatic athlete was owed in large part to the rise in sportswriters who made it their business to transform inconsequential events on the field of play into eternally consequential mythologies. As the attention and dollars followed, however, so too did a moral debate about the business of sports, and whether an athlete's charisma was just a smokescreen for separating people from their paychecks.[3]

## Making $ports Hero$

"When a sportswriter stops making heroes out of athletes, it's time to get out of the business," quipped Rice. Among his more notable mythmaking ventures occurred in 1924, when Rice penned what would become a legendary account of a football game between Notre Dame and Army. "Outlined against a blue-gray October sky, the Four Horsemen rode again," he opened, referring to the backfield of Notre Dame's offense. Drawing on distinct Christian imagery and metaphor, he framed accounts of Notre Dame teams with a flare and style that drew national attention. Here and elsewhere, Rice and his literary fellows intentionally sought to take otherwise mundane contests and make them extraordinary.[4]

One of their main strategies was to use attention-grabbing and memorable nicknames for athletes. For three years, Harold "Red" Grange delighted crowds and set records playing football for the University of Illinois. He drew national fame on October 18, 1924, when he collected five touchdowns in a victory over Michigan by a score of 39–14. Rice turned the athlete's accomplishments into poetry:

> A streak of fire, a breath of flame,
> Eluding all who reach the clutch;
> A gray ghost thrown into the game
> That rival hands may never touch.[5]

Red Grange would thereafter become known as the "Galloping Ghost." It was a name that traveled with the athlete when, in 1925, he opted to play professional football, a decision that would breathe an air of legitimacy into the struggling National Football League. However, as Grange barnstormed across America, some sports critics used his celebrity to engage in discussions about the "purity" of the game and, more broadly, the impact of money on intercollegiate athletics. This debate took an interesting turn, moving beyond the confines of newspapers and sports periodicals to find a platform in the emerging high-minded monthly and quarterly journals of the time. In 1926, *Forum* featured Upton Sinclair challenging the defenders of college football, contending that the game undermined the mental and physical well-being of young men and, as such, should be abolished. Similarly, John Tunis became a stout critic of the game, so much so that one historian has called him "the Great Scold of college football."[6]

Tunis had made his career writing about country club sports before publishing *$port$ Heroics and Hysterics* in 1928. Thus Tunis had favorable words for those who loved "real sport" like golf and tennis, which were played by the "sportsman" who understood the value of competitive recreation. But he claimed that much of the sports world had been consumed by the "curious fiction" that organized sports build character, improve health, and lend to healthy international competition. All of this, according to Tunis, equated to "the Great Sports Myth," a dense diversion built on the power of human emotion that obscured the financial realities of organized sports. Tunis likewise charged sportswriters with building this harmful sentiment by penning stories "with an almost religious seriousness," thereby making it so that "the sporting heroes of the nation are its gods."[7]

Tunis's critique leaned on a use of the word "religion" that depicted adherents as mindless followers of authority, easily distracted by emotional appeals to magic and spectacle. Taking a slightly different approach was New York journalist Francis Wallace. Unlike Tunis, who idealized amateurism and had little time for the violence and spectacle of football, Wallace advocated bringing all the underground activities to the surface. For Wallace, all the supposed "reforms" of college football were ultimately hypocritical, because this "semi-professional sport" had become awash in money and commercialism. The mindset around the "purity" of amateurism distorted the reality of what these athletes could become. Wallace asked, "Why is a boy a traitor if he plays a professional game to get enough money to buy clothes for his graduation?" The answer, he supposed, was that schools wanted to continue building stadiums and funding their own operations. As Wallace saw it, universities could either eliminate the "evil of commercialism" by removing gate receipts and other forms of monetary exchange, or they could dispense with the sham that was amateur athletics. To do anything else, he concluded, would be "to shout at athletic revival meetings while living in sin."[8]

## The High Priest of the Gridiron

Wallace was no stranger to religious language and allusions; before coming to New York, he was a student at Notre Dame, where he was a press agent for the football team, which was coached by the legendary Knute Rockne. Beyond on-the-field tactics, Rockne recognized the power of public narratives. Thus press agents like Wallace did the work of building a mythology, of making this team and this coach into living legends. Starting in 1918, the distinctively Catholic university defeated America's finest Protestant and secular universities. Along the way, they became a positive symbol of American Catholicism in an era of rising anti-Catholicism and nativism. Following Rockne's untimely death in an airplane crash in 1931, one tribute from New York labeled the coach the "high priest of the gridiron" and "an evangel of tolerance." "In popularizing the foremost Catholic football team," the author explained, "he used a universal instrument—sport—to break down bigotry. His team each year invaded the Ku Klux belt for a game with Georgia Tech and won a popularity there next only to Yale."[9]

This reference to the Klan played on a perception that the organization thrived principally in the American South. To be sure, the Klan emerged during Reconstruction in the region and reemerged again there after the 1915 release of *Birth of a Nation.* Klan imagery even became part of college football's vernacular in the South. When teams were plagued by leg injuries, journalists would jokingly call these sidelined players members of the "Knee Kap Klan."[10]

But by 1924 Indiana too had become a Klan stronghold, with an estimated 30 percent of native-born White men in the state holding membership. The Klan's leader in Indiana was D. C. Stephenson. He used the tactic of respectability to promote the organization, insisting that it was a social club and fraternity, unified by a shared sense of patriotism and virtue. The Klan, Stephenson insisted, was the people of picnics and parades and not the unruly antics of popular imagination. The campaign was successful, and Stephenson enriched himself through an influx of membership dues and apparel sales. Additionally, Klansmen began taking over state politics, and at the height of their power in 1924, the Klan began targeting South Bend. With rumors circulating that the city's sewer harbored an arsenal for a Catholic uprising, Klan speakers began lecturing on the presumed incompatibility of Catholicism and America. Then, on May 17, 1924, a planned three-day Klan rally drew Notre Dame students to the streets to respond. In the early stages, students gathered around the Klan's headquarters, where they tossed potatoes at a window that held a cross of red lightbulbs, meant to imitate the infamous flaming cross. They managed to destroy all but one lightbulb, which stubbornly evaded their throws. And then, suddenly, Harry Stuhldreher, their quarterback and one of the soon-to-be-declared Four Horsemen, emerged from the crowd, grabbed a potato, and dispatched the final flickering lightbulb.[11]

Tensions between the Notre Dame students and the Klan escalated until Monday, as hundreds of students and Klansmen brawled in the streets. At one point, the Notre Dame men retreated to the courthouse, where Father Matthew Walsh, the university's president, urged them to return to campus. In the aftermath, the administration at Notre Dame attempted to downplay the event, concerned that the riot would feed into preexisting stereotypes about the belligerence of Irish Catholic people. The Klan, meanwhile, went to work creating their own story. One of their publications described an unprovoked attack not only on Klansmen but on local men, women, and children. All the while, the "cursing mob" made sure to stomp on American flags.[12]

Father Walsh's office was inundated with hate mail, but the fury died down when revelations of Stephenson's criminal sexual activity surfaced. In 1925, Stephenson was found guilty of the rape and murder of Madge Oberholtzer. The trial revealed that Stephenson and his associates, all advocates of Prohibition and "Protestant womanhood," were serial drinkers and womanizers. One consequence of the trial was the rapid diminishment of the Klan in Indiana. Meanwhile, Notre Dame underwent its own image rehabilitation project. When Francis Wallace went to New York and began writing about his alma mater, he resisted using a common nickname applied to Notre Dame: "Fighting Irish." But then Wallace took ownership of the team's name, transforming a pejorative label into a badge of honor. In 1927, with more and more people using this label positively, Father Walsh made the nickname official.[13]

The mythmaking of Wallace and others helped propel the Fighting Irish into the national spotlight, thereby enabling a bond to form between American Catholics and the Notre Dame football team. Even in the American South, a place where anti-Catholicism had a deep hold, sportswriters like Fuzzy Woodruff heaped praise on Rockne and his teams for their victories in the Southland. Similarly, the Dothan, Alabama, newsman Scottie McKenzie Frasier held up Rockne as a leader who eschewed religious bigotry and intolerance: "We need men like Knute Rockne, who will call the youth of America to move up three yards out of a lawless and cynical and self-indulgent era on to the line where Honor, Justice and Truth are required as the only worthwhile touchdown in Life's game."[14] Football was a growing sport in the South, and the region's journalistic mythmakers like Woodruff and Frasier were deeply involved in making the game more visible and attractive to a wider audience. They would do this by foregrounding the charismatic appeal of the teams and coaches who were succeeding on the field of play.

## "Centre Saves the South!"

In the early days of college football, journalists and enthusiasts in the South faced a distinct challenge in comparison to their northern counterparts in the form of an evangelical establishment that had been suspicious of the game. In the 1890s, several religiously affiliated colleges in the South disbanded their football teams after starting these programs only a few short years before. Evangelical sensibilities recoiled at what they believed was the debauchery of the game and its fans, nodding in collective agreement with one college president who called football "an evil that the best tastes of the public have rebelled against."[15]

But a few short decades later, a distinctly evangelical discourse came to the surface in the sport, thanks to the Praying Colonels of Centre College in Kentucky. In 1920, the relatively unknown Presbyterian school traveled north to play the mighty Harvard Crimson. Anticipation for the game led to an estimated forty thousand fans and curious onlookers crowding into Harvard Stadium, where they watched Centre's quarterback Bo McMillan direct his team to a 14–7 halftime lead. The Harvard squad had not only entered the game undefeated, but to that point, they were unscored upon. While Centre seemed poised for the upset, Harvard reclaimed the lead in the second half and won 31–14. According to one account, Harvard's captain offered the game ball to McMillan, who promptly refused it and vowed to return the following year to win it properly.[16]

Indeed, in 1921 McMillan and his team made the trip to Boston once more, this time winning by a score of 6–0. While Vanderbilt and Auburn had experienced some success in interregional contests, Harvard was a football powerhouse with very few rivals in the sport. Accordingly, accounts of the game in Boston and throughout the Northeast made note of the momentous victory, emphasizing that this unlikely college from the Bluegrass State had "conquered" a mighty giant thanks in part to the "hero" Bo McMillan. As news of the victory filtered into the Southland, interpretations of the game went even further with the transcendent allusions. With pride and pleasure, the *Atlanta Constitution* announced, "Centre saves the South" and dubbed McMillin a "New Immortal." Moreover, stories about these "pious" southern football players praying before games inspired teams at other Christian schools to follow suit.[17]

The southern blend of playing and praying was not enough to win over some of Centre's critics, even those in the South. The Praying Colonels lost their final game of the 1921 season to Texas A&M in the Dixie Classic by a score of 14–22. Fuzzy Woodruff took delight in the result. An unabashed booster for the southern football cause, Woodruff dismissed the victory against Harvard on the grounds that he believed Centre had enlisted "ringers," or paid players. Additionally, Woodruff objected to Centre's not being a member of the Southern Intercollegiate Athletic Association, a regulatory body he championed for their commitment to the "purification of college athletics." Woodruff and his ilk happily allowed Centre's victory to become a distant memory once Alabama defeated the Washington Huskies in the 1926 Rose Bowl. The victory certainly caused a stir in Tuscaloosa, and it has since become known as "the game that changed the South."[18]

Football in the South had begun to merge with and shape the broader national college football culture, a project that in previous years had been the aim and ambition of John Heisman. A native Ohioan, Heisman brought his coaching skills southward to Auburn and Clemson before taking over in 1904 at Georgia Tech, where he remained until 1919. Woodruff called Heisman the "Dean of the Dixie Gridiron" and a "wizard" who compiled a record of 102–29–7 and won a national championship in 1917. Outside of football, Heisman was a lover of acting and opera, even appearing on stage early in his career to supplement his income. The skills honed on the stage translated to the football field, as Heisman became known for his stirring oratories to his teams and the public. He was also known for his margins of victory. In 1916, his Georgia Tech team defeated the Cumberland College Bulldogs by a score of 220–0. Cumberland had suspended their program beforehand but played anyway with a hastily assembled team to avoid a breach of contract. Heisman was reportedly upset that in the previous year Cumberland had defeated Tech in baseball 22–0. At halftime with a score of 126–0, Heisman cajoled his players to keep pushing. Once the second half resumed, Cumberland players reportedly hid under blankets and jumped the fence to escape. The game would become known as "football's glorious slaughter," and forty years later the teams held a reunion. "Little did we realize we were playing ourselves into immortality that day," remarked a Cumberland player.[19]

In 1919 Heisman and his wife divorced, and as part of the agreement he left Atlanta, where his former wife chose to stay so that she could avoid "social embarrassment." Northern newspapers took notice. One Pittsburgh paper exclaimed, "There is no doubt that wherever he goes Heisman's efforts to establish himself in the east will command much attention from the football men." He quickly found employment at his alma mater, the University of Pennsylvania, and gained additional notoriety with his 1922 book, *Principles of Football*. In it, the coach focused on football's supposedly positive influence on young men, echoing a muscular Christian discourse about the game's ability to inculcate self-control, clean living, honesty, fidelity, and sportsmanship. All of this led to young men who were prepared not only for college and college sports but for service to their country as well. With memories of the Great War in the backdrop, he explained, "The first duty of a soldier is to obey orders. It so happens it's the first duty of a football player as well." The militaristic ethos also applied to coaches, who Heisman urged to be "masterful and commanding" as well as "severe, arbitrary, and little short of a czar."[20]

Heisman retired from football in 1927 and took up residence in New York, where he turned his attention to writing and publishing articles in noted outlets of the era, including *American Liberty* and *Collier's Magazine*, while also serving as the football editor for *Sporting Goods Journal*. By 1930, his elevated status in the football media had led to his being appointed as the first athletic director of New York's Downtown Athletic Club. In this role, Heisman took the lead in creating an award for the most outstanding college football player in the nation. In 1935, the inaugural Downtown Athletic Club Award was presented to Jay Berwanger of the University of Chicago. Heisman passed away the following year, prompting the club to rename the award for him. In the coming years, the Heisman Trophy would become a "sacred trophy" and an "American icon." At the end of each football season, the nation's top players make the "pilgrimage" to New York City for the award ceremony.[21]

The deliberate incorporation of religious language in the interpretation of this trophy bears witness to its magnetic pull, historical significance, and continued importance in college football. But while the Heisman Trophy is an object that speaks to the memory of its namesake and his role in the game, Ray Chapman's enduring emotional resonance in baseball arose from a tragic event.

## Baseball's Martyr

October 1920 roared in Cleveland, with newspapers echoing a spirited chorus: "Do it for Ray!" The fervent cry reverberated as the Indians professional baseball team triumphed through the World Series, ultimately clinching victory over Brooklyn. The rallying call paid homage to Ray Chapman, whose tragic demise on August 16, 1920, captivated the nation after he succumbed to a fatal blow to the head from a pitch by Carl Mays of the New York Yankees. The *New York Times* mournfully observed, "The tragic death of Ray Chapman has thrown a veil of sadness over major league baseball."[22]

While national headlines chronicled the incident, Cleveland's passionate fans commemorated Chapman's life and career in the immediate aftermath of his passing. Flags flew at half-staff, and St. John's Catholic Cathedral became a solemn gathering place as thousands paid their respects during his funeral. The somber occasion saw thirty-four priests participate, with Rev. Dr. William A. Scullen delivering a eulogy. Describing Chapman as "clean, wholesome, gentle, and true," Scullen emphasized the player's impact beyond the field: "[Chapman] was the idol of this city as a ball player—but above all was his gentleness and kindness as a man." Addressing the potential blame cast on Mays for Chapman's demise, Scullen discouraged hasty conclusions, drawing not from religious teachings but from the spirit of baseball. "The great American game of baseball does not develop men who would willingly try to injure another participant in the game," the priest averred. "Chapman, we know, would be the first to decry any thought of revenge if he could but speak."[23]

Following the funeral, fans donated funds for a plaque in Chapman's memory, which was hung at League Park in Cleveland. While the plaque is significant, his gravestone has developed an even more magnetic appeal, with fans through the decades routinely leaving baseballs, poems, books, pennants, and assorted other tokens of tribute at the location. This activity reportedly has increased when the team is doing poorly, indicating that

Chapman has come to represent a kind of intercessor to the gods of baseball. Or perhaps, more accurately, as one sports journalist phrased it, Chapman is "baseball's martyr." This classification took visual form in 2018, when artist Michael Guccione created an icon of Chapman, intentionally patterning it after the Christian martyr St. Stephen, who legend states was stoned to death in 34 CE. Guccione explained, "The sudden fatal events the two men shared were too striking to ignore."[24]

Martyrs like St. Stephen have as their story dying for a cause, persecuted directly by a hostile outside force. But admirers adapted the imagery of the stoned martyr to Chapman, who they have remembered as both a hero of their baseball team and a man whose death forever changed baseball for the better. Blame for Chapman's death was placed partly on the ball itself, which on that gray, dreary day had been practically unseeable. Such was the convention of the "dead ball" era, when a cost-conscious league extended the life of every ball as much as possible. When the 1921 season opened, the "Chapman Rule" mandated the immediate retirement of any baseball that became discolored, scuffed, or dirty during play. The clean, white baseballs became a visual symbol of a new era in the game, in terms of safety as well as the game itself.[25]

On the topic of safety, in addition to the ball, there was also added momentum for the use of helmets. At the outset of the 1921 season, Cleveland players experimented with wearing leather helmets like those worn in football. This was a significant change, because in previous years the helmet had been seen as a sign of weakness. But in 1921 *Spalding's Official Base Ball Guide* announced, "A head helmet for the batter is not to be despised. There is nothing 'sissy' about it."[26] While standardized helmet use was three decades away in Major League Baseball, the death of Chapman brought the issue into the realm of serious consideration.

Serious too were considerations about the moral responsibility of pitchers. Mays insisted that even if he had intended to do harm to Chapman, hitting him directly on the temple exceeded the ability of the best pitchers. "Suppose a pitcher were a moral monster enough to want to kill a batter," he pondered. "Christy Mathewson in the days of his most perfect control couldn't have hit a batter in the temple once in a thousand tries." Mays added that Walter Johnson, one of the hardest throwing pitchers of the era, had hit numerous batters on the head, none of them dying as a result. For his own part, Johnson was aware of the speed of his pitches, going so far as to pitch outside to batters who crowded the plate. "The bean ball is one of the meanest things on earth and no decent fellow would use it," he exclaimed.[27]

The road to Chapman's becoming "baseball's martyr" was laid soon after his death, a time when the conversations around morality and ethics in baseball led to calls to adjust and recalibrate. In prior decades, critics were assured that the sport of baseball was nothing more than a "craze" that would have little staying power. But the money and magnetic allure of baseball and its famed athletes gave the game a deeply entrenched place in American culture. And it would become only more entrenched with the end of the dead ball era, when baseball was characterized by low-scoring games, limited home runs, and an emphasis on pitching, defense, and small-ball strategies. Home runs were a rarity, and several seasons ended with league leaders hitting fewer than ten. The Chapman Rule resulted in firmer balls throughout games, making home runs more possible. In turn, this made space for a new kind of baseball hero, the power hitter, who came in the form of Babe Ruth.[28]

Meanwhile, the accomplished athletes of the dead ball era who had been celebrated for their speed and cunning, faded into obscurity. Such was the case with Ty Cobb. Grantland Rice called Cobb his "first big story," recalling a 1904 account about the then eighteen-year-old Cobb who had just started spring training. "He is a terrific hitter and faster than a deer,". Rice exclaimed, "he is undoubtedly a phenom." Rice and others helped to elevate the status of Cobb, who they described as a fierce competitor with something to prove. In 1936, Cobb became the first inductee in the newly created Baseball Hall of Fame, garnering the most votes of any player. "The famous Georgian," announced one account, "won the distinction as the immortal of immortals today by outscoring even such diamond greats as Babe Ruth, Honus Wagner and Christy Mathewson."[29]

Despite his widespread acclaim, Cobb harbored concerns about his legacy, particularly as baseball shifted its focus from speed to power, raising questions about how he would be remembered or if he would be remembered at all. In 1955, the popular game show *I've Got a Secret* featured Cobb as the "mystery guest," unveiling his secret of holding the highest lifetime batting average in baseball's history. However, the blindfolded panelists failed to identify Cobb or his achievement, and even after the blindfolds came off, they gazed quizzically at the sixty-eight-year-old legend. It was precisely the reaction that Cobb feared most. In response to these worries, he decided to collaborate with sportswriter Al Stump on his autobiography, intending to "set the record straight." Cobb passed away before the book was published, and upon its release it achieved only modest sales. For his part, Stump would claim Cobb wanted the book to portray him as a "wronged person, a Caesar knifed in the back, a martyr." But Stump saw the baseball player differently. In December 1961, he published an article based on his time with Cobb, characterizing the autobiography as a "cover-up" and depicting Cobb as a racist, murderous, violent tyrant who lived in estrangement from family and friends, ultimately dying alone. Stump's article became integral to the prevailing public perception of Cobb's memory, influencing a 1994 film. Subsequent historical analysis has shown that Stump's account was largely embellished and, at times, outright fabricated, leading one writer to conclude that Cobb was "stumped by the storyteller."[30]

Ty Cobb's portrayal by storytellers has changed over time, casting the athlete's nickname, the "Georgia Peach," in both endearing and despicable lights. Coined, perhaps, by Detroit sportswriter Joe S. Jackson in 1906, the name emerged as Cobb prepared for the upcoming season, with Jackson envisioning the entire town rallying behind him. Jackson's anticipation of crowds assembling wherever Cobb went envisioned a scenario wherein a "grand chorus of fans" would flood the streets, singing praises to Cobb, the relocated southerner promising greatness for Detroit.[31] During the Golden Age of Sports, monikers like "Georgia Peach" played a crucial role in capturing the magnetic charm and charismatic appeal of sports celebrities. For athletes whose identities transcended the predominantly White mainstream, these names served a dual purpose. They not only provided a distinctive identity but also signaled difference, representing a mythical persona arising from an unfamiliar corner of the American landscape.

# 10
# The Name of the Game

"[Even] though he has inherited no title, Duke Kahanamoku is a king just the same, a king of the water by the power of his great arms and the rhythmical kick of his sturdy legs," wrote Charley Paddock in 1929. Paddock, an Olympic sprinter and aspiring writer, intentionally linked the renowned swimmer Kahanamoku's name and Hawaiian heritage to royalty in his profile. He also highlighted the swimmer's impressive longevity. Paddock pointed out the lasting impact of sports legends such as Babe Ruth, Jack Dempsey, Bobby Jones, and Bill Tilden, each having enjoyed prolonged success. Kahanamoku achieved championship status earlier than any of these athletes, and his success endured longer than theirs as well. In 1910, Kahanamoku set a swimming record at the 50-yard distance, which he subsequently broke again in 1923. His stellar achievements included winning three gold medals across the 1912, 1920, and 1924 Olympics. Remarkably, at the age of forty, Kahanamoku came close to making the 1928 Olympic team.[1]

Duke Kahanamoku was, in Paddock's estimation, a legend among legends. To mention his name was to conjure images of a transcendent athletic talent with unparalleled longevity and gracious humility. He was also Hawaiian royalty, even though he wasn't. Kahanamoku's father had been named Duke in honor of Prince Alfred, Duke of Edinburgh, who had visited Hawaii. The younger Kahanamoku would take his father's name. But when Kahanamoku became a sports celebrity, his name beckoned interpreters to draw the comparison by leaning on tropes of an exotic island culture, differentiated from the American mainland.

As indicated in the previous chapter, names in the Golden Age of Sports had a mythological weight born out of a common perception of the athlete as superhuman and larger than life. Babe Ruth wasn't just Babe Ruth, after all. He was "the Bambino," "the Sultan of Swat," "the Colossus of Clout," and many other names that helped to elevate his status within the sport of baseball and beyond. "Duke" as a name did a similar kind of symbolic work, connecting the image of royalty to athletic fame and achievement, as well as

*Bodies in Motion*. Arthur Remillard, Oxford University Press. © Oxford University Press 2025.
DOI: 10.1093/oso/9780197789766.003.0011

otherness. Kahanamoku embraced his mythology, thereby enhancing both his own prestige and the reputation of his homeland. Alongside him, other prominent athletes of that era crafted their own mythologies, enriching their own personas and the communities they represented through sports. Interpreters employed their names and nicknames to weave tales of heroic feats, simultaneously making these individuals and groups more recognizable while highlighting the challenges of diversity in an evolving America.

## Duke

To establish a link between Kahanamoku and Hawaiian royalty, Paddock recounted a purported mystical prophecy from the island. According to the author, after the 1912 Olympic Games in Stockholm, Kahanamoku returned to Hawaii. While standing "under the statue of old King Kamehameha," observers began to associate Kahanamoku's "Herculean tapering body" with the legendary king's. Paddock then shared a proclamation attributed to the king: "Some day my people will lose their freedom and their nationality. Some day they will be supplanted in their own islands and sickness will spread among them and their strength will pass away. But before they are entirely gone there will come one in my image who shall have within himself all the glorious strength of a dying race, and he shall be honored throughout the world, and he shall bring fame to my people." Thus it was this great swimmer who became the island's new king. And though some islanders were suspicious, Kahanamoku removed all doubt when he ably manned a replica of the king's surfboard through the water. Heavy and bulky, the watercraft generally took four men to launch. But Kahanamoku did it on his own, further validating his new status.[2]

Paddock's mention of the surfboard was intentional, as Kahanamoku had also become known as the "Father of Surfing." Surfing was a sport unique to Hawaii, likely brought there by Polynesians and Pacific Islanders. Called "wave-riding," it was the recreational activity of kings and chiefs, with handcrafted boards sixteen feet in length and weighing 150 pounds. Surfing was also written into the ritual culture, the board itself a sacred object that was featured at festivities like Makahiki, which honored the god of agriculture and fertility, Lono. Many outside commentators were suitably fascinated by the sport. In 1866, Mark Twain described his unsuccessful attempt at "the national pastime of surf-bathing." Marveling at the speed and agility of Hawaiian surfers, Twain reported having fallen directly into the water. "None but natives ever master the art of surf-bathing thoroughly," he resolved.[3]

Missionaries had a less favorable view of the sport. With riders generally wearing little more than a loincloth, their nakedness registered as sin and barbarity to the Christian onlookers, a sentiment which was further confirmed by the presence of gambling. Some missionaries chopped up surfboards, introducing games like baseball and volleyball as replacements. As a result, surfing witnessed a decline, and by 1892 it was listed as a relic of the past in an account of sports on the island. Missionaries attributed this shift to their efforts in "Christianizing" Hawaii.[4]

However, surfing began returning to favor in the years following Hawaii's annexation in 1898, likely due in part to Kahanamoku's influence and example. He was, in the mind of island admirers, a prototypical gentleman athlete worthy of celebration and admiration. On Kahanamoku's return from the 1912 Olympics, one of the local Hawaiian judges commended him for his "clean life," which stood as a model for other men of the island. Another judge pointed out that the swimmer's unique crawl stroke was a Polynesian institution, not born of Australia as many commentators had said.[5]

While Hawaiian voices were quick to locate Kahanamoku's success in island life and culture, admirers on the mainland made him one of their own. "Duke was 'made in America' and by Americans," proclaimed the *New York Times*. "He learned all he knows about the art of swimming right here in the East, and it was here that he developed the now famous 'Kahanamoku kick.' " The article qualified that while his skill developed stateside, Kahanamoku had "a natural inclination toward the water," eliciting the trope of Indigenous people being "natural" athletes.[6]

Kahanamoku's chosen sports were not at the level of popularity as baseball or prizefighting, but his Hawaiian roots and aquatic exploits became part of his legend that was encoded into his name. Accordingly, Christian references were often found in close proximity to his name and deeds. Following the 1912 Olympics, Kahanamoku capitalized on his fame by staging swimming and surfing exhibitions all along the East and West Coast, as well as in Australia. In one account of his 1915 trip to Australia, the author wrote that "the crowd was enthralled as the Duke glided Christ-like over the waves." The divine allusions continued as accounts told of his growing number of followers. At the end of his demonstration in Australia, he convinced the fifteen-year-old Isabel Letham to try the sport. In the coming years, she would become "the Grande Dame of Australian surfing," as a "disciple" of Kahanamoku.[7]

The Kahanamoku legend also depicted him as a literal savior. In 1925, he and his friends were out for a morning swim at Newport Beach in California, when they noticed a fishing yacht capsizing in the water. The swimmer and his friends grabbed their surfboards and paddled out to help. From there, as one account described it, "Duke Kahanamoku, with his mighty swim strokes, seemed to be all around the boat at all times, and whenever a head bobbed up, he was there, to grab the drowning man and to place him on a surfboard." Although five of the fishermen drowned, twelve survived in no small part due to Kahanamoku's efforts. "The Hawaiian was a wizard," remarked one of the survivors. The police chief of Newport Beach went even further, saying, "Kahanamoku's performance was the most superhuman rescue act and the finest display of surfboard riding that has ever been seen in the world." In 1957, Kahanamoku, who also had a film career in the 1920s and 1930s, appeared on the popular television show *This Is Your Life*, where he reunited with three of the fishermen he saved that day, all of whom expressed their deep and lasting gratitude.[8]

At this stage in his life, Kahanamoku had stepped back from competitive surfing and swimming, dedicating his time to serving as the sheriff of Honolulu from 1934 to 1960 and engaging as a greeter. Despite his shift from active competition, his prominence in the surfing world persisted. In 1963, he co-hosted a surfing championship event with Johnny Weissmuller in Huntington Beach, California, drawing a crowd of approximately thirty thousand, mostly teenagers. The audience rose in unison to cheer when they caught sight of him.

Kahanamoku passed away in 1968, but admirers continued finding ways to commemorate him. In 1990, on the centennial of his birth, a massive bronze statue of him was revealed at Waikiki. Crafted by Jan Fisher, a professor at Brigham Young University–Hawaii, the statue aimed to depict Kahanamoku as more than just a surfer, swimmer, or athlete. Rather, as one admirer phrased it, he was "an international ambassador of aloha and an asset to the state as a humble, majestic individual." For some, the statue's orientation contradicted their memory of Kahanamoku, as his back faced the water. Given his burial at sea, it seemed more fitting for him to be facing the very body of water where his legend was forged. Nevertheless, the statue retained its current position, allowing visitors to capture images with the Hawaiian water as a backdrop.[9]

Even in his afterlife, Kahanamoku was part of a project promoting and selling his home state. He was not just a surfer or swimmer but an emblem of Hawaii, a royal representative of this relatively new member of the United States, with its unique culture and identity. The twentieth century saw numerous athletes following a similar path, with qualities of race, gender, and ethnicity becoming the defining features in interpretations of their movements.

## Big Chief

In 1949, Leslie Mayle made Battle Creek, Michigan, his home after retiring as a lieutenant colonel from the Army. In subsequent years, he became known as "the Colonel" and gained recognition for his unwavering commitment to physical activity. Mayle volunteered with the athletics department at the local Veterans Affairs hospital, showcased his golfing skills with a hole-in-one in 1964, and regularly participated in the noontime volleyball games at the YMCA. Upon his passing in 1974, his obituary highlighted his extensive military service spanning two world wars, his civic contributions, and his family legacies. Additionally, one sentence acknowledged Mayle's representation of the United States in the 1924 Olympic Games in Paris as a heavyweight boxer.[10]

During a distant chapter in his life, in the mid-1920s, Mayle was a rising star in amateur boxing as a member of an Army program for athletes training for international competition. Along with his size, skill, and potential, observers took careful notice of another facet of his identity: he was a Chippewa person from Wisconsin. "The Army is quietly grooming a big strapping young man for heavyweight honors," announced one profile. "His name is Chief Mayle, and he is a true American, being a full-blooded Indian." The article went on to speculate that "the big Redskin" had the advantage of being supported by the Army, thereby liberating him from the money-hungry managers and publicists corrupting the sport. Because of this, the author foresaw Mayle "[pulling] a Custer massacre on the present crop of heavyweights."[11]

Throughout his boxing career, sportswriters opted for generic "Indian" descriptors for "Chief Mayle," only very rarely mentioning his tribal affiliation or even his first name. The dismissiveness spoke to the decided minority status of Indigenous people at the time, as members of the majority freely assigned names to these athletes that were at best unflattering. By this time, circuses, dime novels, and Buffalo Bill's Wild West Show all combined to make Indigenous people into a counterpoint to modernity and a nostalgic relic of the past. Athletic teams also began appropriating Indigenous names and imagery, with youth, college, and professional teams taking on names like Indians, Warriors, and Savages. In most cases, plain imagery became the norm, flattening the realities of tribal diversity into one generic form of Indigenous culture. As for Indigenous athletes themselves, their stories were often interpreted as stereotypes which either denigrated and dehumanized them or identified certain Indigenous athletes as "good Indians" who met the standards of "civilization."[12]

All these social forces were at work in one of the more distinct sporting events of the 1930s: professional wrestling. After the Civil War, wrestling began to take hold as a spectator event at carnivals, where wrestlers adopted the chaos and humor of their surroundings. Complete with colorful costumes, elaborate biographies, and exciting action, wrestling was, for the most part, stagecraft—dramatic performance designed for entertainment. For this reason, the refined class looked askance at the sport. In 1933, the Illinois State Athletic Commission ordered a suspension of professional wrestling, described as "fake matches and other schemes to evade agreements or victimize a gullible public." Sportswriters likewise scorned wrestling as "fake" entertainment that delivered "public thrills galore" but not a true test of athletic skill.[13]

But professional wrestling only grew in popularity, and promoters were always on the hunt for a unique new wrestling star. Such was the case with "Big Chief" Osley Bird Saunooke. Size was a defining feature of Saunooke, with reports listing him as weighing well over three hundred pounds. Stories of his background stressed this feature to signal his superhuman qualities. "Big Chief Sunoco comes from a family of giants," wrote one account, noting the similar stature of his parents and nine brothers and sisters. Saunooke was also revered for his longevity. He participated in 5,217 professional matches during his career, wrestling in every state as well as Mexico and Canada. A graduate of the Haskell Indian Institute in Kansas, where he also played football, Saunooke spent a brief time in the U.S. Marines before returning to the Midwest during the Great Depression and working a range of jobs, from harvesting wheat to driving a cab in Chicago. When Saunooke began going to a gym in Chicago, his size and strength drew the attention of wrestling promoters. His matches were often marked with feats of strength, as he would raise his opponents over his head and hurl them across the ring.[14]

Early in his career, Saunooke went by "Chief Sunoco" because, one writer explained, "his Christian name, Osley Bird Saunooke, was hard to spell and even more confusing to pronounce." This became part of a broader effort to adapt to audience expectations. In the ring, Saunooke sported a giant feathered headdress and performed various "Indian" gestures, including "war whoops." Newspapers added to the mythology, with headlines like "318-Pound Injun Meets White." This account claimed that Saunooke had been "crowned king of wrestlers by his tribesmen" and that soon "pale faces" might also crown him "king of heavyweights." This was precisely what happened when, in 1937, Saunooke defeated Tor Johnson in Boston Garden and launched a fourteen-year career as the heavyweight champion. For his part, Johnson was often referred to as "the mountainous Swede." An account of the match made recurring use of these identities clashing. "When the good Chief whirled the Nordic monument of flesh to the canvas," one author proclaimed, "the reverberation nearly shook the ring lights loose from their moorings."[15]

While Saunooke did play the role that promoters and audiences expected, he also occasionally shed light on his Cherokee identity. In one interview, he told a reporter about "Indian ball," the form of lacrosse played on his North Carolina reservation. He also detailed the annual corn ceremony, which happened as summer turns to autumn. Still, the journalist reporting on Saunooke's background fell back on stereotyping throughout the article, claiming, for example, that winners of the lacrosse game were honored "in a typical Indian dance," which was "wild and unrestrained."[16]

Saunooke retired in 1951 and went on to serve as tribal chief in 1951–55 and 1959–63. In this role, he became known as a skilled political actor both on and off the reservation, taking his talents in showmanship to the public square. But the wrestling arena had been a place for him and others to elevate and exaggerate their perceived differences for the sake of entertainment. At times, matches reached into current events to bring a rivalry to the ring. Such was the case when Hans Schuman, the "Nasty Nazi," faced off against Ignacio Martinez, a Spaniard, in 1937. It was "a little replica of the Spanish Civil War," one article suggested.[17] For its emphasis on showmanship, professional wrestling was an obvious setting for dramatic reenactments of international conflicts. But wrestling was certainly not alone in becoming a stage for such rivalries to unfold.

## Black Moses

In 1935, the rising boxing star Joe Louis defeated the Italian former champion Primo Carnera. Accounts of the match framed it as an American defeat over Benito Mussolini. In Harlem, crowds carrying Ethiopian flags gathered to celebrate Louis's victory. During this time, many Black Americans empathized with Ethiopia, a country that was fending off an invasion from the fascist Italian regime. Also working through this symbolic demonstration was a protest of a distinctly domestic concern: the plague of lynching. As Harlem-born author and playwright Loften Mitchell declared, "The Brown Bomber, appearing in the darkness when Italy invaded Ethiopia and the Scottsboro Boys faced lynching, became a Black hero his history books could not ignore."[18]

While Louis was not a particularly vocal boxer, in contrast to his predecessor Jack Johnson, his skill in the ring advanced his charismatic appeal. Langston Hughes wrote, "No one else in the United States has ever had such an effect on Negro emotions, or on mine." Like other great sports heroes of the era, Louis's otherworldliness was certified by his many nicknames, such as the "Brown Bomber." But Edward Van Every, a White journalist for the *New York Sun*, took the boxer's persona in an explicitly biblical direction. "It is . . . as though the finger of God had singled this youth out for purpose[s] of His Own," exclaimed Van Every in his 1936 book, *Joe Louis, Man and Super-Fighter*. Released just prior to Louis's infamous bout with the German Max Schmeling, Van Every's book proclaimed that the boxer had become the "Black Moses," who through his bodily movements was "lighting the way to a broader tolerance on the part of his white brother." Reviewers took note of Van Every's lofty aspirations. "Van Every sees [Louis] as an amazing apparition, a fighter of good character and ability, and an ambassador of good will between two races," wrote the noted book reviewer Harry Hansen in the *New York World*.[19]

Louis would lose his first match against Schmeling but return in 1938 with a convincing victory. In between, he defeated Jimmy Braddock to become the first African American fighter since Jack Johnson to own the heavyweight title. With a championship in hand and a proxy victory over Nazi Germany, Louis had become a superhuman figure representing American strength and resolve in the form of a Black body. It was a narrative that grew in authenticity when Louis enlisted during World War II. Championing his enlistment, recruitment posters portrayed Private Joe Louis in an Army uniform, proclaiming, "We're going to do our part . . . and we'll win because we're on God's side."[20]

Louis's widespread fame and adulation, while seemingly spontaneous, actually resulted from the deliberate cultivation of his public image. At the time Louis came into public view, White America remained uneasy about watching interracial matches, and even more uneasy with any boxer who reminded them of Jack Johnson. Following Louis's victory over the White fighter Max Baer in 1935, an Oklahoma newspaper expressed unease, stating, "We have never believed a white man should fight with a negro." The author emphasized that while the sporting public may desire such a fight, the social consequences were too significant. "It causes the negro race to believe that they are the equals of the white race," the author declared, ominously adding, "There is but one way to fight a negro, and we of the south know what that way is."[21]

While Johnson's time as champion was nearly two decades in the past, Louis was still hovering in the fighter's shadow and battling the "religion of whiteness" that deemed Johnson a racial heretic. John Roxborough was among Louis's team of managers who made it their task to create a new narrative for the fighter. This started with Roxborough's "Seven Commandments" for Louis, which included never having his picture taken with a White woman and no gloating over fallen opponents—two things that Johnson was particularly noted for doing. At the same time, a photograph circulated in the press of Louis calmly reading his Bible, which his mother had given to him. Stories of Louis's lifestyle also claimed that he didn't drink or smoke, that he remained entirely focused on his training, and that he even performed his capitalist duties by saving money for the future.[22]

In stark contrast to the fast-talking, brash, and spendthrift Johnson, Louis was characterized as laconic, humble, pious, and deeply devoted to his family. Journalists observed this stark difference; Richards Vidmer of the *New York Herald Tribune* declared, "Joe Louis is as different a character from Jack Johnson as Lou Gehrig is from Al Capone." Many other journalists echoed this sentiment, repeatedly praising Louis as a "credit to his race." Meanwhile, Johnson, viewing from the sidelines, harbored a healthy dose of skepticism. Johnson was in Harlem when Louis suffered his first loss to Schmeling. After the match, Johnson reportedly roamed the streets, flaunting his gambling winnings and disparaging the defeated boxer's skills. In response, some embittered residents of Harlem formed a mob to confront Johnson, prompting police intervention to protect the boxer. Despite

Johnson's history as a hero in Harlem, his behavior and rivalry with the emerging champion had eroded his support.[23]

As Louis's fame eclipsed that of Johnson, many Black Americans channeled Louis's status and strength in a time of crushing social injustices. "I'm in death row, and I got only six more weeks to go," a Black man wrote to Louis from a southern penitentiary in 1935. "Your picture hanging on the wall will make me feel better as I wait for the electric chair." The story of this letter likely became the basis for the apocryphal account that told of a condemned man's final words as he choked to death in a North Carolina gas chamber: "Save me, Joe Louis! Save me, Joe Louis!" In 1963, Martin Luther King Jr. repeated these words as he lamented, "Not God, not government, not charitably minded white men, but a Negro who was the world's most expert fighter, in this last extremity, was the last hope."[24]

Though the details of this story are uncertain, for numerous Black individuals in America, particularly in the South, the actualities of existence in a society molded by White supremacy meant facing a life replete with restrictions, humiliations, and perils. In these regions, the notion of Joe Louis carried associations of strength, faith, and an improbable capacity to triumph over life's challenges. It's a sentiment that aligns with historians' use of the phrase "muscular assimilation," capturing how Black leaders and institutions, in particular, framed sports as the "great equalizer" to drive forward social reform. In the 1920s, for example, Black colleges and universities fielded football teams in hopes of replicating the "school spirit" demonstrated by their White counterparts. "Athletics is the universal language," announced a Howard University editorialist. "By and through it we hope to foster a better and more fraternal spirit between the races in America and so to destroy prejudices; to learn and to be taught; to facilitate a universal brotherhood." Paradoxically, the ascent of Black athletes also rendered them vulnerable to the skepticism of White audiences. This became evident in the case of a boxer who, following Louis's successes, decided to change his name to align with his newfound Muslim identity.[25]

## Ali

At the 1960 Rome Olympics, boxer Cassius Clay won gold by defeating Zbigniew Pietrzykowski of Poland. Clay was not ignorant of the Cold War underpinnings of the fight, nor of the racial prejudices that existed in his homeland. After the contest, he remarked to a Soviet reporter, "To me, the U.S.A. is still the best country in the world, including yours." Clay drew widespread admiration back home for playing his role in the symbolic battles between the United States and the Soviet Union, his alliterative name becoming part of his emerging mythology of boxing heroics. But the boxer's status shifted dramatically when he converted to Islam and, in 1964, formally adopted the name Muhammad Ali. Within White circles in particular, the deviation from the Christian norm signaled a possible alliance with, or tacit support of, "godless communism." Ali's very public conversion, punctuated by his name change, became a Cold War battleground featuring a form of American patriotism that expected loyalty to Christian norms and names.[26]

All of this came into sharp focus in 1965, when Ali faced off against former heavyweight champion Floyd Patterson, a recent Catholic convert. The fight assumed the posture of a "holy war," not only between Christian and Muslim but also between "patriotic" and "un-patriotic" America. Doing his part, Patterson, who refused to acknowledge Ali's new name, penned an essay for *Sports Illustrated* explaining his reasons for taking the fight. "I say it, and I say it flatly," Patterson averred, "that the image of a Black Muslim as the world heavyweight champion disgraces the sport and the nation. Cassius Clay must be beaten and the Black Muslims' scourge removed from boxing." As the fight drew near, Patterson became a celebrity for those who shared his fears and convictions, one of whom was Frank Sinatra. On the morning of the fight, Sinatra called the boxer to his room and explained that "many people in America" were counting on him to "win back" the title.[27]

In the ring, Ali pummeled Patterson, drawing out the match for twelve rounds and crushing the hopes of his detractors. After losing the fight, Patterson sought out Sinatra to apologize, who said nothing and promptly walked away. Patterson discovered in that moment that he was valuable to White America only as a counterpoint to Ali's defiant nonconformity. On the other side, this very nonconformity was a source of pride and elation for the likes of Eldridge Cleaver. "Muhammad Ali is the first 'free' black champion ever to confront white America," Cleaver exclaimed, gleeful at the way in which Ali rejected the status quo and paved his own way forward.[28]

From the days of Tom Molineaux to the era of Jack Johnson, boxing has a rich history of encapsulating the complex interplay of racial, religious, and nationalistic tensions prevalent in each period. Fitting neatly into this history, Ali faced a unique twist as his name became entwined with Cold War politics. Standing out from the conformist White majority, Ali drew increasing jeers, particularly when he refused military service in 1967. The consequences were severe, with the loss of his championship, a nationwide ban from fighting, and a criminal conviction resulting in a five-year prison sentence. Despite his being out on bail, it took four years for the U.S. Supreme Court to unanimously overturn his conviction. By this time, Ali had reentered the ring and started a new phase of his career, gaining favor as he shunned the Nation of Islam's separatist message and went on to stage epic battles against Joe Frazier and George Forman. During this time, Ali's name came to mean something new, his brashness now an endearing quality that was not only patriotic but also marketable. Companies began using film footage of the boxer to sell everything from soda to automobiles, as "I'm the greatest" echoed through the marketplace, sometimes in unlikely places. In 1978, DC Comics portrayed Ali teaming up with Superman to defeat an alien invasion, with Ali besting Superman in the ring. The comic cover featured a diverse audience, from Presidents Ford and Carter to the Jackson 5 and Ron Howard. The story concluded with Ali triumphing over the alien boxer, saving the world in the process.[29]

Superman, as a comic book hero, epitomized the ideal Cold War warrior, the powerful embodiment of "truth, justice, and the American way." Ali's placement within this symbolic universe aimed to address a specific Cold War challenge. Whenever racial conflicts arose in the United States, the Soviet Union exploited them for propaganda purposes. By elevating Ali, the comic demonstrated the progress the United States had made in civil rights and showcased how the partnership between a real-life and a fictional American hero was evidence of an evolving racial condition.[30]

When Ali lit the flame at the 1996 Atlanta Olympics, sportscaster Bob Costas deemed the event a "distinctively American moment." Costas speculated that, despite turbulent events in his past, Ali's talent and warm personality had transcended politics, rendering the boxer "beloved by everyone." The acclaim and commercial appeal surrounding Ali's name persisted in 2001, when Michael Mann directed a film about Ali starring Will Smith, aptly titled *Ali*. Mann described the film as depicting Ali's quest for identity, viewing him as a symbol of possibility. Such sentiments resurged strongly upon Ali's death in 2016, with admirers reflecting on his impact not only in boxing but on society at large. In an NPR interview, sports journalist Howard Bryant explained why Ali's name is uttered worldwide "as a kind of prayer," saying simply, "He stood up. He spoke for poor people. He spoke for himself."[31]

Basketball star LeBron James reached a similar conclusion. "The reason why he's the [greatest] is not because of what he did in the ring, which was unbelievable," James stated. "It's what he did outside of the ring, what he believed in, what he stood for. . . . Muhammad Ali was definitely the pioneer for that."[32] Indeed, Ali's career in sports had become that of the pioneer, the boundary-breaking hero who would leave a legacy of smashing prejudice and opening pathways for others to follow. As it happened, Ali operated in a time when pioneers were appearing across the sporting landscape, giving yet another new meaning to the mythological renderings of bodies in motion.

# 11

# Pioneers! O Pioneers!

A month after Jackie Robinson's debut with the Dodgers in April 1947, Brooklyn played the Pittsburgh Pirates, who had recently acquired the aging veteran Hank Greenberg from the Detroit Tigers. One of the greatest power hitters in baseball, "Hammerin' Hank" was Jewish, and in the 1930s he had played in a city where the flames of antisemitism burned hot, due in part to the raging rhetoric of the radio demagogue Father Charles Coughlin and the automobile magnate Henry Ford. Consequently, Greenberg experienced discrimination and hate at a most visceral level. But in time the combination of his success in baseball and serving in World War II led to a change in perception. No longer called "Jew Boy," Greenberg had become the "Hebrew Hammer." When Greenberg and Robinson met on the baseball field, it was now the Black baseball player who was the focusing point of White hostility. During the game, Robinson took to the plate and, amid taunts from the opposing bench and fans, he laid down a bunt and rushed toward first base, where he collided with Greenberg. Later in the game, Greenberg checked in on Robinson before offering words of assurance and encouragement. It was a moment of unstated solidarity and mutual admiration. A grateful Robinson later told reporters, "Class tells. It sticks all over Mr. Greenberg."[1]

In the aftermath of the game, Wendell Smith of the *Pittsburgh Courier*, a Black-owned newspaper, pointed out that in previous years, White opponents of integration would imagine that scene at first base and assert that a race riot would follow. But nothing of the sort happened. Quite the opposite: the collision led to a lasting friendship between the two players. When Greenberg died in 1986, sports journalist Ira Berkow cited this story as a way of emphasizing that the ballplayer was "a special man in special times." Jewish himself, Berkow recalled his family reveling in Greenberg's exploits on the baseball diamond, "as if he were a kind of beacon for them." In 1961, Wendell Smith used similar language about Robinson, calling him "the courageous player who was the pioneer of all Negroes in the majors today."

*Bodies in Motion*. Arthur Remillard, Oxford University Press. © Oxford University Press 2025.
DOI: 10.1093/oso/9780197789766.003.0012

Along these lines, in one scholar's framing, Greenberg and Robinson were "two pioneers," with similar and interlocking stories that led to the transformation not only of baseball but of America as well. "Each was an American hero. Each represented the best that their country stood for: equality of opportunity and fair treatment for all."[2]

In its nineteenth-century form, the American pioneer had been an agent of westward expansion, of breaking soil on the frontier while displacing and removing Indigenous populations. It was a story that was as White, male, and Christian as Manifest Destiny itself. In sports, however, the pioneer has come to represent an athletic standard-bearer of a marginalized group. This label gained currency in the mid- to late twentieth century, as interpreters of sports began identifying individuals and moments that spoke to the diversifying trends in race, gender, religion, and ethnicity that had come to define the century. Put another way, the sports pioneer has been a retroactive designation, assigned in hindsight. In their own time, sports pioneers faced indignities and abuse at every turn. Accordingly, the sacred substance of this term lives in the subtext, as the pioneer would become remembered as the hero who persevered, who transcended the moral limits of an era and suffered for the sake of a more inclusive future—the American melting pot mythology. Thus was the pioneering memory of Greenberg and Robinson, as well as Paul Robeson, who in 2019 was called "a pioneer like no other" by his alma mater Rutgers.[3]

## A Pioneer in Hindsight

In 1915, Paul Robeson earned a scholarship to Rutgers, where he became the first Black football player on their team. After being assaulted on the first day of practice by his own teammates and continually called an assortment of racial slurs, Robeson went on to become one of the best players in the sport, twice earning College Football All-American honors. He also excelled in baseball, basketball, and track, as well as in academics. Robeson was his class valedictorian; in his commencement address, "The New Idealism," he imagined a future where "black and white shall clasp friendly hands in the consciousness of the fact that we are brethren and that God is the father of us all." Following his time at Rutgers, Robeson obtained a law degree from Columbia, concurrently making significant strides in professional football as one of the earliest Black athletes in the league. However, his greatest renown came from the stage, where he became a prominent figure in the Harlem Renaissance and a household name across America as a singer and actor.[4]

As his career took him across the world, Robeson also became more politically aware and vocal in his advocacy for civil rights. In 1943, he led a delegation petitioning Major League Baseball to desegregate the sport, and two years later was part of a group who challenged President Truman to support antilynching legislation. In 1949, Robeson's star began to fade after he spoke in Paris at the communist-led World Congress of Partisans of Peace. With Cold War anxiety as a backdrop, newspapers reported Robeson suggesting that Black citizens in the U.S. would not fight in a war against the Soviet Union. He later protested that he had been misquoted, insisting that he said Black Americans did not seek such a war. But the damage was done, and Robeson received rebukes from all directions.[5]

In the South, White critics braided together criticism of Robeson's remarks with recent news that his son had married a White woman. "We believe the laws of the Southern states against miscegenation are wise and far-seeing," announced one editorialist, before adding, "We do not believe Paul Robeson by his spectacular championing of Soviet Russia, is serving the best interests of his people." There were Black critics too. "I am chagrined at his presumption," exclaimed Mary McLeod Bethune. "I think he has missed his cue and has entered the stage during the wrong scene." Appearing before the House Un-American Activities Committee, Jackie Robinson questioned Robeson's patriotism, while he also stoutly condemned the injustices of Jim Crow, a fact that received much less attention.[6]

Robeson lived out his final years in relative seclusion. It was only after his passing that his image underwent rehabilitation, with posthumous honors including an induction into the College Football Hall of Fame and the American Theater Hall of Fame. Remembered as a pioneer in these settings, the story of his status as a social misfit was but a prelude to the story of a heroic advocate for civil rights. As they had with Greenberg and Robinson, interpreters characterized Robeson's slights and outright bigotry as a necessary struggle for the sake of social transformation. From this perspective, these sports pioneers achieved heroic victories for an America aspiring to be a "melting pot," where individuals could progress based on their own merit. This narrative echoed across different sports, from widely followed activities like football to relatively niche pursuits like bowling.[7]

## Bowling Pioneers

Among the artifacts at the International Bowling Museum and Hall of Fame in Arlington, Texas, is Catherine Menne's "pioneering ball." Menne, the inaugural president of the Women's National Bowling Association in 1916 and one of its founding members, made history and contributed to the broader acceptance of women's bowling. Proud of her achievements, Menne had her bowling ball custom-engraved with her name and title.[8]

The subsequent decades witnessed bowling's surge in popularity, opening doors for individuals and groups previously marginalized in both sports and society. During the postwar boom years, bowling became a favored winter sport for the burgeoning middle class. A Utah advertisement proudly declared, "Bowling is the Great American indoor sport," emphasizing its inclusivity for women and men of all ages. The government even promoted the sport with a Bowling for Health campaign, leading to the establishment of alleys in more cities and on military bases.[9]

Bowling mirrored many of the defining features of the era, with mechanization and low-wage labor creating ease and comfort for players. From ball-return systems to pin-setters, all the details were managed for a population with newfound disposable income, a fact that drew immediate interest from Wall Street. In the late 1950s, bowling manufacturers American Machine Foundry and Brunswick both saw their stocks double as smaller bowling companies soon followed suit and went public. Investors poured roughly $2 billion into the sport; by 1960 there were approximately twelve thousand bowling alleys across the United States and 10 million people bowling at least once weekly. But the "bowling bubble" would soon pop as the 1960s witnessed a slow and steady decline in the sport's popularity. Still, at its peak, bowling alleys had become known as "the people's country club." And like most country clubs of the era, bowling, while heralded for its inclusivity was at the same time a segregated sport.[10]

As Black people from the South migrated to northern cities to work in expanding mills and factories, they encountered systematic exclusion from bowling—both socially and economically. Limited access to loans and funding posed unique challenges for aspiring Black owners of bowling alleys. J. Elmer Reed in Cleveland emerged as an advocate for African American bowling, negotiating with White owners for after-hours tournaments. Reed opened his own alley in 1941, and a year later Joe Louis helped fund Detroit's Paradise Bowl. With bowling gaining popularity in Black communities, efforts intensified to desegregate national contests. In 1945, the National Negro Bowling Association rebranded as the National Bowling Association (NBA) and joined forces with the NAACP to petition the American Bowling Congress (ABC) to lift its long-standing "Caucasian-only" policy. This alliance resonated with many, as one Brooklyn bowler later remarked: "In the beginning, the NBA meant the same as the NAACP and the Bill of Rights to the Negro bowler . . . freedom in bowling."[11]

These Black-led organizations had an ally in Betty Hicks, a golfer who had been incensed by the fact that Black women were barred from the links. Determined to integrate bowling as well, in 1948 she was co-chair of the National Committee for Fair Play and, speaking to her mostly White audience, denounced the "un-American" policy of "Caucasian only" bowling. That same year, Father Charles Carow made a similar argument at the annual gathering of the ABC. Carow came as a representative of the Catholic Youth Organization of the Brooklyn Diocese. In 1945, the organization was denied membership in the ABC because they had two Black teams. This led Carow to petition the ABC to revoke its policy of racial segregation. The 1949 convention was his third effort to sway the membership to change their ruling. He emphasized that integrating bowling would not only benefit the sport "but would also contribute much to American social and sport life." The Catholic priest added, "Today the eyes of the world are turned to the United States to see if our principles of democracy are working in practice."[12]

Despite multiple efforts, the ABC upheld its ban on interracial bowling in 1949. The National Committee for Fair Play took the case to court the following year, leveraging antidiscrimination clauses in northern states, including New York, against the policy. Faced with mounting legal costs and a membership primarily from the North, the ABC voted to integrate in 1950. After a five-year struggle, Carow declared that the organization was "American not only in name but in practice."[13]

The news was greeted with cheers in Pittsburgh, particularly by Ted Page and the bowlers at his Hillview Lanes. In 1937, Page retired from baseball after a successful career in the Negro leagues. After settling in Pittsburgh, he turned his attention to bowling and training bowlers, while also writing about the sport in the local newspapers. For Page, bowling was special because it was an "inspiration" for Black organization and advancement. Among those he trained was Louise Fulton, who in 1964 became the first Black woman to win the Professional Women's Bowling Association title. The victory kicked off a distinguished career, and in 2001 Fulton was inducted into the

U.S. Bowling Congress Hall of Fame, the opening words of the announcement calling her a "bowling pioneer." Similar proclamations accompanied her inductions into the National Bowling Association Hall of Fame and the Pennsylvania State Women's Bowling Hall of Fame, as well as her receipt of the Joyce Deitch Trailblazer Award in 1999.[14]

For those well-versed in bowling, Fulton's name would be mentioned alongside other pioneers like Charlie Sifford in golf and Arthur Ashe in tennis, all navigating landscapes entrenched with a "Caucasian-only" structure and culture. Tackling this required addressing the profound prejudices woven into the fabric of American society. What made these athletes additionally noteworthy is that, unlike pioneers in team sports, athletes in individual sports lacked a built-in support network. This was particularly significant for Black women, including Fulton, who faced the additional challenge of negotiating gender norms—an issue shared by athletes in track and field.[15]

## Pioneers on the Track

In the 1940s, Louise Stokes of Massachusetts became a noted bowling pioneer when she founded the Colored Women's Bowling League. Prior to her extensive career in bowling, Stokes excelled as a track athlete, participating in the Olympic 4x100 relay at the 1932 Los Angeles Games alongside her fellow Black teammate, Tidye Pickett. Their reception from White teammates and the sports community, however, was far from cordial. During the train journey from Denver to Los Angeles, the Black athletes were segregated in their sleeping and dining arrangements. Adding to the animosity, Babe Didrikson out of spite reportedly threw ice water on Pickett and Stokes while they slept. Eventually, the U.S. Olympic Committee decided to replace Stokes and Pickett with two White sprinters. Although never provided with a reason, journalist Rus Cowan of the *Chicago Defender* succinctly attributed the decision to "lily-whiteism." The NAACP likewise sent a telegram to the U.S. Olympic Committee protesting their exclusion, but it was met with silence.[16]

In 1936, Pickett and Stokes once again qualified for the Olympic team. Pickett achieved the milestone of becoming the first Black American woman to compete in an Olympic event. Unfortunately, her journey was cut short as she suffered a severe foot injury during a qualifying heat of the 80-meter hurdles, preventing her from continuing. Meanwhile, Stokes faced a familiar disappointment reminiscent of the 1932 Games. As a member of the 400-meter relay squad, she traveled to Berlin but was replaced by a White sprinter just before the race, forced to watch from the stands as the U.S. team won gold. While the outcomes left Pickett and Stokes disheartened, their presence at the Games held significance for future Black female Olympians. "The girls who came on later didn't have to face the same things," Pickett would recall decades later, adding, "We really opened the door for them, but I was glad it was opened."[17]

The 1936 Olympics also marked a pivotal moment for Black sportsmen, providing an opportunity for recognition and breaking barriers. In total, eighteen Black men secured fourteen of America's fifty-six medals in male sports. The *Pittsburgh Courier* affectionately dubbed them the "Black Eagles," accompanied by an illustration of them soaring to Berlin on an eagle. One athlete highlighted by the *Courier* was John Woodruff, the surprise winner of the 800-meter event and a student at the University of Pittsburgh at the time. Jesse Owens emerged as arguably the most noteworthy athlete of the Games, securing convincing victories in the 100-meter, 200-meter, 4x100-meter relay, and the long jump. Over time, both Woodruff and Owens would be recognized as pioneers in both sports and society. However, both athletes faced substantial injustices and mistreatment prior to and following their Olympic triumphs.[18]

Some White interpreters of Owens, for instance, portrayed him as an embodiment of their ideal Black person, complete with a litany of backhanded compliments. One Harrisburg editor exclaimed that Owens's speed was matched only by his humility, refusing to get "a swelled head" over all the acclaim coming his way. "He declined to say any harsh things about Herr Hitler," the article continued, "or to indicate in any way that he felt snubbed by the failure of Der Fuehrer to welcome him, personally, at the games." Owens additionally drew praise for pledging to return to Ohio State to finish his degree. The article concluded, "He is a credit to his race and to his Nation."[19]

Woodruff received similar racially tinged praise following his gold medal win in the 800-meter event. Florence Fisher Parry, a drama critic from Woodruff's hometown of Pittsburgh, wrote, "It would be interesting to know from what primeval source young John derived the Miracle of his legs." The author recounted Woodruff's impoverished background, emphasizing that his parents were hardworking and would never have sought "charity." Despite societal limitations, Woodruff inherited their determination, ultimately achieving greatness. The author emphasized, "It didn't matter to America that he was lowly-born. It didn't matter to America that his skin was bronze and his father was a lowly laborer and his home a scant, bare shack. All that mattered to America was that he had a Talent for covering distance." Consequently, she labeled Woodruff a "Prince of Privilege," likening him to Joe Louis, Henry Ford, and Fred Astaire.[20]

In White circles, Owens, Woodruff, and the others became superhuman athletes who embodied America's values and showed these values through Olympic victory. But once the parades in their honor concluded, these athletes reentered the racial status quo, without congratulatory calls from the president or monetary rewards. Woodruff's hometown held a parade for him, but when he returned to the University of Pittsburgh he lived at the YMCA and worked as a groundskeeper. Then in 1937, he posted a world-record time of 1:47.8 in the 800-meter event at the Pan-American championships in Dallas, Texas, only to find three days later that the American Athletic Union negated the record after measuring the track and determining that it was six feet short. Woodruff and others immediately suspected that Jim Crow bigotry was at play, and the athlete later wondered how the chief engineer had measured the track within 1/1,000 of an inch just days prior yet declared it short once a Black man claimed a world record.[21]

Owens faced his own racial obstacles after the Olympics. "I came back to my native country, and I couldn't ride in the front of the bus. I had to go to the back door. I couldn't live where I wanted." With few opportunities in front of him, Owens began cashing in on his celebrity. He teamed up with Black baseball teams like the Pittsburgh Crawfords and the Indianapolis Clowns and, before games, staged races with horses and dogs. "People said it was degrading for an Olympic champion to run against a horse, but what was I supposed to do? I had four gold medals, but you can't eat four gold medals."[22]

In the coming years, corporate sponsorship would help Owens to make ends meet. As the 1952 Olympics drew near, he signed an endorsement deal with Coca-Cola, and his image would soon appear on advertisements with the slogan "Quality you can trust." Standing alongside Owens in these advertisements was Alice Coachman, the first Black woman to earn an endorsement from the beverage giant.[23] While racial bigotry was alive and well in the United States, this advertisement featuring two Black athletes was both groundbreaking, and inspired by the political climate of the era. Showing the athletes in their Olympic uniforms, the advertisement bundled capitalism, sports, and American exceptionalism as a volley back at the Soviet Union, which had been a frequent critic of America's record on race relations.

Coachman grew to fame when she became the first Black American woman to win Olympic gold, taking top honors in the high jump at the 1948 London Olympics. Black newspapers celebrated her victory and framed it as a win for the race. In contrast, the *New York Times* mentioned Coachmen's gold in one sentence at the end of an article on the Games. The *Atlanta Constitution* printed a longer article but made sure to emphasize that this great athlete was not a great student. And then there was her return to her hometown of Albany, Georgia. A parade awaited the athlete when she arrived, and community leaders led a celebration in her honor. Among the speakers was the mayor, James Smith, and newspaper editor James H. Gray. "It is this girl's spirit that Albanians honor today," Gray proclaimed. Aaron Brown, the president of Albany State College, where Coachman was enrolled, added that the parade was evidence that "all races can work together for a better, happier world in which to live."[24]

And yet the event was segregated, and the same mayor who spoke glowingly of Coachman refused to shake her hand. The indignity was compounded by the fact that when she won gold in England, she received the award directly from King George VI. As Coachman remarked later in life, "To come back home to your own country, your own state and your own city, and you can't get a handshake from the mayor?" She eventually moved on from track and field and became an educator and noted figure in her community. "At a time when there were few high-profile black athletes beyond Jackie Robinson and Joe Louis," read her obituary in the *New York Times*, "Coachman became a pioneer."[25]

Coachman emerged as an Olympic hero during an era when the Olympics served as a battleground for nations to symbolically vie for global supremacy through their athletes. The track, in particular, played a crucial role in this unfolding drama and served as a stage for other pioneers to make their mark. Between 1958 and 1985, the United States and the USSR engaged in nineteen outdoor dual meets and seven indoor meets, with American sports and political leaders contending that these competitions would showcase the superiority of democracy and market capitalism to the Soviets and the world. While the Olympics were built on the premise of international competition, these track meets featured only two countries in a scored event. The advent of television technology further amplified the visibility of these competitions. Drawing inspiration from popular televised sports like roller derby and professional wrestling, known for their stylized contests between good and evil, the television industry was poised to apply a similar approach to track and field. As decathlete Rafer Johnson later described it, this wasn't just an ordinary athletic contest; it was a battle between "Communism vs. the Free World."[26]

The growth and popularity of this meet spotlighted the relative underdevelopment of American women in track and field events. While the men's team won the first six contests, the Soviet women convincingly defeated their American counterparts. Additionally, while the American Athletic Union scored the men and women separately, the Soviet scorekeepers combined the scores, which gave them a combined victory for the first five events. Some in the United States chose to dismiss their opponent's results, often downgrading the importance of the women's meet. Additional charges were leveled against the Soviets for fielding a team composed of "mannish" athletes.[27]

But the American sports public still had a deep interest in surpassing the Soviet team on every inch of the track. Thus emerged the significance of the historically Black college Tennessee State, dubbed "the Notre Dame of women's track" by *Sports Illustrated*. Among the great athletes from this program was Wilma Rudolph, winner of three gold medals in the 1960 Olympics. At the 1961 dual meet in Moscow, "Wilma the Wonderful" anchored the 400-meter relay and pulled off a surprise victory for the American team. She also took top honors in the 100-meter race, tying her own record of 11.3 seconds. While it wasn't enough to win the women's team title, the White press applauded the progress. Rudolph and other successful Black women in track and field became positive images of American democracy, in contrast to the communists. She would also go on to have a distinguished career as a leader in civil rights and women's rights, prompting *Sports Illustrated* to announce in 2020, "Her legacy as a pioneer lives on."[28]

At the peak of her athletic career, Rudolph played a role in paving the way for the American team to secure a combined victory in 1964. This meet also featured an unexpected pioneer in the form of Gerry Lindgren, a short and slightly built eighteen-year-old from Washington State. A late addition to the roster, Lindgren competed in the 10,000-meter run against the Soviet favorites, Leonid Ivanov and Nikolay Dutov. For the first half of the race, he tucked in behind the leaders until the team coach, Sam Bell, told Lindgren to take the lead. Described as having a look of fright and terror, the teenager obeyed and surged ahead of the leaders. The laps passed, and Lindgren steadily widened his lead, causing the crowd to erupt with wild cheers with each lengthening stride. As Lindgren entered the homestretch, he believed the stadium noise meant that his competitors were gaining ground. Bursting through to the finish line, Lindgren looked back and discovered that he had won by a convincing 150-meter margin. Bobby Kennedy, who was in the crowd of thousands, was reportedly reduced to tears, as were many others in the stands. As newspapers scrambled to discover more about Lindgren, he told them plainly, "I knew people would judge our system by this one race. I couldn't let America down. I had to do my best."[29]

When Lindgren returned to Washington, his hometown newspaper exclaimed that the "Spokane pioneer" had become an "inspiration" to runners throughout the state and beyond. *New York Times* journalist Arthur Dailey likewise praised Lindgren's character, adding, "This young man can be the inspiration to a new generation of Americans to start a boom in distance running such as this country never has had."[30] As it happened, a "running boom" was just on the horizon, with Lindgren and other famous runners bringing the sport into popular focus. Meanwhile, women as well as Black pioneers in this sport would remain conspicuously absent in the origin story of the running boom, despite their significant influence.

## Pioneers of the Running Boom

The mythology of America's running boom generally begins in the 1940s, when noted New Zealand distance running coach Arthur Lydiard posited that long, slow distance running for average people could offer a range of health benefits. In the following years, Lydiard built up a community of "joggers" who trotted through the countryside when, in 1962, University of Oregon track coach Bill Bowerman visited New Zealand and was astonished by Lydiard's innovation. Returning to the United States, Bowerman begin teaching jogging classes to university students and distributing a pamphlet to community members. Then in 1972, as more people were identifying as joggers, American Frank Shorter won marathon gold at the Munich Olympics, thereby thrusting him and the sport of distance running into the national spotlight. Seizing on all this momentum, Bowerman and his former University of Oregon athlete Phil Knight started what would become the Nike Corporation, which marketed athletic shoes to a rapidly growing number of distance runners.[31]

As marketing dollars and public interest collided, the sport of distance running had become no mere "fitness fad." In 1978, medical doctor and philosopher of running George Sheehan published *Running and Being.*

A regular writer for the expanding print culture for running in the 1970s, Sheehan often made comparisons between his sport and religion. In one article, he recalled visiting Anchorage, Alaska, where he met a skeptical reporter who asked, "Is running your religion?" Pausing thoughtfully, Sheehan replied, "Running is not a religion, it is a place." Sheehan elaborated by likening running to "a monastery—a retreat, a place to commune with God and yourself."[32]

In the running boom era, Sheehan and others developed a frame for the sport that went beyond physical fitness into life's meaning and purpose. One prominent runner from the era explained that "running filled a void." Woven into this theme was also an emphasis on the sport's natural inclination toward inclusion. "Jogging is free. It is convenient and enjoyable. It is safe," wrote Bowerman in his 1967 book, *Jogging*. "And it can benefit nearly everyone who is not ill or disabled." Bowerman's jogging mentor Lydiard agreed. "Anyone can jog," remarked the New Zealander as he gave talks on the sport in the United States.[33]

While jogging might have had limited restrictions on participation, the emerging sport of distance running had clearly marked boundaries. In 1966, Roberta "Bobbi" Gibb completed the Boston Marathon, albeit unofficially. Not permitted to formally enter the race, Gibb hid in the bushes at Hopkinton Common and jumped out to join the runners when it began. She finished in a time of 3:21, fast enough to beat 290 of the 415 male competitors. "I did want to make people see something different that would shake them up a little bit, maybe change some traditional attitudes," Gibb would explain afterward. *Sports Illustrated* was among the many news outlets that took note of the moment, arguing that her marathon finish would put to rest the "old-fashioned notion that a female is too frail for distance running." At the same time, the article elicited domestic stereotypes, announcing that "Boston was unprepared for the shapely blonde housewife who came out of the bushes to crush male egos." One particular male ego that remained solidly uncrushed was that of race official Will Cloney, who insisted that Gibb did not run the marathon: "She merely covered the same route as the official race while it was in progress."[34]

The following year, Katherine Switzer entered the race, eluding gender detection by registering as "K. V. Switzer." Like many young women of her time, Switzer had been cautioned throughout her life that engaging in sports like distance running could lead to excessive muscularity and, worse yet, the feared consequence of her uterus falling out. As the marathon kicked off, Switzer joined a crowded field of men, catching the attention of race official

Jock Semple, who realized that a woman had infiltrated the event. Semple tracked down Switzer on the race course, aggressively attempting to tear off her number. In a dramatic turn of events, Switzer's burly boyfriend and running partner intervened, forcefully knocking the race official to the ground. A cameraman captured the entire incident, and the photo quickly circulated through the national media. Despite the controversy, Semple asserted that he was justified in trying to stop Switzer. This sentiment was echoed by Cloney, who declared, "Women can't run in the Marathon because the rules forbid it. Unless we have rules, society will be in chaos.... If that girl were my daughter, I would spank her."[35]

In the days and years that followed, the image of Semple's crumpling body and Switzer running past him came to symbolize the broader inclusion of women into American society. Switzer would in her lifetime earn the title of "pioneer." But her status as a first official female finisher would be subject to revision. Almost ten years earlier, in 1959, Arlene Pieper was the only woman among the twelve runners who competed in the Pikes Peak Marathon in Colorado, a sanctioned event that directed runners up the 14,115-foot mountain for thirteen miles and then back down. Pike's Peak never had a prohibition on women running, so when the story of Bibb and Switzer began to develop, the race organizer argued that the marathon barrier had been broken years earlier. The problem was that no one could locate Pieper. It wasn't until the fiftieth anniversary of her finishing the marathon that organizers were finally able to find Pieper in California; she had taken her husband's name, Stine, and was shocked to learn that she was a barrier-breaking athlete. It had been her only marathon, done in part to promote her women's health club in Colorado Springs. In the years that followed, her story became part of the lore of the Pike's Peak Marathon, particularly how, when passing men on the course, she would remark, "Isn't this a beautiful day for a race?" Once they found her, race organizers made a point of flying Pieper Stine out to the race each year. And on the sixtieth anniversary of her race a group of women runners commemorated the moment by summiting the mountain wearing white shorts, hats, shoes, and shirts, Pieper Stine's clothing in her race. In February 2021, Pieper Stine passed away at the age of ninety. "Without pioneering efforts like Arlene's, we would have no history nor legacy in our sport," remarked Nancy Hobbs, executive director of the American Trail Running Association.[36]

Arlene Pieper Stine's story is of a forgotten pioneer whose memory would be recovered in a time when celebrating the accomplishments of women in sports had become a priority. While Pieper Stine was trekking up and down a Colorado mountain, a Black runner named Ted Corbitt was winning races all along the East Coast. But despite his looming presence in the distance running scene, his name would also be erased from the story of the running boom.

Corbitt was quite literally a pioneer in American distance running. After attending the University of Cincinnati and serving in the Army during World War II, Corbett became a physical therapist and moved to New York City. In 1947, he joined the New York Pioneers Club, established by three Black men in 1936 to provide health and fitness opportunities for youth. Joe Yancey, one of the founders, was particularly focused on promoting interracial cooperation. In 1942, the club expanded its membership to include White athletes, stating in its new constitution a commitment "to work toward a better racial understanding through the medium of education and sports." The American Athletic Union had been known to tacitly condone segregation, a practice the Pioneers actively resisted. But Black runners also faced racism away from the race competitions. Running through the streets of New York City, Black Pioneers frequently were met with racial slurs from disapproving White onlookers. Furthermore, the broader distance running community showed little interest in including Black members. In a 1955 *Saturday Evening Post* story about long-distance runners, one participant featured in the article expressed a particularly prejudiced view of Black Americans. When reminded that noted runner Lou White was Black, the man dismissively responded, "Oh, that doesn't count. . . . Lou's not really a Negro in my mind. He's a real gentleman, a marathoner."[37]

As a member of the Pioneers, Corbitt became the first Black American Olympic marathoner when he competed in the 1952 Helsinki Games. In the years that followed, the Pioneer ethos was grafted onto his efforts to build an interracial culture of distance running in New York City and beyond. In 1958, he was among the founders of the Road Runners Club of America, and he served as the first president of the New York Road Runners. He also established a program for certifying racecourses, a process that guaranteed the accuracy of distances. And then he popularized a term that became a new classification in distance running, "ultrarunning," signifying races of distances over 26.2 miles. Calling these a true "spiritual test," Corbitt became an ultramarathoning legend, training two hundred to three hundred miles per week.[38]

But still, Corbitt's place within this broader culture faced racial limitations. In 1958, after he placed third in the International Trade Marathon in New Jersey, a two-page article in the *Jersey Journal* featured pictures of the first-, second-, and fourth-place finishers but failed to show Corbitt's image or even mention him. It became something of a pattern in his career. Despite his presence in the sport, rare was the mention of Corbitt in stories of the running boom.[39]

Sportswriter Robert Lipsyte posited that the absence of reporting on Corbitt was the result of his withdrawn personality. "Corbitt was the inside man during the running boom," Lipsyte explained. Still, people needed to see Corbitt as "the last surviving spiritual elder of the modern running clan." At the time this 1993 article was published, Corbitt was seventy-five and still incredibly physically active. His longevity and contributions to distance running would soon be more visible, as he would be recognized as a pioneer of the sport. But the road he and others had to take to gain notice was paved with exclusion and omission.[40]

Marathoner Marilyn Bevans faced many of the same barriers Corbitt did in distance running circles. In 1975, she became the first Black woman to win a marathon, and in 1977 she finished second in Boston, at 2:51:12. Bevans was the only Black woman training alongside a group of White men who comprised the Baltimore Road Runners. Her presence in this White world sometimes drew negative attention, such as when someone chastened her for celebrating after a race, or well-intentioned comments about her being "articulate" and a "credit" to Black America. The insults were part of her experience. "When some runners ran, there were cheers," she commented on her rise in the distance running ranks. "When I ran, you heard crickets. I was called the N-word sometimes." Decades later, *Runner's World* would count her as a pioneer of the sport, and Bevans was among the first class of inductees into the National Black Marathoners Association's Distance Runner Hall of Fame. Corbitt was also inducted. He would receive another boost in the summer of 2020, when the New York City Parks Department renamed the main loop in Central Park after the runner. Now millions of runners each year encounter the "father of distance running" on the "sacred ground" that is this loop.[41]

# 12
# Sacred and Profane

"A great many people have been searching during ever so many years for the religion of democracy," declared Simeon Strunsky in 1914. "I believe I have found it." Writing in the *Atlantic Monthly*, one of the premier magazines of the time, Strunsky assured readers that this religion would not be found in any institutional church, which he characterized as being hopelessly mired in internal politics and misdirected priorities. "What I have in mind is a great democratic rite," he announced, "a ceremonial which is solemnized on six days in the week during six months in the year by large masses of men with such unfailing regularity and such unquestioning good faith that I cannot help thinking of it as essentially a religious performance." What he had in mind, of course, was baseball.[1]

In the eight pages that followed, the Russian-born Jewish American used an array of Christian allusions and comparisons to develop his argument. But Strunsky also did something unique for the time by referencing insights from the Scottish anthropologist James Frazer's book, *The Golden Bough*, first published in 1890, and later expanded into twelve volumes. Frazer collected and analyzed a range of myths and rituals from so-called primitive cultures. His intent was to trace the evolution of humanity from magic to religion and finally to a scientific worldview. Frazer became enormously popular in Europe and America among the intellectual class, as he represented a new way of understanding and studying religious behavior, one that attempted to unveil the origins and purposes of religion through meticulous examination.[2]

With *The Golden Bough* in mind, Strunsky posited that instead of "primitive" cultures, Frazer could have found plenty of "raw material" for his study in America among the legions of baseball fans: "If religious ceremonial has its origin in the play instinct of man, why go back to remote origins like the Australian corroboree and neglect Ty Cobb stealing second? If religion has its origin in primitive man's worship of the eternal rebirth of earth's fructifying powers with the advent of spring, how can we neglect the vivid stirring in the hearts of millions that marks the departure of the teams for

*Bodies in Motion*. Arthur Remillard, Oxford University Press. © Oxford University Press 2025.
DOI: 10.1093/oso/9780197789766.003.0013

spring training in Texas?"[3] Continuing his exploration, Strunsky delved into detailed analyses of the game's structure and mythology and its power to influence the emotions of fans. Based on these considerations, the author ultimately asserted that "the religion of baseball" was the genuine religion of America.

Strunsky was by no means the first to make such a claim. On May 28, 1910, for example, the Philadelphia sports publication *Sporting Life* printed the headline on their opening page "Religion of Baseball," with the subtitle "Our National Sport Founded upon the Same Principles as Underlie All True Religion and All Essentials to Moral and Physical Welfare to Rightful Conduct in This Life." The author was John Heydler, a baseball executive with the National League and the son of a Lutheran clergyman, which no doubt influenced his interpretation of America's pastime. Similarly, decades earlier, some clergymen began leaning into comparisons between their faith commitments and baseball. In 1889, Reverend Forest E. Dager of Holy Trinity Episcopal Church in Philadelphia preached a sermon titled "The Moral Lessons of Baseball."[4]

In contrast, Strunsky was not seeking to identify the "lessons" that baseball could teach about one's faith life. Nor was he, like Heydler, a baseball insider writing to other baseball insiders. Instead, Strunsky pivoted in a scholarly direction, speaking directly to the high-minded thinkers of his time. In the coming decades, other intellectuals would follow his lead, picking up threads from Frazer and his intellectual heirs to make similar arguments. Instead of developing theological inquiries about God and faith, these scholars shifted their attention toward exploring how individuals have found meaning in sports by examining the interplay between the realms of ultimate reality and everyday existence—the sacred and profane.

## The Church of Baseball

In 1919, *The Dial*, one of New York's most noted highbrow publications, featured a curious article from Morris Cohen titled "Baseball as a National Religion." A professor at the College of the City of New York, Cohen's academic work fit within *The Dial*'s scope, with a focus on democracy, pragmatism, law, and academic freedom. But this article seemed profoundly out of place, or at least that was Cohen's opening observation. "Do not be shocked gentle and learned reader!" he begged. "I know full well that baseball is a boy's game, and a professional sport, and that a properly cultured, serious person always feels like apologizing for attending a baseball game instead of a Strauss concert." But Cohen insisted that if one were to understand religion in terms of "mystic unity with a larger part of which we are a part," then baseball was worth considering. Cohen was aware that not everyone would agree, particularly those from his intellectual class. He recalled once asking his "friend and teacher" William James if baseball might just be the "moral equivalent to war." James quickly and firmly demurred. But Cohen found this shortsighted: "National rivalries could find their intensest expression in a close international pennant race, and yet such rivalry would not be incompatible with the establishment of the true Church Universal in which all men would feel their brotherhood in the Infinite Game."[5]

The tone of Cohen's article was no doubt ironic, but many more intellectuals would follow his path in the coming years. In 1954, the French American cultural historian Jacques Barzun, who, like Cohen, expressed an intellectual debt to William James, echoed similar sentiments in his ruminations on the game. "Whoever wants to know the heart and mind of America had better learn baseball, the rules and realities of the game," he surmised. This particular quote would find its way into baseball's lore, appearing on a plaque in the Baseball Hall of Fame.[6] It also graced the pages of Michael Novak's 1976 bestselling book, *The Joy of Sports.*

A Catholic intellectual with a broad public following, Novak offered thoughts on baseball and sports more generally that drew widespread attention. Consequently, his book on religion and sports introduced many readers to the idea of "American civil religion." In the late 1960s, sociologists and historians recovered the idea of "civil religion" from the French philosopher Jean-Jacques Rousseau to argue that throughout American history there has existed an unidentified, yet objectively real, system of symbols, rituals, and beliefs that has held together the diverse nation. This conversation blossomed in the years surrounding the bicentennial, as scholars examined parades, monuments, and civic celebrations using the tools and language of religious studies to interpret these so-called secular spaces and activities.[7] For Novak, there was a ball-shaped hole just waiting to be filled in this conversation.

"In the study of civil religions, our thinkers have too much neglected sports," he wrote in the opening pages of *The Joy of Sports*. "Sports are an almost universal language binding our diverse nation, especially its men, together." Novak saw baseball as being particularly effective in bringing about this end, since it was "an enactment of the white Anglo-Saxon Protestant myth." According to Novak, baseball's origin story was eminently rooted in individualism and the tacit agreements that people make to cooperate to advance their mutual interest. Novak also argued that the game was distinctly rural in a way that could be true only in America: "If baseball holds the secret to national character, that character is far removed from Hollywood, or Broadway, or Madison Avenue."[8]

In addition to baseball, Novak provided mythic interpretations of two other members of the "holy trinity" of American sports: basketball and football. All this fed into his broader argument of sports functioning as what he called a "natural religion." While distinct from traditional religions, "sports flow outward into action from a deep natural impulse that is radically religious: an impulse of freedom, respect for ritual limits, but has zest for symbolic meaning, and a longing for perfection."[9]

While the topic of sports still carried a degree of stigma in intellectual corners, Novak's status in this community put the literary world on notice. In his syndicated review, Dartmouth professor and noted conservative commentator Jeffrey Hart was particularly taken by Novak's discussion of baseball. The *New York Times* featured an excerpt of the book, while also printing two reviews, the first from Christopher Lehmann-Haupt—who, interestingly, in 1986 published his memoir, *Me and Joe DiMaggio: A Baseball Fan Goes in Search of His Gods*. Lehmann-Haupt opened by confessing that his "Protestant conscience" had difficulty considering sports a "natural religion": "It tells me that Mr. Novak has gone a bit too far in his enthusiasm." Similarly, John Leonard poked at Novak's religious affiliation, claiming that he "appropriates my pleasure for the purposes of his Catholicism." The *Times* reviewers were not alone. "Novak is a commentator of enormous ability and insight," wrote William Bennett in his review for *Commentary*, "but from time to time he becomes excessive and self-indulgent." A review in *CrossCurrents* took exception to Novak's standing as an "intellectual," and after dismantling the book for three pages ridiculed the title for its close mirroring of the 1972 bestselling book *Joy of Sex*. Sports fans, the author assured readers, "will find the book a tedious humbug and as joyless as a rainout."[10]

Interestingly, appraisals from specifically academic corners were largely positive. A review in the *Journal of the American Academy of Religion* concluded, "Novak has made an important contribution to a growing new field of academic philosophy." And another in the *Journal of Sports History* suggested, "Novak's work stands in sharp relief to that of the sports critics who have been attacking the very fiber of sport during the past ten years." Even those who largely disagreed with Novak took his arguments seriously. Before his time as a professor of literature and American studies at Amherst College in Massachusetts, Allen Guttmann lived in Germany, where he began to wonder about the differing German and American sports cultures. The result was his 1978 book, *From Ritual to Record: The Nature of Modern Sports*. Like Novak's, Guttmann's book drew broad interest and set a course for more intellectual engagement with sports and religion. Academics were well-prepared to give serious consideration to Guttmann's arguments, as reflected in comprehensive reviews in the *American Journal of Sociology* and the *Journal of American History*, as well as in popular outlets.[11] Unlike Novak, though, Guttmann argued for a separation of religion and sports.

Guttmann derived his foundational theoretical insight from the sociologist Max Weber and his ideas about the progressive rationalization of society. Accordingly, Guttmann proposed that while games in ancient contexts were played as expressions of religious ritual, modern games had evolved to be characterized by secularism, an equal opportunity to compete, specialization, rationalization, bureaucratic organization, quantification, and a pursuit of records. On the topic of religion, he drew aim specifically at Novak's conclusion that sports represent a "natural religion," arguing instead, "We do not run in order that the earth be more fertile. We till the earth, or work in our factories and offices, so that we can have time to play."[12]

Significantly, in later sections of the book Guttmann would shift attention to baseball, providing a comprehensive exploration of American exceptionalism and seeming to be open to the suggestions of Novak and others. "If our argument is valid," Guttmann posited, "baseball has retained something of the primitive connection between sports and the sacred. It is a secular activity with adumbrations of the mythic." With baseball as a possible exception, Guttmann added a new dimension to the intellectual discussion surrounding sports, aided by a secularization thesis that perceived society's progressive distancing from the language of enchantment. In the next few decades, more scholars would join this conversation, invoking these and other theoretical insights, particularly from Émile Durkheim and Mircea Eliade.[13]

Durkheim's *Elementary Forms of the Religious Life* was first published in 1912; there the French sociologist set forth to interpret the social behaviors of Australian Indigenous people. Religion, in his view, was not simply about a "belief" in God or gods. Instead, he focused on the work done in communities to negotiate a place between the transcendent realms and the ordinary—or to put it more precisely, the sacred and the profane. This approach to framing religious activity was a major influence on Eliade's 1959 book, *The Sacred and the Profane*. Additionally, Eliade, a novelist as well as a scholar, wondered about the broad-ranging implications of such a methodology: "A whole volume could well be written on the myths of modern man, on the mythologies camouflaged in the plays that he enjoys, in the books that he reads." Eliade's invitation to examine secular society for signs of mythic activity served as an invitation for scholars interested in sports. It was even enough to prompt some authors to see this venture as an exercise in heretical thinking and idolatry.[14]

Thus, as the twenty-first century began, there was very little novelty in seeing scholars bantering about religion and sports. And while they have taken to examining a range of athletic activities, some scholars have continued privileging baseball, arguing that this sport in particular "serves as a distinctive symbol of American identity." To this end, New York University president John Sexton published *Baseball as a Road to God*, which grew out of an undergraduate course he taught. With a background in American religious history and law, Sexton also professed to a youth shaped by dual allegiances to his Catholic faith and his hometown Brooklyn Dodgers. With ample references to theological concepts such as grace, conversion, and saints, Sexton also drew from his religious studies background, all in service of locating baseball as an "important thread" of American civil religion. On this point Sexton insisted that the civil religious elements of baseball were not just the result of committed fans and cathedral-like ballparks: "It is that baseball has the capacity to elevate and transform, that it has a power to bring people together in expanding levels of relationships."[15]

It was 2014 when Sexton's book was published, precisely one hundred years after Strunsky made a similar argument. Both writing from New York, they represent bookends to an intellectual discourse that brought together the discipline of religious studies with the fervor and intensity of America's pastime. It has become a conversation largely focused on national character—or at least a national character as translated through the majority White lens.

Indeed, two years after Sexton published his thoughts on baseball, Onaje X. O. Woodbine offered an examination of the "lived religion" of street basketball, particularly among Black men in urban settings. Eschewing framings of basketball as an escapeway from the streets, Woodbine examined how the game had become its own religious experience for these young men. It can serve, for example, a ritual function when giving players a way to deal with communal injury and loss, while also making space for hope and healing. Woodbine belongs to an emerging generation of Black scholars who have directed their focus to sports, narrating a tale of America and its sporting landscapes that encompasses the impact of racial marginalization and the ongoing struggle for civil rights. Some scholars involved in this conversation have told this story by examining the movements of Black athletes in sporting spaces as well as their acts of protest beyond the field.[16]

## Countercreeds

At the 1968 Olympics in Mexico City, Americans Tommie Smith and John Carlos took gold and bronze, respectively, in the 200-meter sprint. While their accomplishments on the track were noteworthy, it was what happened next that would cement their names in public consciousness. At the awards ceremony, Smith and Carlos stood silently as the "Star-Spangled Banner" played, their heads bowed and their gloved fists raised into the air in a Black Power salute. In addition, neither athlete wore shoes, signifying the impoverished state of Black America. Smith wore a black scarf as a tribute to racial pride, and Carlos wore beads, "for those individuals that were lynched, or killed, that no one said a prayer for." Their intention, simply, was both to draw awareness to the plague of racism in America and to hold their nation to a higher standard. "If I win," remarked Smith in a press conference after the event, "I am an American, not a black American. But if I did something bad, then they would say 'a Negro.' We are black and we are proud of being black."[17]

A photograph of the protest quickly circulated through the newspapers, which generated widespread outrage and condemnation aimed at the athletes. The Olympic governing body immediately ejected the sprinters from the Olympic Village and suspended them from the Games. White sports journalists howled in disapproval, echoing Brent Musburger, who dubbed Smith and Carlos "black-skinned storm troopers." Even the Australian Peter Norman, the silver medalist in the event, became subject to scrutiny. Smith and Carlos had informed Norman of their plan before the ceremony. In a show of solidarity, Norman—reportedly acting from a place of Christian conviction—remarked simply, "I will stand with you." He wore the badge of the Olympic Project for Human Rights, the organization that had given inspiration to the protest. Norman faced denunciations from his homeland as a result, punished additionally by being left off the 1972 Olympic squad.[18]

The architect of the Olympic Project for Human Rights was Harry Edwards, a civil rights leader and sociologist who at the time was at San Jose State, where Smith and Carlos were students. Edwards wanted the athletes to boycott the Olympics, but he fully understood the significance of their staged Black Power salute. The infamous image would be on the cover of Edward's 1969 book, *The Revolt of the Black Athlete.* Their story would also receive attention in his 1973 book, *Sociology of Sport,* where Edwards made unique use of the language of religion to advance his arguments about race, sports, and politics. He wrote, "If there is a universal popular religion in America it is to be found within the institution of sport." Using comparisons to familiar forms of religious expression, he listed eleven characteristics of this "quasi religion": formally stated beliefs, saints, ruling patriarchs, gods, high councils, scribes, true believers, devotees and converts, shrines, houses of worship, and symbols of faith. Edwards moved swiftly through these points before coming to his final one, setting it up with a lengthy citation by French sociologist Roger Bastide on race and Christianity. According to Bastide, the history of Christianity has seen the colors of white and black used as representations of good and evil, that which has been embraced and incorporated and that which has been rejected and despised. In turn, this combination has been imposed on Christian depictions of race.[19]

Edwards channeled Bastide's insight to argue that this color dichotomy had deeply influenced American culture (for example, white hats and black hats) and sports as well. Thus, as Edwards saw it, "there is little ground for the expectation that this society, which does not tolerate an image of its sacred God cast in a Semitic body, would be strongly predisposed to tolerate black heroes and 'gods' in its secular religion of sport." While talking specifically about White fans in this instance, Edwards did admit that the elevated status of Black athletes could possibly serve as a basis for widespread acceptance. But even here the author was skeptical. He was witnessing a world where Black people were dominating in sports like basketball, baseball, boxing, track and field, and football. Moreover, in international contests against Cold War foes, Black Americans repeatedly played significant roles in securing victories. Yet discrimination continued. "It is my judgment," Edwards concluded, "that the pride derived by black society from the black athlete's domination of whites in certain sports is an 'empty' and 'phony' pride."[20]

Edwards's observations on religion flowed into the book's broader point about what he called the "American sports creed," an umbrella term for the ideological goals of sports, which included character, discipline, competition, physical fitness, mental fitness, religiosity, and nationalism. Edwards explained that these values were reflections of the dominant American culture that had been heavily influenced by a form of White Protestantism that prized individual effort and achievement. But the author proposed that America also has "counter-creeds," such as what he called the "humanitarian creed," which stressed cooperation and community over competition and individual achievement. Edwards also identified an "equalitarian creed," which had its ideological center among Black athletes who have made demands for equality and opportunity. For Edwards, these countercreeds had been resisted and rejected by the dominant American creed, thereby reflecting a broader social pattern of meeting dissent with derision.[21]

Unlike Novak and others, Edwards revealed the competing civil religious discourses at work in American sports, stressing that a White creed had consistently suppressed Black voices, unless they performed in a certain way. In advancing his arguments, Edwards was figuring into a broader scholarly discussion over the ways in which sports played a role in forming political communities in America. Meanwhile, other groups of academics were considering another religious dimension to sports, one that avoided social questions and aimed instead at the individual's quest for a "peak experience."

## Peak Experience

In 1926, newspaper accounts of the Penn Relays—a premier collegiate track and field event in Philadelphia—detailed the extraordinarily dramatic finish in the two-mile relay. As the race entered its final leg, the favorite, Boston College, was poised for victory with a lead of a dozen yards over the nearest competitor. But Columbia's Joe Campbell refused to concede victory. Over the next two laps, he chipped away at the gap, and in the final stretch Campbell took the lead and broke the tape for a victory. It was the first time that Columbia had won this event at Penn since 1907, and much of the credit went to Campbell's performance. "Joe Campbell, New Lion Hero," exclaimed one headline.[22]

As headlines go, this one could not have been more ironically predictive of the future. In the coming decades, Joe Campbell the "Lion Hero" would become Joseph Campbell, the scholar known for developing "the hero's journey." In examining the mythologies of an assortment of cultures, Campbell identified what he saw as an archetypal pattern for hero stories: "A hero ventures forth from the world of common day into a region of supernatural wonder: fabulous forces are there encountered and a decisive victory is won: the hero comes back from this mysterious adventure with the power to bestow boons on his fellow man." This framework would become central in the storytelling of fiction and film, most notably through the *Star Wars* franchise. But Campbell maintained that "the hero's journey" was ultimately about self-discovery, giving individuals a tool for understanding their own lives, and, specifically, those key "moments" that people use to tell their own story. For Campbell, those years of running track at Columbia remained formative. He remarked in an interview, "I think I learned more about living then, what it takes to win, and what it takes to lose." He would point to his relay victory specifically when expanding on psychologist Abraham Maslow's notion of "peak experience," "moments in your life when you experience your relationship with the harmony of being." Campbell elaborated, "Nobody could beat me that day. . . . [I]t was the experience of really being at my full and doing a perfect job."[23]

Among Campbell's other influences was the American philosopher William James, who, while not a sports fan himself, would leave an intellectual mark on others who considered the deeper meaning of sports. The author of *The Varieties of Religious Experience*, James was the principal articulator of the philosophical school known as pragmatism, which emphasized that "truth" ought to be defined in terms of "practical results." James credited another American philosopher, Charles S. Peirce, with first coining the term. Coincidentally, another philosopher who had come under the influence of Peirce and James was Morris Cohen, who in turn would leave a combined intellectual fingerprint on the work of his student, Paul Weiss. For the majority of his career, Weiss was a leading philosopher at Yale. As he reached retirement, he became increasingly interested in character formation, publishing *The Making of Men* in 1967. In the preface, Weiss focused on the role of coaching in sports, leading him to resolve, "[W]e need a philosophy of sport."[24]

This led to the 1968 publication of *Sport: A Philosophical Inquiry*. Like Cohen and others, Weiss saw in sports a "semireligious" quality insofar as athletic events "pivot about national songs and symbols, and are expressed in conventionally approved gestures." But the bulk of his attention went to the athlete himself—with emphasis on the *him*—and how playing sports offers a promise of "becoming excellent." He asserted that women simply lacked the intuitive drive to become athletes. Their identities were "more firmly established" as "wives and mothers." Weiss was also apparently imagining White men in his philosophical deliberations, suggesting, "If there is a real difference in the bodily capacities of Negroes and whites, we out to handicap one or the other." He insisted that this would not be a move to weaken civil rights but a means for assuring fair play, just as men and women competed separately.[25]

The book's essentializing claims were the principal criticism of a review in the *Journal of Philosophy*. Describing it as "a tedious, pompous, ill-written book," the reviewer explained that Weiss largely disregarded the "rich lore of the sports world," missing out on its "magic." To leave no doubt about his opinion, the review concluded, "Anyone fond of either sport or philosophy can spare themselves from a thoroughly distasteful experience by avoiding Weiss's book."[26]

Despite this criticism, *Sport: A Philosophical Inquiry* would become a fixture in scholarly discussions about sports, marked as being the first "serious" philosophical examination of an individual's athletic experience by a credentialed scholar. Then in 1967 another philosopher approached the world of sports from an intellectual perspective. In *Man, Sport, and Existence*, Howard Slusher from the University of Southern California similarly explored how sports serve as a vehicle for understanding human existence. In a chapter on the religious aspects of athletics, Slusher referenced the existentialist insights of Paul Tillich, contending that sport "has the potential to assist man in a demonstration of meaningful concern." Thus he concluded that sports, much like religion, was a vehicle for individuals to develop their "inner self."[27]

A review from the noted Associated Press religion reporter George W. Cornell gave close attention to the book's inward focus. Similarly, a Methodist weekly took notice of Slusher's examination of ritual: "Sport simply wouldn't be sport without the toss of the coin or the seventh-inning stretch. Indeed, this element of ritual may meet a profound need in the human psyche." But Slusher certainly had his detractors. English analytical philosopher Anthony Quinton reviewed this book along with Weiss's and found the entire topic of sports to be unworthy of the discipline of philosophy.[28]

While reviewers covered these books and linked them together, another sports philosopher was dealing with similar themes and receiving less mention. Eleanor Metheny was a professor of physical education at the University of California. She studied English and mathematics at the University of Chicago in the mid-1920s, where she was introduced to a line of thinking developed by Ernst Cassirer, who advanced the philosophical understanding that human beings make meaning of their life and the world through symbolic expression. Metheny's other main influence was the American philosopher Susan Langer, who applied Cassirer's philosophy to the arts. During her career, Metheny adapted these insights to her own "movement theory," which was characterized by three neologisms. The "kinestruct," she proposed, is the simple fact of a physical body in motion; the "kinescept" is about perception, how one experiences or witnesses the movement; and the "kinesymbol" indicates the diffuse meanings that these movements can have.[29]

All of this was outlined in her 1968 book, *Movement and Meaning*. "No form is innately meaningful," Metheny wrote. "Rather, this conception becomes meaningful to us as we seize upon it, take it into ourselves, and become involved with it." In her analysis of sports, she too drew comparisons to religion, noting that the athlete might pursue "wholeness" through their movements. She additionally advocated women in sports, acknowledging that many games had been designed with men in mind. In the author's view, both men and women could equally derive enjoyment and value from sports.[30]

Later scholars would credit Metheny for her trailblazing work, but in her own time she received limited attention in comparison to male scholars of similar stature. Metheny was undeterred. Throughout her career, she wrote five books, more than 150 articles, papers, and research studies, and thirty book chapters. Additionally, she made a point of connecting with audiences outside of the academy, delivering over six hundred lectures to community organizations and schools of all varieties. As a result, her influence extended far beyond her corner of academia. When Metheny died in 1982, one former student took the opportunity to reflect on how her professor influenced her life and career, remarking, "She sensitized me to movement as creativity, as expression, and as essential to being."[31]

In Metheny we find an example of a professor whose ideas were absorbed by her many hearers and adherents, who then took these ideas into the broader world. Similarly, academic voices at this time were central in inspiring students to produce another religious interpretation of sports, one linked to an interest in "Eastern religions."

## Zen Sports

Frederic Spiegelberg was born into a Jewish family in Hamburg, Germany. As a student, he came under the influence of Rudolf Otto and Paul Tillich before fleeing Hitler's Germany and eventually landing at Stanford in 1941. It was there he grew a reputation as an expert in Eastern religions, and in the spring semester of 1950 sophomore Michael Murphy reportedly wandered into one of Spiegelberg's lectures by accident. Almost immediately, Murphy was entranced as Spiegelberg drew parallels between what he believed were the intersecting principles of Eastern and Western religions. Murphy reoriented his studies as a result and started practicing meditation, a decision that led to his having "an experience" one evening confirming that his life should be spent exploring "the inner world." After finishing his degree and serving in the Army, Murphy traveled to India and spent eighteen months studying meditation at Sri Aurobindo's ashram. When he returned, Murphy and his fellow Stanford graduate Dick Price enlisted Spiegelberg's assistance to co-found a retreat center in Big Sur, California, called the Esalen Institute, a name reportedly derived from an ancient Indigenous population that had once occupied the area. As the counterculture movement of the 1960s grew, Esalen would become a central location for what was called the Human Potential Movement. Bringing together philosophical and psychological insights alongside Eastern-inflected ideas and practices (as well as hallucinogenic drugs and free love), the advocates of this movement sought to achieve "self-actualization."[32]

By the 1970s, Murphy began to apply the unconventional Esalen philosophy to the entirely conventional world of sports, specifically golf. He had played and watched the game for most of his life. As a young man, he had watched Ben Hogan during a practice session, and the image stuck with him. "There was a Zen aspect to it," Murphy reflected later. "He was so focused it was like he was in a meditative state."[33]

Hogan served as the inspiration for the mysterious character Shivas Irons in Murphy's 1971 novel, *Golf in the Kingdom*. In the story, Murphy's protagonist, resembling himself, aspires to study at an ashram in India but ends up playing an unplanned round of golf during a layover in Scotland. This chance encounter leads to the protagonist gaining wisdom and insight from Shivas Irons. The narrative structure, from the accidental meeting with a spiritual sage to the eventual transformation of the lead character's mind, body, and spirit, distinctly echoes Campbell's "hero's journey." Campbell, a regular lecturer at Esalen since 1965 and one of Murphy's favorite scholars, influenced *Golf in the Kingdom* not only in structure but also in Murphy's comparative approach, referencing such diverse sources as Plato, St. John of the Cross, the *Bhagavad Gita*, and Jean-Paul Sartre. Moreover, the name Shivas Irons bears an obvious resemblance to Shiva, the Hindu god of destruction and redemption. Irons's aphorisms and advice throughout the book resemble lessons in meditation, instructing the young golfer, for example, to "let the nothingness into yer [*sic*] shots."[34]

Almost immediately upon publication, the book became "holy scripture" for golfers. One professional golfer observed, "It gave us the language to talk about the spiritual side of the game." In 1992, the book took institutional form through the nonprofit Shivas Irons Society, "dedicated to furthering golf as a mindful pursuit and as a tool for personal growth and development."[35]

Murphy also wrote on sports more generally. In 1978, he teamed with the parapsychologist Rhea White to publish *The Psychic Side of Sports*, which would later be retitled *In the Zone: Transcendent Experience in Sports*. In the introduction, the authors drew upon James's ruminations on the phenomenon of the "second wind," citing instances of the ways that ordinary people possess supposedly hidden energy reserves that allow them to transcend their limits. In their discussion of "uncanny suspension," the authors described the basketball standout Michael Jordan as someone who defied the laws of gravity.[36]

At the time of the book's new edition, Jordan was playing for the Chicago Bulls, where he was coached by Phil Jackson. A practitioner of Zen meditation, Jackson had long been an admirer of Murphy, particularly *Golf in the Kingdom*, a book that he gave to Jordan as a reading assignment. Nicknamed "the Zen master," Jackson had made a coaching habit of referencing teachings and symbolism from an amalgam of spiritual resources, including the Christianity of his youth, Zen Buddhism, and the traditions of the Lakota Sioux. Jackson would go even further and interpret his coaching philosophy in religious terms. When he started coaching the Bulls in 1989, he inherited the rising superstar Jordan and a team content with feeding him the ball and letting him take over. But Jackson knew that a fully functioning team would always rival a singular talent. So he implemented an offensive strategy known as "the Triangle." Adapted from the legendary Kansas State coach and Bulls consultant Tex Winter, the Triangle emphasized moving the ball to empty spaces. In his 1995 book, *Sacred Hoops*, Jackson called it "five-man tai chi" and wrote that "it embodied the Zen Christian attitude of selfless awareness." For his part, Jordan expressed little interest in Jackson's "Zen stuff." But that didn't stop Jackson from imparting Zen meaning onto his superstar, writing, "Michael had attained a quality of mind few Zen students ever achieve."[37]

As Jackson was contemplating the Zen qualities of his non-Zen star athlete, other athletes—especially in endurance sports—were developing similar attractions to Buddhism. Mark Allen, also nicknamed "the Zen Master," won the Hawaii Ironman (2.4-mile ocean swim, 112-mile bike race, 26.2-mile run) six times, the first coming in 1989. That year would become known as the "Iron War," as Allen dethroned the "Lord of the Lava" Dave Scott after finishing behind Scott six times prior. As Allen rose to triathlon fame, interest in his spiritual practices followed, as was true for eight-time Hawaii Ironman winner Paula Newby-Fraser. She too credited her performances to Zen meditation, as she elaborated in the foreword to Shane Alton Eversfield's 2004 book, *Zendurance*.[38]

And then there was Tiger Woods, who Murphy believed was the embodiment of "Eastern ideas of superphysical energies and actions." Unlike Murphy or Jackson, Woods had a family connection to Buddhism through his mother and her homeland of Thailand. In 1996, a *Sports Illustrated* feature article focused on Woods's Buddhism, folding it into a broader story of the athlete's unique background and exceptional talent. "I believe in Buddhism," Woods remarked. "Not every aspect, but most of it." He explained, "I can enjoy material things, but that doesn't mean I need them."[39]

Alas, in 2009 revelations of extramarital affairs prompted Woods to take a brief hiatus from the sport. Despite successfully resuming his golf career some years later, Woods grappled with a series of injuries, and in 2017 he faced arrest and DUI charges. Reflecting on this tumultuous period, golf journalist Curt Sampson noted, "Death, ego, and the fame machine knocked Tiger on his ass a decade or so ago, and a lot of people who'd cheered for him now sneered at him." Sampson added, "Woods seemed suddenly to personify something or other, like pride goeth-ing before a fall, or Icarus, or King Lear." By 2019, however, the Icarus of the golf world had transformed into a phoenix, rising from the ashes with a victory at the Masters tournament in Augusta, Georgia. Sampson enthusiastically remarked, "As he tapped in for the win, Tiger tapped into our intense and undying interest in tales of redemption." Echoing these sentiments, Murphy observed, "It's the classic hero's journey. That he has made it back to the top is a great American story."[40]

After Woods's 2019 Masters victory, an image of the golfer in his trademark red shirt, arms outstretched, clutching his putter in celebration, soon became *the* image of the moment. "What will we remember 30 years from now, when the story is conveyed to a new generation," asked one reporter. This was no mere documentation of a moment on the golf course. To this interpreter of Woods's movements, it was an "iconic" image of an "iconic" athlete.[41]

# 13
# Making Icons

As the 2016 Olympic Games in Rio neared, American Olympians voted to have the swimmer Michael Phelps carry the flag into the opening ceremonies. While Phelps was perhaps the most visible and discussed athlete during the lead-up to the games, the second-place vote-getter was African American fencer Ibtihaj Muhammad. Coming into the Games, Muhammad was a media point of focus for being the first American Muslim to compete in the Olympics while wearing a hijab. According to Muhammad, this came with a unique set of challenges in an America where the sight of a hijab could stir anti-Islamic sentiments, intensified by her race and gender. "[I feel unsafe] all the time," she told reporters. "I had someone follow me home from practice and try to report me to police." For one sports journalist, the fencer's rise in the public's eye made her the ideal candidate to carry the flag instead of Phelps: "Ibtihaj Muhammad is a pioneer who may soon become an icon, and nothing would have said more about the meritocracy and egalitarianism of America than a Muslim woman carrying our flag."[1]

Incidentally, the author's prediction that the fencer would soon become an "icon" arguably happened in 2017, when the toy company Mattel introduced a new doll to their "Barbie Shero" line, which replicated the fencer's likeness, duly noting her attire, sport, and skin color. "I'm proud to know that little girls everywhere can now play with a Barbie who chooses to wear hijab," Muhammad stated after the release of her doll. The fencer's attire was again highlighted in 2018, when Nike released the "Pro Hijab." The new item intentionally aimed to push back on the growing trend of hijab bans in sports. Muhammad celebrated the new product's statement to the world, as well as its functionality in athletics. In competitions, her previous hijab would obstruct her hearing and movement, a limitation that the Nike design corrected. Therefore the Nike hijab was marketed as a product for Muslim athletes, by Muslim athletes.[2]

Muhammad's narrative follows familiar framings, portraying her as both a hero (shero) and a pioneer. In American history, the sports hero is nothing new, often carrying sacred undertones as the person or group representing

*Bodies in Motion*. Arthur Remillard, Oxford University Press. © Oxford University Press 2025.
DOI: 10.1093/oso/9780197789766.003.0014

their sport and more. The hero-as-pioneer, as illustrated earlier, adds a trailblazing dimension to this narrative form. Muhammad introduces yet another layer to this mix: the athlete-as-icon. The Greek root of "icon" refers to votive statues of victorious Olympic athletes, local heroes revered for their accomplishments. Fast-forward to the present, and we observe a similar sports iconography at arenas and civic spaces featuring the likenesses of favored athletes, often as statues. From antiquity to today, these icons connect to values such as persistence, forbearance, excellence, beauty, and courage. So while the hero and the icon share many similarities, icons are dynamic images that shape and are shaped by the community that creates them.[3]

Uniquely, the contemporary practice of designating athletes as icons started gaining prominence in the 1990s and continued to evolve in subsequent decades. This trend coincided with the rise of digital media, whereby images can easily circulate and be created or replicated with minimal skill and effort. Moreover, the technology employed in this process adopted the terminology "icons." Beginning in the 1970s, computer interfaces incorporated icons—small graphical representations of programs, files, folders, or other objects. Over the following decades, icons became ubiquitous on keyboards and touch screens of digital devices. Consequently, people began leveraging these computer icons to conceptualize cultural icons, offering a new perspective on subjects ranging from the Alamo to the Zipper.[4]

Digital media provided global corporations with an efficient avenue to expand their brand presence into new markets, turning sports icons into potent marketing tools. This transformation of ordinary individuals into extraordinary figures required a particular artistry—a creative endeavor to craft an image that could promote products without overly emphasizing this commercial intent. Nike, in particular, excelled in this realm, skillfully utilizing their advertisements to elevate bodies in motion into revered symbols of both sports and global capitalism.

## Icons of Global Capitalism

Before co-founding Nike with his former college coach, Phil Knight attended Stanford Business School, where he studied how Japanese camera makers had streamlined production costs to undercut German companies and dominate the market. Intrigued by the possibility of applying a similar approach to running shoes, Knight journeyed to Japan. There he established a partnership with a shoe manufacturer and underwent two profound awakenings. The first pertained to global capitalism, wherein market forces and profit-seeking behavior would lead to the efficient circulation of capital, goods, and labor across national boundaries. His second awakening was spiritual, influenced by an encounter with Zen Buddhism. The emphasis on self-negation, simplicity, and nonlinear thinking resonated with Knight, who was dissatisfied with the prevailing business culture in the United States. Continuing his spiritual journey, Knight traveled to Greece, drawing inspiration from the Temple of Nike, the goddess of victory. Upon returning to the United States, these diverse experiences became the foundation for his new company. The missing piece was finding an athlete who could embody this ethos and propel Nike into the public spotlight.[5]

In other words, Knight needed a sports icon, and conveniently found one in his former University of Oregon teammate, Steve Prefontaine. At his zenith, Prefontaine, often known as "Pre" by his fans, held every American record from 2000 to 10,000 meters. He drew crowds to tracks wherever he competed, captivating audiences with his talent, bold energy, and authenticity. Prefontaine was also known for his outspokenness, both words and actions, earning him the moniker of "the James Dean of distance-running." His career met a tragic end when he died in a car accident just outside of Eugene in 1975. After his death, tributes to Prefontaine and what he symbolized poured in abundantly, continuing for decades. Even today mourners visit "Pre's rock," located at the site of his accident, which has become a pilgrimage site for distance runners worldwide who admire and pay homage to the late athlete.[6]

Nike has actively fueled this fascination, primarily because Prefontaine served as Knight's inaugural icon. "Pre was a rebel from a working-class background, a guy full of cockiness and guts," Knight emphasized. "Pre's spirit is the cornerstone of this company's soul." This sentiment is palpable on Nike's Oregon campus, where a statue of Prefontaine in full stride commands attention. Nike's myth-building around Prefontaine is further evident in its advertising efforts. In 1997, Nike sponsored *Fire on the Track*, a documentary spotlighting the athlete, broadcast ahead of a track meet named in his honor. Although ostensibly centered on Prefontaine, Nike is featured in 15 percent of the fifty-eight-minute documentary, with Knight narrating the company's origin story interwoven with Prefontaine's narrative. The outcome was an idealized portrayal of both Prefontaine and Nike, together packaged as rebellious entities designed to captivate audience attention.[7]

At this juncture in Nike's history, the company had firmly established its prowess in advertising. In its early days, however, Nike was primarily recognized for capitalizing on the "running boom" of the 1970s. This strategy proved lucrative, with sales soaring from $10 million to $270 million by the end of the decade. Despite this initial success, profits soon began to decline, leading to employee layoffs by the mid-1980s. Seeking a resurgence, Knight aimed for more and found it when Nike signed basketball standout Michael Jordan in 1984. The company swiftly crafted an advertising campaign around Jordan, kicking off with the "Jordan Flight" commercial. This advertisement featured Jordan in slow motion approaching a basketball hoop, accompanied by the sound of revving jet engines and a voice declaring, "Who said man was not meant to fly?" The ad struck a chord with audiences, propelling Nike to sell over $100 million worth of their Air Jordan line in its inaugural year on the market.[8]

In the years that followed, the image of Jordan soaring above the earth, legs spread, aiming for the basket, would soon need no explanation. It was iconic in the most literal sense, an image of athletics and commerce that had become instantly recognizable, not just in the United States but around the world. "Now the experience of sports is everywhere," Knight asserted, adding that the ubiquity of sports had made it "the culture of the world." By the mid-1990s, Nike's sales would ride the wave of this culture and reach nearly $10 billion in this global market, enabled by a communications revolution that included fiber-optic cables and direct-broadcast satellites that brought his sports icons to every corner of the earth.[9]

The elevation of Jordan to icon status certainly was not lost on the media of the time, nor was Nike's role in building his mythology. *Time* magazine quipped, "If Michael Jordan is God, then Phil Knight put him in heaven." And yet while Nike branded itself as the revolutionary force that was more than just a shoe company, its willingness to wade into challenging social issues was tempered at best. In the Jordan era, Nike would enlist several Black athletes to represent their products, while avoiding any of the activism of the past. Both athletes and the company seemed to agree on this point. In 1990, Jordan declined to endorse Harvey Gantt, the Black Democrat who was running against North Carolina senator Jesse Helms, a Republican with a record of standing in the way of racial justice that included opposing the Voting Rights Act and the Civil Rights Act. "Republicans buy sneakers, too," Jordan reportedly remarked, although he has since said this comment was made "in jest." At the same time, Jesse Jackson was leading a Black boycott of

Nike after revelations of the company's inequitable hiring practices. Jordan again remained neutral.[10]

Jordan's pose had a historical parallel. In 1968, the same year as the Black Power salute at the Olympics, O. J. Simpson achieved acclaim by winning the Heisman Trophy as a running back at USC. Soon Simpson's outstanding professional career and friendly persona garnered numerous high-profile endorsements. As reported in 1968, he distanced himself from racial controversy by stating, "I'm not black, I'm O.J." In his autobiography two years later, Simpson clarified that this was his way of addressing racial discrimination, expressing the hope of being as influential as Tommie Smith, Jim Brown, and Jackie Robinson.[11]

Tiger Woods would take an approach similar to Jordan's and Simpson's. But Woods's trajectory had a unique angle, due in large part to the deeply embedded whiteness of his chosen sport. After two years of college, Woods joined the professional tour in 1996, when Nike signed the athlete to a $40 million endorsement. Knight knew he had something special in Woods, an icon in the making. "The world has not seen anything like what he's going to do for the sport," said Knight. "I wasn't alive to see Claude Monet paint, but I am alive to see Tiger play, and that's pretty great."[12]

No other athlete prior to Woods had ever become so wealthy so quickly. As such, anticipation and interest peaked at his first press conference, where he opened by saying simply, "I guess, hello, world." The journalists were unaware of it, but Woods was giving a nod to an ad campaign that Nike had planned to roll out later that week. In it, the refrain "Hello world" punctuated a montage of images and achievements banked by the golfer in his short life, set to an emotionally charged score in the background. Then, as the ad ended, the text read, "There are still courses in the U.S. where I am not allowed to play because of the color of my skin. . . . Hello world. I've heard I'm not ready for you. Are you ready for me?"[13]

The commercial caused a stir for both Nike and Woods, which only intensified with the release of Nike's next advertising campaign, "I am Tiger Woods." With no Nike products in view, the commercial instead depicted a world where boys and girls of all backgrounds were uniting around the game of golf. It was a commercialized packaging of an emerging narrative for Woods as "the Chosen One." This particular moniker started with a curious comment made by his father, Earl: "Tiger will do more than any other man in history to change the course of humanity." When asked if he meant "sports history," Earl Woods stood firm in his wording. Because his son played an international sport, and because of his charisma, and because of his unique racial identity, "he is the Chosen One. He'll have the power to impact nations. Not people. Nations. The world is just getting a taste of his power."[14]

The grandiose expectations announced by the father were nothing new in the life of Tiger Woods. It was a message that Earl had been repeating to him since his earliest days. Now the golf world was inscribing this onto his emerging mythology. When Woods won his first Masters tournament in 1997, analysts and observers lifted the moment up as a marker of racial progress. Woods himself noted the occasion by situating his win within the game's history, referring to the Black golfers who came before him, including Lee Elder and Charlie Sifford. Meanwhile, Nike was doing the work of, as one journalist phrased it, "creating a style icon as much as an athletic one." In addition to the advertisements and products, for the final day of the tournament Nike had outfitted Woods in a red shirt and black pants. The visual would come to signify the intensity of the athlete, the single-minded focus of a champion. In a short time, weekend golfers seeking to model Woods's game and persona wore their Nike-branded red shirts too.[15]

Nike's challenge was in finding a balance between the template that they had created with Jordan, of the globally famous icon who does not offend the majority's sensibilities, and acknowledging the success of a Black athlete in a very White sport. It was a challenge that only grew in the wake of Woods's Masters victory, when an interview with golfer Fuzzy Zoeller began circulating through the media wherein he made a series of racist comments about Woods, complete with references to "fried chicken" and "collard greens." Woods initially did not respond to the golfer, refusing to return Zoeller's calls. Woods also had another problem on his hands. After winning the Masters, President Bill Clinton called to congratulate and invite him to Shea Stadium to celebrate the fiftieth anniversary of Jackie Robinson's breaking the color barrier in baseball. Woods declined, despite the president's offer to transport him on an air force plane. Instead, Woods, who took it as a slight that he hadn't been invited earlier, went to Cancun and enjoyed a vacation with his friends. The press reaction was quick and harsh.[16]

Amid this swirl, Woods finally sat for an interview with Oprah Winfrey. When the conversation reached the topic of race, he explained that his racial identity was a unique blend of Caucasian, Black, and Asian—what he called "Cablinasian." More criticism piled up after the interview, with several commentators weaponizing Woods's neologism and his emphatic "I'm just who I am." And yet, outside of the media ecosystem, Woods's popularity experienced a significant rise. Polling at the time showed that he had become the most popular athlete in America, surpassing Jordan. He received a negative rating of only 2 percent from respondents. Fans, in other words, didn't care about his perceived social missteps. They wanted to see him on the golf course. Nike's forthcoming advertisements took the hint, magnifying his accomplishments and generating an iconography for the athlete that became inseparable from the Nike swoosh.[17]

## Iconic Controversies

"The trinity of O.J., Michael and Tiger, and the wealth they tapped, had created a new template for a new generation, which had no personal memory of when athletes took principled stands on issues." This was journalist Howard Bryant's assessment of these successful and inoffensive athletes and the era that they represented. But then in 2012, basketball great LeBron James of the Miami Heat circulated an image on social media of him and his teammates donning hoodies, their heads bowed in support of and solidarity with Trayvon Martin, a Florida teenager whose killing had become national news. In the coming years, James continued voicing support for racial justice while simultaneously hearing chants of "Shut up and play" from his detractors. Colin Kaepernick faced even more scrutiny when he entered the activism stage, or rather, took a knee. Starting in 2016, the San Francisco 49ers quarterback drew widespread attention for initially sitting, and later kneeling, during the national anthem. "I am not going to stand up to show pride in a flag for a country that oppresses Black people and people of color," he announced, adding: "When there's significant change and I feel like that flag represents what it's supposed to represent in this country, I'll stand."[18]

The context for Kaepernick's gesture had deep roots in the history of Black activism in sports. The noted sociologist Harry Edwards had been serving as a consultant for the 49ers, and Kaepernick counted him as a "good friend" and conversation partner. A driving force behind the 1968 Olympic Black Power salute, Edwards knew the power of symbolic imagery, the way in which the right image at the right time could bring about awareness and change. Perhaps this is why John Carlos, one of the gloved protesters at that Olympics, compared Kaepernick to Muhammad Ali, calling the quarterback "this generation's iconic civil rights leader."[19]

While an icon of racial progress to some, Kaepernick faced criticisms that echoed those deployed following the 1968 Olympic protest. "America—let's sack this ungrateful punk," declared former Alaska governor and 2008 Republican vice-presidential candidate Sarah Palin on her Facebook page. The 2016 Republican nominee for president Donald Trump advised that Kaepernick "should find a country that works better for him." Even the former NFL quarterback and football analyst Boomer Esiason piled on, declaring that he was "disgusted" by the protest and that Kaepernick was a "disgrace."[20]

Kaepernick quickly found himself without a team in the NFL. But he would soon be playing for another team: Nike. In 2018, Nike released an ad that featured Kaepernick, showing only his face accompanied by the words, "Believe in something. Even if it means sacrificing everything." Edwards was among those commending the corporate giant, saying in a formal statement, "Thank you NIKE for taking a corporate leadership role and a progressive stand on the right side of history in this enduring American struggle." This was a point Edwards would make repeatedly during the controversy, drawing comparisons between Kaepernick and the Black athletes of the 1960s.[21]

Indeed, by 2020, following the police murder of George Floyd in Minneapolis and the ensuing protests, public sentiment started to align more with Kaepernick. The NFL issued a statement that essentially echoed Kaepernick's convictions, the league's commissioner, Roger Goodell, publicly apologizing "for not listening to NFL players earlier." Edwards, in the meantime, advocated for Kaepernick to either play for an NFL team or work with the league to advance their social justice initiatives. Edwards also proposed the idea of nominating Kaepernick for the Nobel Peace Prize, not only recognizing his individual efforts but also acknowledging the broader history of protests by Black athletes, dating back to Jesse Owens and Jackie Robinson. At Kaepernick's alma mater, the University of Nevada, Reno, a group of alumni and supporters began advocating for a statue of the football player to be erected on the campus. This initiative coincided with a nationwide movement to replace and remove various controversial statues in public spaces.[22]

Despite receiving admiration from various quarters, Kaepernick faced challenges in restarting his NFL career, fostering suspicion that the league's apologies and gestures toward racial justice were merely performative, lacking substantive change. One year earlier, Nike had encountered similar criticism, particularly concerning the treatment of female athletes under its sponsorship. In 2019, middle-distance runner Alysia Montaño wrote an op-ed for the *New York Times* titled "Nike Told Me to Dream Crazy, Until I Wanted a Baby." The opening line starkly declared, "Many athletic apparel companies, including Nike, claim to elevate female athletes, but that's just advertising." Montaño listed numerous female athletes signed by Nike whose pregnancies resulted in a loss of support from the company. One of these athletes was distance runner Kara Goucher, who continued training during her high-risk pregnancy, fearing the loss of sponsorship. Goucher even delayed revealing her pregnancy to friends and family for four months because Nike wanted to announce it on Mother's Day. She intended to fulfill her sponsorship commitment by participating in a half-marathon three months after giving birth. However, when her son fell ill and required hospitalization, Goucher found herself torn. She confessed, "I felt like I had to leave him in the hospital, just to get out there and run, instead of being with him like a normal mom would. I'll never forgive myself for that." Sprinter Allyson Felix joined the chorus of critics, applauding Montaño and Goucher for "heroically breaking their nondisclosure agreements with the company to share their pregnancy stories."[23]

Nike immediately went into damage control, pledging to include contractual protection for pregnancy. The company received a boost from one of its most noted athletes, tennis standout Serena Williams, who commended Nike for "learning from mistakes." Williams had recently become a mother, but her status and longevity in the sport shielded her from financial concerns. In 2018, *Forbes* listed Williams as the highest-paid female athlete that year, which came less from her earnings on the court and more from her $18.1 million in endorsements and business ventures.[24]

Williams's iconic status is a result of both her exceptional talent and her distinctive form of activism. Throughout her career, she showcased a willingness to challenge the conventional norms of the tennis court, particularly through her unconventional attire choices. In 2002, she garnered attention for wearing a skintight black catsuit, sponsored by Puma, at the U.S. Open. In 2018, she sported another catsuit, this time created by Nike for the French Open. While the outfit was partly chosen for style, it also served a functional purpose. Following the birth of her daughter, Williams faced health complications, including blood clots, which compression gear helped alleviate. Beyond the practical benefits, the sleek look also provided a mental advantage for Williams. "I feel like a warrior in it, a warrior princess . . . from Wakanda, maybe," referencing the Marvel comic and film *Black Panther*. She added, "I've always wanted to be a superhero, and it's kind of my way of being a superhero." However, the French Tennis Federation failed to recognize the significance and imposed a dress code explicitly banning Williams's outfit.[25]

The decision prompted an immediate backlash, in which Nike took a leading role. A black-and-white advertisement from the company features Williams in a powerful stance on the court, with the words, "You can take the superhero out of her costume, but you can never take away her superpowers" overlaid on the image. Here and elsewhere, Nike's advertising machine stepped into the middle of a controversy by using the iconic imagery that they had created to make a positive statement about race, gender, and sports. In other words, Nike had developed an apparatus for handling its own controversies, as well as the controversies confronting their athletes—something it had spent years refining with Tiger Woods.[26]

In the early months of 2009, Tiger Woods's life and career were both soaring. In March, nine months removed from knee surgery, Woods launched a historic comeback to win the Arnold Palmer Invitational in Orlando, Florida. It was one of his seven wins for the season after playing a total of nineteen tournaments. Meanwhile, he became the first athlete in history to reach $1 billion in career earnings. And then there was Woods's family, as he and his wife welcomed their second child. But by November, Woods's life took a significant and unexpected turn. When a tabloid story emerged that detailed his extramarital affairs, he initially denounced and dismissed the claims. But shortly after these revelations, he was found unconscious in his wrecked car near his home. The public soon learned that Woods was fleeing his house following a heated confrontation with his wife, who used a golf club to smash out the back windows of Woods's car.[27]

As more details emerged and the media prodded for answers, more women came forward claiming to have had affairs with the golfer. By December, when the number reached fourteen, new reporting additionally raised questions around Woods's association with a physician known for dispensing performance-enhancing drugs. Woods, meanwhile, remained largely silent and withdrawn as one by one his sponsors dropped him. Nike was one of the rare exceptions. After a stint in rehab, Woods focused on returning to the sport and repairing his image. Nike took up the latter task. In April, as the Masters tournament approached, Nike released a black-and-white commercial with Woods's face staring silently into the camera. In the background was the voice of his father, who had died in 2006 and seemed to be speaking to his son from beyond the grave. At the end of the commercial, the father's voice asks, "Did you learn anything?" The camera focuses on Woods's eyes, then fades to black before showing a Nike swoosh. The minimalistic thirty-second ad relied on the audience knowing about Earl and Tiger's long and complicated relationship. Disappointment, shame, and love all mixed together in this story of a father and son, and sin and redemption. All of this, without Woods saying a word.[28]

The cynics were not impressed. One sports journalist chided, "A real man, Tiger, wouldn't use his dead father's voice in a commercial to make it seem like his father is rebuking him for cheating on his wife." Another said, "What's most interesting to me about the ad is how it plays as an act of both personal and corporate penance." The author reasoned that Nike's loyalty to Woods allowed it to be a "surrogate scold" for him, seemingly absolving the golfer from misdeeds.[29]

Still, the ad demonstrated Nike's ever-expanding role in the creation and maintenance of its iconic athletes. And the company's loyalty to Woods would prove profitable, despite his uneven career trajectory. Following the 2009 scandal, Woods spent the next decade struggling with injuries and other assorted physical and psychological ailments. A DUI arrest in 2017 only brought more voices into the chorus of critics who proclaimed his career tragically complete. Through it all, Nike continued producing ads that supported the athlete. Then in 2019, Woods won the Masters after an eleven-year drought in major tournaments. Nike quickly posted a social media ad with highlights from the win, punctuated by their "Just do it" slogan. Sports analysts estimated that Nike gained $22 million worth of exposure from Woods's win in Augusta.[30]

The story of Woods and Nike points to the ways in which corporations can not only produce icons but also re-create them when they fall from grace. While certainly not everyone finds these mythologies of rising from the ashes compelling, the marketplace on balance has certainly rewarded Nike for its effort. The repair of an icon, in other words, can deliver both monetary gain and symbolic capital for the athlete and the company. Unless, of course, that icon is a proven cheater—a dirty athlete.

## Dirty Icons

In a 1999 Nike advertisement titled "Chicks Dig the Long Ball," pitcher Tom Glavine ponders alongside his teammate Greg Maddux, "How long are they going to worship this guy?" The object of their combined scorn is slugger Mark McGwire, who had recently broken Roger Maris's home run record. The commercial depicted McGwire taking swings while surrounded by adoring female fans. Inspired to earn similar acclaim, the two pitchers decide to enhance their hitting skills, leading to a training montage where they are transformed from hapless to capable batters. But in the final scene, actress Heather Locklear walks by, giving a suggestive glance and asking, "Have you guys seen Mark?"[31]

Indeed, one year earlier, all eyes were on Mark McGwire as well as Sammy Sosa of the Chicago Cubs as the two chased Major League Baseball's home run record. The excitement was what one journalist called "a godsend for baseball," which, the standard story presumed, had been a game in decline since a strike in 1994 that culminated in the cancelation of that year's World Series. But the lure of the long ball brought the masses back, in part because of the powerful mythology of the home run. As we have seen, the story of the home run starts in 1921, with the end of the dead ball era and the emergence of the power hitter. No one embodied this role more thoroughly than Babe Ruth, whose sixty home runs in 1927 stood as the standard until Roger Maris hit sixty-one in 1961. The objects, actions, and memories attached to home runs have taken on a gravity that extends far beyond the game. As one baseball admirer summarized, "[N]othing else in professional team sports quite symbolizes the American competitive culture of free enterprise, success, and failure as the home run does." The 1998 home run chase marked a significant chapter in American sports mythology, reaching its climax during a September series between the two players' teams. It was in this series that McGwire smashed his record-breaking sixty-second home run.[32]

The presence of these two rivals and friends provided a refreshing break from the dominant news story of the time: the Clinton-Lewinsky scandal. McGwire, reflecting on their impact, said, "I definitely think we've brought the country together and helped make baseball a sport that people care about and talk about again." With McGwire and Sosa both standing atop the sports world, their public images and mythologies expanded further as advertisers capitalized on the moment. In the minutes after McGwire knocked his record-breaking home run, he hugged his ten-year-old son on the field and then looked into the television camera and announced that he was going to Disney World. Mastercard featured both hitters in their "Priceless" campaign, with flashes of McGwire and Sosa hitting home run after home run before declaring the record-breaking shot "priceless." Predictably, McDonald's ran an ad playing off McGwire's nickname, declaring, "Congratulations from one Big Mac to another."[33]

As the story of the home run chase grew on several different fronts, one feature of both athletes that had been venerated by admirers was their physique, and specifically their bulky bodies. When *Sports Illustrated* honored McGwire and Sosa as the 1998 "Sportsmen of the Year," the magazine's cover featured the two men adorned in Olympic robes and laurels, showcasing their well-defined muscles.[34] They had become icons in the truest sense, just as the images of athletes in Ancient Greece were chiseled in stone. But the size of these athletes, which was once so admired, was about to come under scrutiny, as the conversation in baseball and throughout sports shifted to performance-enhancing drugs (PEDs).

It was a problem that was hiding in plain sight. One year before the home run chase, *Sports Illustrated* ran a feature article calling PED use "the dirty and universal secret of sports." This was confirmed in a *Sports Illustrated* investigation in 2002, which had as its centerpiece the testimony of former baseball player, Ken Caminiti, who confessed to using steroids during his 1996 National League MVP season. He asserted that he wasn't alone, as he estimated that half of the players during his time were using PEDs. Caminiti's success that season gave credence to the argument that steroids could bolster performance. Previously, his highest home run number for a season was twenty-six. But during his MVP season, Caminiti hit forty home runs, while also averaging .326 in the batter's box. An image of Caminiti holding a baseball bat graced the front page of this article, the subtitle reading, "Coming Clean."[35]

The story of baseball and sports more generally in the early 2000s was a story of "dirty athletes." "Dirt offends against order," wrote the anthropologist Mary Douglas. "Eliminating it is not a negative movement, but a positive effort to organize the environment." In the backdrop of the early 2000s doping scandal, the imagery of dirt played a crucial role in emphasizing specific sacred boundaries within sports—boundaries that sports interpreters aimed to safeguard and fortify. While steroids might have contributed to remarkable performances, the imperative was to cleanse the "polluted record books." Congressional hearings and legal investigations emerged as avenues through which American society sought to purify and rectify the state of sports.[36]

As a result, dirty athletes faced monetary and reputational consequences, as well as legal punishments. Olympic champion Marion Jones eventually got jail time for lying to federal investigators about PED use and a check-fraud scheme. But Jones was not alone. An investigation found twelve other track athletes who had been associated with the Bay Area Laboratory Co-operative (BALCO), a nutritional supplement company that had supplied Jones, Barry Bonds, and several other high-profile athletes with performance enhancers. The group of track athletes collectively came to be known as "the dirty dozen." Bonds, who later won the home run title, has not been elected to the Baseball Hall of Fame, and the same holds true for McGwire and Sosa.[37]

Ken Griffey Jr., however, did earn a spot in the Hall of Fame in 2016, securing immediate induction upon eligibility. Despite the absence of explicit references to the steroid era during his induction, his nickname, "the Natural," took center stage. The ceremony highlighted his impressive twenty-three-year career, marked by resilient perseverance in the face of numerous challenges and injuries. Originally bestowed by *Sports Illustrated*, the moniker "the Natural" drew inspiration from a baseball novel and film of the same name. The PED scandal added a new layer of significance to this title. Amid a backdrop of fellow baseball players experiencing remarkable physical growth, Griffey maintained a lean and sinewy physique. His 1998 season, featuring fifty-six home runs, initially played second fiddle to the exploits of McGwire and Sosa but gained retrospective recognition. A year after his induction, the Mariners unveiled a statue of Griffey outside their stadium. Described by an observer as capturing his "iconic swing," the statue also captures Griffey's physique—a poignant symbol of his unwavering dedication to a pure and honorable pursuit of excellence.[38]

While physical size became visual evidence of a boundary violation in baseball, unusual stamina raised speculation in endurance sports. As 2002 ended and it became clear just how widespread PED use had become, *Sports Illustrated*, the same publication that sounded the alarm about steroid use in baseball earlier that year, named cyclist and cancer survivor Lance Armstrong their "Sportsman of the Year." The magazine announced, "For his courage and commitment—not to mention his fourth straight Tour de France victory—SI salutes the ultimate road warrior." Rick Reilly wrote the feature piece on this "All-American hero." Reilly acknowledged the rumors of Armstrong's PED use but asserted that the U.S. Doping Agency had made Armstrong "pee in front of more people than a zoo panda" and that the cyclist never tested positive. The journalist was not alone, as armies of supporters repeated Armstrong's contention that the French press just couldn't accept that an American was dominating their premier bicycle race.[39]

Nike was also among Armstrong's strongest defenders. In 2001, the company released a commercial that opened with Armstrong having his blood taken for a drug test, with a crowd of reporters and others surrounding him. From there, we see images flashing across the screen of the athlete training, sleeping, and fully committing himself to his sport. The ad closed with Armstrong's voice defiantly narrating, "Everybody wants to know what I'm on. What am I on? I'm on my bike, busting my ass six hours a day. What are you on?" Nike and Armstrong were both firmly asserting that hard work, determination, and dedication are what makes an athlete great, not drugs.[40]

Armstrong's relationship with Nike started early in his professional career. In 1996, Phil Knight inked a deal with the Tour de France organizers, establishing Nike as the supplier of the renowned yellow jersey worn by the race leader. This marked Nike's initial foray into the $2 billion cycling market, coinciding with the signing of Armstrong that same year. With his career on the climb, Armstrong then received news that he had stage-3 testicular cancer. Despite the bleak prognosis, he successfully battled back to health and triumphed in the 1999 Tour de France. The moment was custom-made for Nike. Armstrong immediately embarked on a global media tour, flying on Nike's personal jet. Meanwhile, the company released a "Just do it" commercial showing the cyclist riding across America, giving hope to onlookers, including a group of children receiving cancer treatment. Then in 2004, Nike and Armstrong introduced their most "iconic" collaboration: a yellow bracelet inscribed with the word "Livestrong." Beyond a clever play on Armstrong's name, the term embodied a worldview and an approach to overcoming challenges, notably cancer: persevere and conquer. Initially skeptical, Armstrong and his then-partner Sheryl Crow donned the bracelets during an interview with Oprah Winfrey. The response was immediate, with an estimated 900,000 viewers purchasing the bracelets on the same day. While the proceeds contributed to Armstrong's foundation, both he and Nike witnessed their reputations soar, as this "iconic accessory" became a ubiquitous symbol on the wrists of millions of ordinary individuals.[41]

Journalists were likewise captivated by Armstrong, viewing him not just as a sports icon but as a figure transcending the realm of athletics. Robert Lipsyte, himself a cancer survivor, proclaimed, "Lance Armstrong burst out of Cancerland last week . . . to win the Tour de France." The journalist emphasized that Armstrong had swiftly earned spots "in several different icon queues," as a cancer survivor and athlete, asserting that "[Armstrong] had actually completed the mythological hero's journey." This theme continued to gain momentum as Armstrong achieved successive victories. After Armstrong's seventh Tour de France triumph, sportswriter Berry Tramel proclaimed, "He's an icon for more than just what he does in the French mountains."[42]

And all that time, Armstrong and his team were engaged in a widespread, organized, and highly effective doping program. While Armstrong had gotten several suspicious results in drug tests, he and his team managed to evade consequences. This enabled him to deflect eyewitness accounts of his drug use by claiming that he had never been found guilty of doping. Additionally, as his stature in the sports world grew, so too did his feelings of invincibility. He used all his financial, legal, and political connections to intimidate and threaten the livelihood of anyone who spoke out against him. But his tendency to make enemies eventually backfired, as the evidence of his extensive doping regime came to light. On August 24, 2012, the U.S. Anti-Doping Agency issued a lifetime ban against Armstrong in competitive cycling. In October he stepped down from his Livestrong Foundation and the International Cycling Union erased his Tour de France wins from the records. Finally, in January 2013 Armstrong was ready to "come clean," agreeing to be interviewed by Oprah Winfrey. While he admitted to using a list of banned substances, he became defensive and evasive when Winfrey pressed him on the details. "The definition of 'cheat' is to gain an advantage on a rival or foe that they don't have," Armstrong lectured Winfrey. "I didn't view it that way. I viewed it as a level playing field." The viewing audience was unmoved; 3.2 million viewers tuned in for the first installment, but only 1.8 million returned for the second half of the interview the next day.[43]

Much like the general public, media champions and sponsors swiftly distanced themselves from Armstrong. Reflecting on his defense of Armstrong in an August 2012 *Newsweek* cover story, Buzz Bissinger candidly admitted, "I completely fucked the duck." Bissinger was not the only one who ardently supported Armstrong until the bitter end, only to retract that support after the Oprah interview. Rick Reilly expressed his dismay at Armstrong's initial ban in September 2012 with the headline "Lance Still Worth Revering," urging readers to wear yellow in support. However, after the Oprah interview, Reilly reversed his stance, acknowledging, "It's partially my fault. I let myself admire him. Let myself admire what he'd done with his life, admire the way he'd not only beaten his own cancer but was trying to help others beat it." All of this was personal for Reilly, whose sister was also a cancer patient and had been moved by Armstrong's life and example. It was a disillusionment that Reilly speculated was felt by millions worldwide.[44]

In contrast to the journalists, Nike only marginally preceded the trend. In October, following Armstrong's lifetime bans, the company finally terminated its sponsorship of the cyclist. It also quietly removed Armstrong's name from a fitness center on their Oregon campus, previously adorned with a plaque praising the athlete's "fearlessness and confidence." Meanwhile, the Livestrong Foundation, no longer affiliated with Armstrong, found itself with a surplus of approximately 100,000 yellow wristbands still packaged with the cyclist's name. These were eventually directed to a recycling project. Livestrong continued the production of bracelets, still featuring the Nike swoosh, but with no reference to Armstrong.[45]

It was only a yellow silicon bracelet. But it wasn't only a yellow silicon bracelet. From its very introduction, it was an "iconic" bracelet that told the story of an athlete who battled back from the brink of death to reach the pinnacle of his sport—several times over. The critics had been just naysayers, those who didn't believe, those who didn't trust that one person could inspire and give hope to millions. He could also give resources. Armstrong's foundation no doubt brought greater awareness to cancer treatment and research, raising over $500 million, which included $6.5 million of his own funds.[46]

But it was all built on a lie. And Armstrong was a cheater. Or, perhaps more accurately, a "spoilsport." It's a distinction made by Dutch cultural historian Johan Huizinga. The cheater is deceptive and pretends to play the game but ultimately respects the world created by the players, a world that is utterly meaningless and entirely meaningful. In contrast, the spoilsport literally spoils the sport by making their own rules and seeking their own gain. As Huizinga states, "The spoilsport breaks the magic world, therefore he is a coward and must be ejected."[47]

This was Armstrong's fate, to be remembered as someone who shattered the magic of his sport—the *something* of his sport. His story shows that the sports icon occupies a particular place in the sacred images of American life and culture. The icon can be great, the icon can be heroic, the icon can falter, and the icon can profit. But when the icon spoils the very world cherished by those who made the icon, then the icon gets sent to the recycling bin.

# Afterword

## Why Do I Care?

The Pittsburgh Steelers nearly broke Terry O'Neill's heart.

On January 15, 2006, O'Neill went to a sports bar on the South Side of Pittsburgh to watch his beloved Steelers play the Indianapolis Colts in a divisional playoff game. The winner would move on to the AFC Championship Game and then, if they won again, the Super Bowl. For three quarters, the Steelers dominated the game, bolting ahead to a 21–3 lead.

Victory seemed inevitable.

Then, less than a minute into the fourth quarter, the Colts scored a touchdown. The Steelers' offense was unable to respond. The vaunted Black and Gold defense also faltered until late in the final quarter, when Steelers' safety Troy Polamalu intercepted a pass from Colts' quarterback Payton Manning. While Polamalu appeared to have caught, fumbled, and recovered the ball, the referee ruled it an incomplete pass. The Colts resumed the drive and scored another touchdown, cutting the Steelers' lead to 21–18. Pittsburgh's defense rose to the occasion with 1:20 remaining in the game, sacking Manning on fourth down on the Colts' two-yard line. The offense took over with running back Jerome Bettis standing in the backfield. Known as "the Bus," Bettis was a perennial clutch performer on short yardage.

Victory, once more, seemed inevitable.

Then the unthinkable happened. When quarterback Ben Roethlisberger handed off to Bettis, the Bus absorbed a crisp hit and the normally surehanded running back fumbled the ball—his first fumble of the season. The Colts' Nick Harper scooped up the loose ball and sprinted for his end zone, only to get tripped up by Roethlisberger, who saved the day with a shoestring tackle. Meanwhile, Terry O'Neill watched in disbelief. Bettis was his hero. O'Neill's heart throbbed. Then his arm tingled. Suddenly, his chest hurt, and he fell off his barstool. His friends thought he was joking until they saw him turn blue.

Death seemed inevitable.

*Bodies in Motion*. Arthur Remillard, Oxford University Press. © Oxford University Press 2025.
DOI: 10.1093/oso/9780197789766.003.0015

Two firemen who happened to be in the bar hurried to O'Neill and performed emergency CPR. An ambulance arrived and medics hit him five times with a defibrillator. For a brief moment, Terry O'Neill was clinically dead. But he recovered and awoke in a hospital bed. Dazed and groggy, he spoke his first three words:

"Did we win?"[1]

The Steelers did win. After the fumble, Indianapolis moved the ball within field goal range but missed from forty-six yards. The following week, the Steelers won the AFC Championship, and two weeks after that, Terry O'Neill returned to his favorite sports bar to watch the Steelers win their fifth Super Bowl. He was admittedly in poor health. So the fumble didn't cause his heart failure as much as it overstressed an already weakened circulatory system. But the story largely sidestepped this physiological nuance and went viral with headlines like, "Fan's Heart Aches for Beloved Steelers."[2]

When I'm talking to groups about religion and sports, I often begin with Terry O'Neill's story because audiences immediately identify with the misfortune of a man whose fandom nearly killed him. Many of us who call ourselves fans have had that experience of allowing the frenzy of a game to overwhelm the better angels of our nature. This is, after all, what it means to be a "fan," a word derived from the Latin *fanaticus*, "possessed by a deity." The spirit of an athletic contest is otherworldly. It controls us without our consent. Terry O'Neill's story typifies the meaning of fan possession.

But this certainly isn't just a Pennsylvania thing. In his book *Rammer Jammer Yellow Hammer*, journalist Warren St. John tells the story of following his beloved Alabama Crimson Tide football team for the 1999 season, all the while attending pre- and postgame festivities in his fuel-inefficient motor home. An Alabama native who was educated at Columbia, St. John confesses to his irrational passion for the Tide, admitting that there is no good reason for him to be obsessed by the doings of these anonymous young men and their coaches. And yet throughout his adult life, wins and losses on a random patch of grass in the American South had become a matter of life or death in his mind. It was enough to lead St. John to wonder, "Why do I care?"[3]

*Rammer Jammer Yellow Hammer* and the story of Terry O'Neil both resonate with me, in part because I have often asked myself this same question. Truth be told, I have a hard time caring about the Pittsburgh Steelers. But college football is an entirely different story. I grew up watching Penn State games. Some of my most vivid memories as a youth are of the celebrations that followed their national championships in 1982 and 1986. And to this day, as a grown adult who has no educational connection to Penn State, I have been known to yell at my television and experience a fitful night of sleep after a losing effort. Allegiance to a college football team was something that I grew up with, and it remains a centerpiece of my conversations with my family. We are, in the truest sense, college football "fans."

All of this became severely challenged in 2011, when revelations of a sex abuse scandal rocked the Penn State community. Readers might notice that I didn't write about this, even though it would have fit well in this book's discussion of fallen icons. I think that this story was just too close in every respect. But proximity to a specific sport didn't stop me from writing quite a bit about another sport that I am connected to: distance running.

In addition to being a regular part of my daily routine, it's also the case that many of my most meaningful life memories involve running, as do the bulk of my closest relationships, including my wife of over two decades. For all the value that running adds to my life, there are innumerable bizarre habits that I engage in that make little to no sense outside of my own mental meanderings. For example, I still participate in races occasionally, even though my fastest times are far, far behind me. These *should* be fun and festive events, opportunities to stress my body and test my current state of fitness. Instead, I find myself locked in competition with those around me, as well as myself, as if the Bunny Dash 5k had some kind of real consequence.

Then there was the time that I dropped out of a marathon after an Achilles tendon began flaring up in the second half. I made the decision at mile 19, aware that hobbling through the next seven miles would lead to more damage. It was a good decision. But it was also a decision that left me with overwhelming feelings of shame and regret, as if somehow, somewhere the world was judging me.

In moments like these, the "Why do I care?" question reemerges. Of football I am a passive observer, but in running I am an active participant. In both settings, I have witnessed myself behaving in ways that make sense only from the inside. I have also found myself returning to the question that so many before me have asked: Is this thing that we call sports a positive moral force, or does its power to incite the passions lead us into dark and unproductive places? It's the "Alypius Problem," harking back to the story of Augustine and his student who couldn't resist the circus. I certainly wrestle with the Alypius Problem when I watch Penn State football games—which I have continued to watch over the past decade, leading to plenty of self-loathing. Irrespective, it seems that, for me anyway, the sacred matters of sports inevitably come entangled with moral concerns over their use and propriety.

When I started writing this book, I was very much intent on figuring out my irrational obsessions with sports and their moral implications. After all, I firmly believe that the discipline of religious studies offers a unique lens for understanding human behavior, for how we interact with, and make sense of, questions related to what Paul Tillich called "ultimate concern." I had come to this project after writing a civil religious history of the American South after the Civil War and Reconstruction. This revealed to me a history of people doing religious activity that was on its surface irrational, counterproductive, and even sometimes dangerous and destructive. These same patterns appeared in my study of sports, which led me to believe that I could finally answer the question of *why* anyone would care about this otherwise nonutilitarian and superfluous physical activity.

Before too long, I came to realize that my approach to studying sports was not best suited to answering this question. Scientists with brain scans and assorted other technologies have better tools and backgrounds for understanding the biological and neurological motivations of fans and players.[4] Instead, through writing this book I have come to realize that rather than explaining *why* people care about sports, my task is to show *how* people have cared about sports. I have sought to do this by shining a bright light on the very intentional decisions that people have made about what matters most to them—about what is "deeply cherished and violently defended."[5]

Since I ascribe to an approach to the study of religion that stresses what people do, rather than what they might or might not believe, it makes sense that "How?" became this book's driving question. To this end, the chapters presented here take seriously the creative and unpredictable ways that people have made sports meaningful, moral, or immoral for themselves and for others. Sometimes their words and gestures pivoted directly toward those ideas and activities that most people would quickly define as religion. A post-touchdown prayer might aim to imprint sacred meaning onto physical activity, to single out what is important in that moment to an individual or group. But other times, the traces of transcendence have been subtler, captured in the mythmaking of a journalist or in a photograph of two Olympians with their gloved fists raised in the air. I don't, as I stated before, assert that sports is a religion. But I have shown in the pages of this book that where we see sports talk, we will certainly also see religion talk alongside it.

In recent years, with the advent of digital photography, more images of athletic moments have come into circulation, giving us more places to identify sacred matters in sports. In 2013, the seventy-eight-year-old Bill Iffrig was nearly finished with his third Boston Marathon when a deafening explosion knocked him to the ground right in front of photographer John Tlumacki of the *Boston Globe*. Likewise confused and unaware of what was happening, Tlumacki reflexively began taking pictures—one of which became what observers would quickly call the "iconic" image of Iffrig surrounded by smoke and scrambling police officers.[6]

Miraculously, Iffrig was not seriously injured. Shortly after the explosion, he walked a few blocks back to his hotel, all the while entirely unaware that a picture of him was spreading through social media. *Sports Illustrated* would soon feature the image on the cover of their issue about the bombings. The managing editor explained, "[W]e felt it truly captured the horrific moment at the end of the race." The word "capture" appears frequently in reflections on images and their importance. In the wake of the 1995 Oklahoma City bombings, for example, the defining image of that tragedy was that of fireman Chris Fields gently cradling the limp body of one-year-old Baylee Almon. "It captured the horror of the murder of innocent children," wrote historian Edward Linenthal. "It captured the tenderness of rescuers." He added, "There are certain images that both capture the essence of an event and transcend the event, expressing through their eloquence what seem to be eternal human feelings, principles, truths."[7]

Looking at the image of Iffrig, I wonder what it captures. What "eternal human feelings" does it evoke? I suppose it brings to the surface the stark contrast of both the joys and harsh realities of life. In the fallen competitor we are reminded that only moments before, he was engaged in the serious pursuit of finishing a marathon. And not just any marathon. As one journalist and runner explained, "Just as Jews pray to celebrate Passover 'next year in Jerusalem' and Muslims pledge to visit Mecca, marathoners want to 'run Boston.'" Boston's mythical quality draws from many sources. It's the oldest marathon in America, started one year after the inaugural modern Olympics. The course itself is "sacred ground" to runners, with notorious landmarks such as "Heartbreak Hill" and "Scream Tunnel." Then there is the race's exclusivity. Runners must meet specified time standards, based on age and gender. Only a precious few marathoners "qualify" for Boston.[8]

However, the action surrounding Iffrig in that image shows another, much more tragic story. While running for leisure had been the order of the day, the explosion sent the yellow-vested police seen in the image's background running toward danger. Their movements had nothing to do with the marathon. Rather, their aim was to quell the chaos, protect the innocent, and apprehend the offenders.

Captured in that image are both the life-affirming celebration of the Boston Marathon—the "Holy Grail" of distance running—and the ways in which ordinary people can act with extraordinary courage. Then there is what is unseen in the story of the image. In the surreal moments separating the bomb blasts from their collective comprehension, Iffrig picked himself up and finished the race in 4 hours, 3 minutes, and 47 seconds. As this veteran of forty-five marathons explained, "After you've run 26 miles, you're not going to stop there."[9]

Imagining Iffrig, who passed away at 89 in 2024, completing the race amid the smoke and chaos has significant value for me.[10] It encapsulates a commendable sense of perseverance, serving as a poignant reminder for all of us to confront life's challenges and persist in finishing what we start. In the midst of great horror, sometimes hope can break through. This is, of course, my interpretation of this unseen image—I'm doing something that I have spent years examining, describing, and critiquing in my sources. The act of interpreting sports and elevating sacred moments, individuals, events, and ideas appears to be an inherent tendency for enthusiasts and participants like me. *Why* we do it is a question that I have stopped asking, or perhaps I'm satisfied outsourcing it to others. Instead, I will continue focusing on the *how*, satisfied that examining the ever-changing nature of sports allows me to gain insight into the most crucial aspects of how both I and others make sense of the world we share.

# Notes

## Introduction

1. Epigraph: Johan Huizinga, *Homo Ludens: A Study of the Play-Element in Culture* (Boston: Beacon Press, 1955), 7.Chris Beneke and Arthur Remillard, "Is Religion Losing Ground to Sports," *Washington Post*, February 2, 2014.
2. Albert Mohler, "The New American Religion," AlbertMohler.com, February 4, 2014, http://www.albertmohler.com/2014/02/04/the-new-american-religion-the-rise-of-sports-and-the-decline-of-the-church/. Some reprints include *The Week*, February 5, 2014; *Town Hall*, February 6, 2014; *Dallas Morning News*, February 6, 2014.
3. Arthur J. Remillard, "Holy War on the Football Field: Religion and the Florida State University Mascot Controversy," in *Horsehide, Pigskin, Oval Tracts, and Apple Pie: Essays in Sports and American Culture*, ed. James Vlasich (Jefferson, NC: McFarland, 2005), 104–18.
4. Jonathan Z. Smith, *Imagining Religion: From Babylon to Jonestown* (Chicago: University of Chicago Press, 1982); David Chidester, *Savage Systems: Colonialism and Comparative Religion in Southern Africa* (Charlottesville: University of Virginia Press, 1996); Robert A. Orsi, *Between Heaven and Earth: The Religious Worlds People Make and the Scholars Who Study Them* (Princeton, NJ: Princeton University Press, 2005); Michael Schellenberger, "Why Wokeism Is a Religion," Public.Substack.com, November 11, 2021, https://public.substack.com/p/why-wokeism-is-a-religion.
5. Courtney Bender and Ann Taves, eds., *What Matters? Ethnographies of Value in a Not So Secular Age* (New York: Columbia University Press, 2012); Talal Asad, *Formations of the Secular: Christianity, Islam, Modernity* (Redwood City, CA: Stanford University Press, 2003); Tracy Fessenden, *Culture and Redemption: Religion, the Secular, and American Literature* (Princeton, NJ: Princeton University Press, 2007); Chad Seals, *The Secular Spectacle: Performing Religion in a Southern Town* (New York: Oxford University Press, 2013).
6. I adopt Jay Coakley's definition of sports as "well-stablished, officially governed competitive physical activities in which participants are motivated by internal *and* external rewards." As Coakley explains, this definition helps to separate sports from "play" and "dramatic spectacle." The former is "an expressive activity done for its own sake," and the latter is "a performance meant to entertain an audience." Sports certainly incorporate both play and spectacle, but the pursuit of rewards sets sports apart. Coakley acknowledges that this definition is not without debate (e.g., is rhythmic gymnastics a sport or a spectacle?). Accordingly, he proposes approaching the topic with the following three questions: (1) "What activities are defined as sports in a particular group or society?"; (2) "Whose sports are most strongly supported and funded, especially with public facilities and money?"; and (3) "Who is advantaged and disadvantaged by the accepted definition of sports and the priorities used to allocate resources to sports?" For Coakley, these questions allow the researcher to better understand the cultural, social, and historical conditions that are at work when people and groups define, experience, and participate in sports. Jay Coakley, *Sports in Society: Issues and Controversies*, 10th ed. (New York: McGraw-Hill, 2009), 6–7, 8.
7. Tom Verducci, "The Left Arm of God," *Sports Illustrated*, July 12, 1999.
8. Emile Durkheim, *The Elementary Forms of Religious Life*, trans. Karen E. Fields (New York: The Free Press, [1912] 1995), 38.
9. Huizinga, *Homo Ludens*, 1, 13; Mary Douglas, *How Institutions Think* (Syracuse, NY: Syracuse University Press, 1986), 97.
10. For the sake of brevity and convenience, I will be using the words "America" and "American" as shorthand. I understand that these terms can be broad and may refer to the continents of North and South America, but my specific context solely pertains to the United States.
11. David Chidester, *Authentic Fakes: Religion and American Popular Culture* (Berkeley: University of California Press, 2005), 10.

12. Courtney Bender, "Things in Their Entanglemets," in *The Post-secular in Question: Religion in Contemporary Society*, ed. Philip S. Gorski, David Kyuman Kim, John Torpey and Jonathan VanAntwerpen (New York: New York University Press), 43–76; David Morgan, "Emotion and Imagination in the Ritual Entanglement of Religion, Sport, and Nationalism," in *Feeling Religion*, ed. John Corrigan (Durham, NC: Duke University Press, 2018), 222–41. I am using the term "sacred matters" in a way similar to Gary Laderman, *Sacred Matters: Celebrity Worship, Sexual Ecstasies, the Living Dead, and Other Signs of Religious Life in the United States* (New York: New Press, 2009).
13. Jill Gordon, *Plato's Erotic World: From Cosmic Origins to Human Death* (New York: Cambridge University Press, 2012), 58–59; Stephen Amidon, *Something Like the Gods: A Cultural History of the Athlete from Achilles to Lebron* (New York: Rodale, 2012), 21.
14. Michael Meyer, *Philosophy and the Passions: Toward a History of Human Nature* (University Park: Pennsylvania State University Press, 2000); Andreja Novakovic, "Hegel on Passion in History," in *International Yearbook of German Idealism*, ed. Dina Emundts and Sally Sedgwick (Boston: De Gruyter, 2020), 143–66; Robert J. Vallerand and Céline M Blanchard, "The Study of Emotion in Sport and Exercise: Historical, Definitional, and Conceptual Perspectives," in *Emotions in Sports*, ed. Yuri Hanin (Champaign, IL: Human Kinetics, 2000, 3–37).
15. Emile Durkheim, *The Elementary Forms of Religious Life* (1912), trans. Karen E. Fields (New York: Free Press, 1995), 228; Arthur Remillard, "Regions and Civil Religion(s) in America," in *Civil Religion Today: Religion and the American Nation in the Twenty-First Century*, ed. Rhys H. Williams, Raymond Haberski Jr., and Philip Goff (New York: New York University Press, 2021), 76–94.
16. Caroline Walker Bynum, *Fragmentation and Redemption: Essays on Gender and the Human Body in Medieval Religion* (New York: Zone Books, 1992). The reference to "fragments" comes from Bynum, who wrote, "[M]y understanding of the historian's task precludes wholeness. Historians, like fishes of the sea, regurgitate fragments. Only supernatural power can reassemble fragments so completely that no particle of them is lost, or miraculously empower the part to be the whole" (14).
17. See Randall Balmer, *Passion Plays: How Religion Shaped Sports in North America* (Chapel Hill: University of North Carolina Press, 2022).
18. David Chidester and Edward T. Linenthal, "Introduction," in *American Sacred Space*, ed. David Chidester and Edward T. Linenthal (Bloomington: Indiana University Press, 1995), 15.
19. I am adapting this distinction from S. B. Rodriguez-Plate, *A History of Religion in 5½ Objects: Bringing the Spiritual to Its Senses* (Boston: Beacon Press, 2014).

## Chapter 1

1. John Fox, *The Ball: Discovering the Object of the Game* (HarperCollins, 2012), 113–14.
2. Charles H. Long, *Significations: Signs, Symbols, and Images in the Interpretation of Religion* (1986; Aurora, CO: Davies Group, 1999), 101.
3. Warren D. Hill and John E. Clark, "Sports, Gambling, and Government: America's First Social Compact?," *American Anthropologist* 103, no. 2 (2001): 331–45.
4. Peter E. Siegel, "Contested Places and Places of Contest: The Evolution of Social Power and Ceremonial Space in Prehistoric Puerto Rico," *Latin American Antiquity* 10, no. 3 (1999): 209–38.
5. Ricardo E. Alegría, "Ball Courts and Ceremonial Plazas in the West Indies" (New Haven, CT: Deptartment of Anthropology, Yale University, 1983), 8, 9–10, 12–13.
6. Richard E. Alegria, "The Ball Game Played by the Aborigines of the Antilles," *American Antiquity* 16, no. 4 (April 1951): 348; José R. Oliver, *Caciques and Cemí Idols: The Web Spun by Taíno Rulers between Hispaniola and Puerto Rico* (Tuscaloosa: University of Alabama Press, 2009); Alegria, "Ball Courts and Ceremonial Plazas in the West Indies," 12.
7. Andrés Pérez de Ribas, *History of the Triumphs of Our Holy Faith amongst the Most Barbarous and Fierce Peoples of the New World* (1645), trans. Daniel T. Reff, Maureen Ahern, and Richard K. Danford (Tucson: University of Arizona Press, 1999), 495.
8. Ibid.
9. Ibid., 496; John Andrews and Todd Bostwick, *Desert Farmers at the River's Edge: The Hohokam and Pueblo Grande*, 2nd ed. (Phoenix, AZ: Pueblo Grande Museum and Archeological Park, 2000); Theodore Stern, *The Rubber-Ball Games of the Americas* (Seattle: University of Washington Press, 1949), 88–90.
10. Frederic B. Perkins, ed., *Narrative of Le Moyne, an Artist Who Accompanied the French Expedition to Florida under Laudonnière, 1564* (Boston: J. R. Osgood, 1875), 13.

11. John Dillenberger, ed., *John Calvin: Selections from His Writings* (New York: Oxford University Press, 1975), 334; Susan Hardman Moore, "Calvinism and the Arts," *Theology in Scotland* 16, no. 2 (2009): 75–92; Perkins, *Narrative of Le Moyne*, 3; David Richards, *Masks of Difference: Cultural Representations in Literature, Anthropology, and Art* (New York: Cambridge University Press, 1994), 46.
12. Michiel van Groesen, *The Representations of the Overseas World in the De Bry Collection of Voyages, 1590–1634* (Boston: Brill, 2008), 112–16.
13. Ibid., 241.
14. Ibid., 176.
15. Ibid., 249–79, 377–88.
16. Reuben Gold Thwaites, ed., *The Jesuit Relations and Allied Documents: Travels and Explorations of the Jesuit Missionaries in New France, 1610–1791* (Cleveland, OH: Burrows Brothers, 1908), 184–85, 88–89.
17. Thomas Vennum Jr., *American Indian Lacrosse: Little Brother of War* (Washington, D.C.: Smithsonian Institution Press, 1994), 9–72.
18. Ibid., 9–10.
19. John Swanton, "An Early Account of the Choctaw Indians," *Memoirs of the American Anthropological Society* 4, no. 2 (1918): 61–62, 68.
20. Ann Laura Stoler, *Haunted by Empire: Geographies of Intimacy in North American History* (Durham, NC: Duke University Press, 2006), 142; Harry Liebersohn, *Aristocratic Encounters: European Travelers and North American Indians* (New York: Cambridge University Press, 1998), 54–60; Antoine Simon Le Page du Pratz, *The History of Louisiana* (London: T. Becket, 1774), 347.
21. John Reed Swanton, *Source Material for the Social and Ceremonial life of the Choctaw Indians* (Tuscaloosa: University of Alabama Press, 2001), 140–41.
22. John Gatta, *Making Nature Sacred: Literature, Religion, and Environment in America from the Puritans to the Present* (New York: Oxford University Press, 2004), 48–54; William Bartram, *Travels through North and South Carolina, Georgia, and East and West Florida* (Philadelphia, PA: James and Johnson, 1791), 268, 497–98, 456.
23. Ibid., 508–9, 369–72.
24. Kathryn E. Holland, "James Adair: His Life and History," in James Adair, *The History of the American Indians* (1775) (Tuscaloosa: University of Alabama Press, 2005), 1–53.
25. Elizabeth Fenton, *Old Canaan in a New World: Native Americans and the Lost Tribes of Israel* (New York: New York University Press, 2020), 55–84; Adair, *The History of the American Indians*, 399–400.
26. Adair, *The History of the American Indians*, 400–401.
27. Ibid., 401–2.
28. William R. Reynolds Jr., *The Cherokee Struggle to Maintain Identity in the 17th and 18th Centuries* (Jefferson, NC: McFarland, 2015), 19–20; Bernard Romans, *A Concise Natural History of East and West Florida* (1775; Tuscaloosa: University of Alabama Press, 1999), 110.
29. Romans, *A Concise Natural History of East and West Florida*, 111, 112, 39, 128, 134, 80–81.

## Chapter 2

1. Saint Augustine, *Confessions*, trans. Edward B. Pusey (Grand Rapids, MI: Christian Classics, 1999), 73–76.
2. Brian Stock, *Augustine the Reader: Meditation, Self-Knowledge, and the Ethics of Interpretation* (Cambridge, MA: Harvard University Press, 1996), 86.
3. Nathan Whiting, ed., *The Works of That Eminent Servant of Christ, John Bunyan*, 3 vols. (New Haven, CT: Nathan Whiting, 1831), 1:17–18.
4. Ibid., 1:21.
5. Frederic J. Haskin, "Sport of Kings in Evil Lines," *Indianapolis News*, April 23, 1907; Bruce C. Daniels, *Puritans at Play: Leisure and Recreation in Colonial New England* (New York: Palgrave Macmillan, 1995); Timothy Lamer, "The Puritans Weren't Puritanical," *Wall Street Journal*, March 4, 1998, https://www.wsj.com/articles/SB888960902942775500.; John Winthrop, *The Winthrop Papers*, 6 vols. (Boston: Massachusetts Historical Society, 1929–47), 1:201–2.
6. Thomas Shepard, *Theses Sabbaticæ* (London, 1650), 62–63; William Bentley, *The Diary of William Bentley, 1784–1792* (Salem, MA: Essex Institute, 1905), 254.
7. William J. Baker, *Sports in the Western World* (Champaign: University of Illinois Press, 1988), 73, 74.

8. Daniels, *Puritans at Play.*
9. David Hackett Fischer, *Albion's Seed: Four British Folkways in America* (New York: Oxford University Press, 1991), 158–66; Thomas Foxcroft, *A Serious Address to Those Who Unnecessarily Frequent the Tavern* (Boston, 1726), 24, 3, 6, 8, 11.
10. Fischer, *Albion's Seed*, 158–66.
11. Alice Morse Earle, *Customs and Fashions in Old New England* (New York: Scribner, 1893), 224.
12. Sarah Kemble Knight, *The Journals of Madam Knight, and Rev. Mr. Buckingham* (New York: Wilder & Campbell, 1825), 39.
13. Herbert William Keith Fitzroy, "Richard Crosby Goes to Court, 1683–1697: Some Realities of Colonial Litigation," *Pennsylvania Magazine of History and Biography* 62, no. 1 (1938): 13.
14. John Blair Linn, ed., *Charter to William Penn, and Laws of the Province of Pennsylvania* (Harrisburg, PA: Lane S. Hart, State Printer, 1879), 107, 114.
15. William Penn, *No Cross, No Crown* (1669; Philadelphia, PA: Collins, 1853), 196–99, 212–23.
16. Rufus M. Jones, *The Quakers in the American Colonies* (New York: Macmillan, 1911), 498; Curtis Miner, "And They're Off: Pennsylvania's Horse Racing Tradition," *Pennsylvania Heritage*, Spring 2005.
17. Benjamin Rush, *Sermons to Gentlemen upon Temperance and Exercise* (Philadelphia, PA: John Dunlap, 1772), 27.
18. Ibid., 30–32, 35, 38.
19. Ibid., 42–44.
20. Benjamin Rush, *Thoughts upon the Amusements and Punishments Which Are Proper for Schools* (Philadelphia, PA, 1791), 2–3.
21. Benjamin Rush, *Thoughts upon Female Education* (Philadelphia, PA: Prichard & Hall, 1787).
22. David Block, *Baseball before We Knew It: A Search for the Roots of the Game* (Lincoln: University of Nebraska Press, 2006); John Locke, *Some Thoughts concerning Education* (1693), ed. Charles W. Eliot, 3 vols., The Harvard Classics (New York: P. F. Collier & Sons, 1909–14), 1:346, 178.
23. John Newbery, *A Little Pretty Pocket-Book* (1744; Worchester, MA: Isaiah Thomas, 1787), 7, 8, 43.
24. Derek H. Davis, *Religion and the Continental Congress, 1774–1789* (New York: Oxford University Press, 2000), 67; George Bancroft, *History of the Colonization of the United States*, 17th ed. (Boston: Little, Brown, 1859), 1:234.
25. Philip Alexander Bruce, *Social Life of Virginia in the Seventeenth Century* (Richmond, VA: Whittet & Shepperson, 1907), 172; Wolfgang Mieder, *Proverbs: A Handbook* (Westport, CT: Greenwood, 2004), 1.
26. Hugh Jones, *The Present State of Virginia* (1724; New York: Sabin's Reprints, 1865), 48–49.
27. James D. Rice, *Tales from a Revolution: Bacon's Rebellion and the Transformation of Early America* (New York: Oxford University Press, 2012); Francis Nicholson, "Proclamation about the College and Orders for Prize Games for Bachelors," *William and Mary Quarterly* 11 (October 1902): 87.
28. Mary Newton Stanard, *Colonial Virginia: Its People and Customs* (Philadelphia, PA: J. B. Lippincott, 1917), 252.
29. T. H. Breen, "Horses and Gentlemen: The Cultural Significance of Gambling among the Gentry of Virginia," *William and Mary Quarterly* 34, no. 2 (1977): 239–57.
30. Bruce, *Social Life of Virginia in the Seventeenth Century*, 207.
31. Dan Parker, *The ABC of Horse Racing* (New York: Random House, 1947), 5; Francis Marion Bush, *Colonial Downs and More* (Bloomington, IN: iUniverse, 2011); Charles E. Trevathan, *The American Thoroughbred* (New York: Macmillan, 1905), 4–5.
32. Allen J. Davie, "Quarter Racing of the Olden Time," *American Turf Register*, May 1832, 451.
33. Edward McCracy, *The History of South Carolina under the Royal Government, 1719–1776* (New York: The Macmillan Company, 1899), 522–23; John Williams, ed., *Philip Vickers Fithian: Journal and Letters, 1767–1774* (Carlisle, MA: Applewood Books, 2007), 236.
34. Michael P. Branch, *Reading the Roots: American Nature Writing before Walden* (Athens: University of Georgia Press, 2004), 172–73; J. F. D. Smyth, *A Tour in the United States of America* (London: Robinson, 1784), 23; Andrew Burnaby, *Burnaby's Travels through North America* (1798; Carlisle, MA: Applewood Books, 2007), 44; Abbé Claude Robin, *New Travels through North America* (Philadelphia, PA: Robert Bell, 1781), 50, 52.
35. Trevathan, *The American Thoroughbred*, 19–22.
36. Katherine C. Mooney, *Race Horse Men: How Slavery and Freedom Were Made at the Racetrack* (Cambridge, MA: Harvard University Press, 2014).

## Chapter 3

1. Barry Schwartz, *George Washington: The Making of an American Symbol* (New York: Free Press, 1987), 93; Catherine Albanese, *Sons of the Fathers: The Civil Religion of the American Revolution* (Philadelphia, PA: Temple University Press, 1976); Petra Gardella, *American Civil Religion: What Americans Hold Sacred* (New York: Oxford University Press, 2014), 160, 136–37.
2. John Cowie Reid, *Bucks and Bruisers: Pierce Egan and Regency England* (London: Routledge, 1971).
3. Luke G. Williams, *Richmond Unchained: The Biography of the World's First Black Sporting Superstar* (Gloucestershire: Amberley, 2015).
4. Pierce Egan, *Boxiana*, vol. 2 (London: Sherwood, Jones, 1824), 126–27, 129, 133.
5. Pierce Egan, *Boxiana*, vol. 1 (London: George Virtue, [1823] 1830), 444–47.
6. Ibid., 1:392.
7. Ibid., 1:392, 454–56; Williams, *Richmond Unchained.*
8. Williams, *Richmond Unchained*, 214–17.
9. Bill Calogero, "Tom Molineaux: From Slave to American Heavyweight Champion," in *The First Black Boxing Champions: Essays on Fighters of the 1800s to the 1920s*, ed. Colleen Aycock and Mark Scott (Jefferson, NC: McFarland, 2011), 9–21; Nat Fleischer, *Black Dynamite: The Story of the Negro in the Prize Ring from 1782 to 1938* (New York: C. J. O'Brien, 1938).
10. Frank P. Fury, "Designs of Identity and Images of American Boxing Tradition in Faulkner's *Absalom, Absalom!*," *Studies in Popular Culture* 29, no. 2 (October 2006): 69–86; Fred Henning, *Fights for the Championship* (London: Victuallers' Gazette, 1902); Eliot J. Gorn, *The Manly Art: Bare-Knuckle Prize Fighting in America* (Ithaca, NY: Cornell University Press, 1986), 34–35; Calogero, "Tom Molineaux."
11. Egan, *Boxiana*, 1:360–62, 454–56.
12. Calogero, "Tom Molineaux"; "Boxing," *The Times* (London), August 23, 1810; Egan, *Boxiana*, 1:367.
13. Egan, *Boxiana*, 1:368.
14. Ibid., 1:401; Carl B. Cone, "The Molineaux-Cribb Fight, 1810: Wuz Tom Molineaux Robbed?," *Journal of Sports History* 9, no. 3 (1982): 83–91; "Boxing," *Evening Post* (New York), February 18, 1811.
15. Cone, "The Molineaux-Cribb Fight, 1810."
16. Bill Calogero, "Tom Molineaux: From Slave to American Heavyweight Champion," *The Times* (London), September 30, 1811.
17. Egan, *Boxiana*, 2:340, 346; 1:492.
18. "From the Metropolitan," *Evening Post* (New York), November 13, 1820.
19. "Tom Cribb's Final Triumph," *New York Herald*, March 20, 1910.
20. "John Henry Lewis Wants Heavy Title," *Prescott (AZ) Evening Courier*, December 21, 1935; "John Henry Lewis Traces Line Back to American Challenger," *Gallup (NM) Independent*, January 18, 1939.
21. "American Eclipse," *Evening Post* (New York), August 7 and 16, 1824; "Balloon," *Sandusky (OH) Clarion*, September 4, 1824, reprinted from the *Brooklyn Star*; Richard Holmes, *Falling Upwards: How We Took to the Air* (New York: Pantheon Books, 2013).
22. John Eisenberg, *The Great Match Race: When North Met South in America's First Sports Spectacle* (New York: Mariner Books, 2007); Paul E. Johnson, "Northern Horse: American Eclipse as a Representative New Yorker," *Journal of the Early Republic* 33, no. 4 (Winter 2013): 701–26.
23. Hamilton Busbey, "The Running Turf in America," *Harper's Magazine* 41 (June–November 1870): 94, 97.
24. "The Races," *New-York Commercial Advertiser*, May 28, 1823; "The Great Race," *Fayetteville (NC) Weekly Observer*, June 5, 1823, reprinted from unknown source in New York, May 28; James Douglas Anderson and Balie Peyton, *Making the American Thoroughbred* (Norwood, MA: Plimpton Press, 1916), 163.
25. Quoted in Eisenberg, *The Great Match Race*, 232.
26. William Gilmore Simms, *As Good as a Comedy* (Philadelphia, PA: A. Hart, 1852), 113–14, 120.
27. Augustus B. Longstreet, *Georgia Scenes*, 2nd ed. (New York: Harper & Brothers, 1850), 112–13, 152; Kenneth Silverman, "Longstreet's 'The Gander Pulling,'" *American Quarterly* 18, no. 3 (1966): 548–49; John Mayfield, "The Theatre of Public Esteem: Ethics and Values in Longstreet's *Georgia Scenes*," *Georgia Historical Quarterly* 75, no. 3 (Fall 1991): 566–86.
28. "Review of *Georgia Scenes*," *Southern Literary Messenger* 2, no. 4 (March 1836): 289.
29. "A Georgia Gander Pulling," *Vermont Watchman and State Journal* (Montpelier), August 7, 1845.

30. "Notes of Travel at the South, No. II," *Anti-Slavery Bugle* (Lisbon, OH), April 20, 1850; Charles Grandison Parsons, *Inside View of Slavery* (Boston: Jewett, 1855), 135–40.
31. "Rev. Mr. Marks, of Georgia, Our Man," *Brooklyn (NY) Evening Star*, June 3, 1856.
32. William Wells Brown, *My Southern Home: The South and Its People* (Boston: A. G. Brown, 1880), 62–63.
33. "Shooting Match and Gander Pulling," *Fayetteville (NC) Weekly Observer*, September 1, 1836; "Gander Pulling at 'Old Man Hinkles,'" *Luzerne Union* (Wilkes-Barre, PA), November 3, 1846; "The Tournament," *Richmond (VA) Dispatch*, October 2, 1854.
34. "How It Came About That 'the Goose Hung High,'" *Pittsburgh (PA) Daily Post*, September 14, 1869; "Gander Pulling," *The Tennessean* (Nashville), October 10, 1873.

## Chapter 4

1. Edward S. Sears, *George Seward: America's First Great Runner* (Lanham, MD: Scarecrow Press, 2008), 47–48.
2. "Pedestrianism in America," *The Era* (London), November 17, 1844, reprinted from *The Spirit of the Times*; "Race against Time," *Weekly Wisconsin* (Milwaukee), August 11, 1847.
3. Daniel Lieberman, *Exercised: Why Something We Never Evolved to Do Is Healthy and Rewarding* (New York: Pantheon Books, 2020), 10–14; Walter Hough, *The Hopi Indians* (Cedar Rapids, IA: Torch Press, 1915), 107–9, 113.
4. Rob Hadgraft, *Deerfoot: Athletics' Noble Savage* (Essex: Desert Island Books, 2007).
5. Quoted in ibid., 47.
6. Edward S. Sears, *Running through the Ages* (Jefferson, NC: McFarland, 2015), 119; "Deerfoot and His War-Whoop," *Freeman's Journal* (Dublin), April 19, 1862.
7. Peter Lovesey, *The Kings of Distance: A Study of 5 Great Runners* (London: Eyre and Spottiswoode, 1968); Timothy Noakes, *Lore of Running*, 4th ed. (Champaign, IL: Human Kinetics, 2002), 363–64.
8. Hadgraft, *Deerfoot*, 56, 82.
9. Ibid., 92.
10. Quoted in ibid., 39.
11. Ibid., 156; *Bell's Life*, March 1, 1863; quoted in Sears, *Running through the Ages*, 121.
12. "Race Types at the World's Fair," *Chicago Daily Tribune*, July 30, 1893; "Red Mean at Chicago," *Democrat and Chronicle* (Rochester, NY), July 25, 1893; Sears, *Running through the Ages*, 120.
13. Hadgraft, *Deerfoot*, 198.
14. "To Sleep with Comrades," *Ottawa Citizen*, April 9, 1900; "Memorial to 'Deerfoot,'" *Democrat and Chronicle* (Rochester, NY), December 24, 1899.
15. Hadgraft, *Deerfoot*, 10.
16. John R. McKivigan, *Forgotten Firebrand: James Redpath and the Making of Nineteenth-Century America* (Ithaca, NY: Cornell University Press, 2008), 108–9; David Blight, "The First Decoration Day," *Star Ledger* (Newark, NJ), April 27, 2015, https://www.davidwblight.com/public-history/2015/4/27/the-first-decoration-day-newark-star-ledger.
17. McKivigan, *Forgotten Firebrand*, 108–9; Blight, "The First Decoration Day".
18. Whitelaw Reid, *After the War: A Southern Tour* (New York: Moore, Wilstach, and Baldwin, 1866), 69; "A Yankee Custom Borrowed by Rebels," *Gallipolis (OH) Journal*, June 13, 1867; "The Origin of Memorial Day," *Lawrence (KS) Daily Journal*, June 17, 1905; McKivigan, *Forgotten Firebrand*, 108–9; William Justin Mann, "Little Walks about Boston," *Boston Post*, June 1, 1921.
19. "Imported Stock," *Charleston (SC) Daily News*, December 28, 1866.
20. Edward J. Blum, *Reforging the White Republic: Race, Religion, and African Nationalism, 1865–1898* (Baton Rouge: Louisiana State University Press, 2005).
21. "The New Race Course at Fordham, N.Y.: An Aid to Reunion," *Daily Picayune* (New Orleans, LA), September 16, 1866; Lonnie A. Burnett, *The Pen Makes a Good Sword: John Forsyth of the Mobile Register* (Tuscaloosa: University of Alabama Press, 2006).
22. "The New Race Course at Fordham, N.Y."; "Leonard Jerome," *Harper's Weekly*, March 14, 1891; Edwin G. Burrows and Mike Wallace, *Gotham: A History of New York City to 1898* (New York: Oxford University Press, 1998), 954–55.
23. "The New Race Course at Fordham, N.Y."
24. Francis Trevelyan, "The Status of the American Turf," *Outing* 20, no. 1 (April 1892): 37; Steven A. Riess, *The Sport of Kings and the Kings of Crime: Horse Racing, Politics, and Organized Crime in New York, 1865–1913* (Syracuse, NY: Syracuse University Press, 2011).

25. Henry William Herbert, *Frank Forester's Horse and Horsemanship of the United States and British Provinces of North America* (New York: George E. Woodward, 1871), 1:363–64.
26. Maryjean Wall, *How Kentucky Became Southern: A Tale of Outlaws, Horse Thieves, Gamblers, and Breeders* (Lexington: University Press of Kentucky, 2010), 25; Edward Hotaling, *They're Off! Horse Racing at Saratoga* (Syracuse, NY: Syracuse University Press, 1995), 67–68.
27. Herbert, *Frank Forester's Horse and Horsemanship of the United States and British Provinces of North America*, 1:365, 366.
28. Ibid., 1:380.
29. Ibid., 1:369–71.
30. Ibid., 1:285, 395, 398.
31. "The Jockey Club Meeting," *New York Times*, September 26, 1866; Hotaling, *They're Off!*, 56; "From Saratoga," *New York Daily Tribune*, August 11, 1865; Edward Hotaling, *The Great Black Jockeys: The Lives and Times of the Men Who Dominated America's First National Sport* (Rocklin, CA: Forum, 1999), 179–207; "Death of Old Abe," *Daily Picayune* (New Orleans, LA), May 19, 1867, reprinted from *Turf, Field, and Farm.*
32. William C. Rhoden, *Forty Million Dollar Slaves: The Rise, Fall, and Redemption of the Black Athlete* (New York: Three Rivers Press, 2007), 63–98.
33. Quoted in Dale A. Somers, *The Rise of Sports in New Orleans: 1850–1900* (Baton Rouge: Louisiana State University Press, 1972), 93; "Public Morals," *New Berne (NC) Daily Times*, November 29, 1865.
34. "The City: Things Generally," *Daily Picayune* (New Orleans, LA), December 22, 1866.
35. *Raleigh (NC) Episcopal Methodist*, November 24, 1869; Ben Ellet, letter to the editor, *Raleigh (NC) Episcopal Methodist*, December 22, 1869; "North Carolina Agricultural Society and the Next State Fair," *Raleigh (NC) Christian Advocate*, August 23, 1871.
36. Francis Trevelyan, "Racing at Southern Fairs," *Outing* 12, no. 6 (September 1888): 492, 493, 494.

## Chapter 5

1. "Base-Ball on the Brain," *Gallipolis (OH) Journal*, October 24, 1867. Also printed around the same time in the *Cecil (MD) Whig*, *Easton (MD) Journal*, and *Montana Post* (Virginia City). Peter Dreier and Robert Elias, *Baseball Rebels: The Players, People, and Social Movements That Shook Up the Game and Changed America* (Lincoln: University of Nebraska Press, 2022), 7–20, 157–206.
2. Balmer, *Passion Plays*, 13–33.
3. "The Great Contest at Hoboken Yesterday," *New York Times*, August 4, 1865.
4. Jon Kelly Yenser, "On Dirt and Baseball," *Aethlon* 30, no. 1 (2013): 117; Bryan Le Beau, "'Colored Engravings for the People': The World According to Currier and Ives," *American Studies* 35, no. 1 (1994): 131; Dave Jamieson, *Mint Condition: How Baseball Cards Became an American Obsession* (New York: Atlantic Monthy Press, 2010).
5. John Thorn, *Baseball in the Garden of Eden: The Secret History of the Early Game* (New York: Simon & Schuster, 2012), 142–54.
6. R. Terry Furst, *Shaping the Image of the Game: Early Professional Baseball and the Sporting Press* (Jefferson, NC: McFarland 2014), 129–44; Balmer, *Passion Plays*, 25–26.
7. "Base Ball," *Daily Phoenix* (Columbia, SC), September 10, 1867; Peter Morris, William J. Ryczek, Jan Finkel, Len Levin, and Richard Malatzky, *Base Ball Pioneers, 1850–1870: The Clubs and Players Who Spread the Sport Nationwide* (Jefferson, NC: McFarland, 2012), 308.
8. Andrew J. Schiff, *"The Father of Baseball": A Biography of Henry Chadwick* (Jefferson, NC: McFarland, 2008); Henry Chadwick, "Baseball in the South," *Outing* 12, no. 6 (September 1888): 538–39.
9. Schiff, *"The Father of Baseball,"* 120–22; "Another Base Ball Match Yesterday," *Memphis (TN) Daily Appeal*, May 30, 1867; "Welcome to the Southerners," *Daily Picayune* (New Orleans, LA), August 29, 1869; Morris et al., *Base Ball Pioneers*, 308.
10. *Gallipolis (OH) Journal*, October 10, 1867; *Atchison (KS) Daily Patriot*, August 2, 1870, reprinted from *St. Louis Times*; *Star Tribune* (Minneapolis, MN) April 16, 1872.
11. William Cathcart, ed., *The Baptist Encyclopædia* (Philadelphia, PA: Louis H. Everts, 1881), 670; "Sunday Ball-Tossing," *Public Ledger* (Memphis, TN), July 11, 1877.
12. "Sunday Base Ball Apologists" *Public Ledger* (Memphis, TN), July 9, 1877.
13. "Concerning Athletic Sports," *Cleveland (OH) Daily Leader*, August 2, 1864.
14. Mark Dyreson, *Making the American Team: Sport, Culture, and the Olympic Experience* (Urbana: University of Illinois Press, 1998); Thomas Wentworth Higginson, *Out-Door Papers*

(Boston: Lee and Shepard, 1886), 14, originally published as "Saints, and Their Bodies," *Atlantic Monthly* 1, no. 5 (1858): 582–95.

15. Theodore L. Cuyler, *Sermon on Christian Recreation and UnChristian Amusement* (New York: E. D. Barker, 1858), 12, 13.
16. "Muscular Christianity," *Cincinnati (OH) Daily Press*, August 23, 1860.
17. Moses Coit Tyler, "Muscular Christianity," *Herald of Health*, September 1866, 99; Robert Allen Skotheim, *American Intellectual Histories and Historians* (Princeton, NJ: Princeton University Press, 1966), 31–47.
18. "Muscular Christianity," *Clearfield (PA) Republican*, November 21, 1860, reprinted from the *Chicago Journal.*
19. "Muscular Christianity," *Leavenworth (KS) Times*, November 11, 1865, reprinted from the *Denver News.*
20. Thomas Hughes, *Tom Brown at Oxford* (Boston: Ticknor and Fields, 1868), 170.
21. "An Unsolved Problem," *Chicago Tribune*, November 23, 1867; "A Plea for Prize Fighting," *New York Times*, September 9, 1870.
22. William J. Baker, *Playing with God: Religion and Modern Sport* (Cambridge, MA: Harvard University Press, 2007), 42–63; Paula Lupkin, *Manhood Factories: YMCA Architecture and the Making of Modern Urban Culture* (Minneapolis: University of Minnesota Press, 2010).
23. John Boyle O'Reilly, *Ethics of Boxing and Manly Sport* (Boston: Chasman, Keating, 1888), 84, xix, 86.
24. "The Pilot Poet on Muscle and Skill," *Brooklyn (NY) Daily Eagle*, May 6, 1888; Somers, *The Rise of Sports in New Orleans*, 176–79.
25. Mark Twain, *The Letters of Mark Twain* (Middlesex: Echo Library, 2007), 388, 389; "News and Comment on Sports," *Buffalo (NY) Evening Times*, May 30, 1898.
26. "Minister Gives Boxing Lessons," *The World* (New York), November 11, 1902; "Teaches Boxing in His Church," *The World* (New York), November 12, 1902; "Preacher, Football and Baseball Player," *Boston Globe*, October 2, 1897.
27. David E. Sumner, *Amos Alonzo Stagg: College Football's Greatest Pioneer* (Jefferson, NC: McFarland, 2021), 96.
28. Caspar Whitney, *A Sporting Pilgrimage* (London: Osgood, 1894), 301, 302; Ronald A. Smith, *The Myth of the Amateur: A History of College Athletic Scholarships* (Austin: University of Texas Press, 2021); David C. Young, *The Olympic Myth of Greek Amateur Athletics* (Chicago: Ares, 1984); S. W. Pope, "Amateurism and American Sports Culture: The Invention of an Athletic Tradition in the United States, 1870–1900," *International Journal of the History of Sport* 13, no. 3 (1996): 290–309.
29. "Workingman Will Be the Worst Sufferer," *Indianapolis (IN) News*, February 2, 1903.
30. "Sixty Ministers Are against Sunday Ball," *Indianapolis (IN) News*, February 2, 1903; "A Protest against Sunday Baseball," *Indianapolis (IN) News*, February 14, 1903; "A Workingwoman on Baseball," *Indianapolis (IN) News*, February 14, 1903.
31. "The 'Poor Workingman' and His Money," *Indianapolis (IN) News*, February 14, 1903; "Next to the Sunday Saloon," *Indianapolis (IN) News*, February 14, 1903; "Has Lived in a Sunday Baseball Town," *Indianapolis (IN) News*, February 14, 1903.
32. "Chartrand Indorses [*sic*] Sunday Baseball," *Indianapolis (IN) Journal*, February 1, 1903.
33. "The Ministers and Sunday Ball," *Indianapolis (IN) News*, February 4, 1903; "Wants Sunday Baseball," *Indianapolis (IN) News*, February 14, 1903; "Working Men and Sunday Baseball," *Indianapolis (IN) News*, February 9, 1903.
34. "A Blow at the Saturday Half-Holiday," *Indianapolis (IN) News*, February 2, 1903; "Arguments for and against Sunday Ball," *Indianapolis (IN) News*, February 9, 1903.
35. "Majority Favors It," *Indianapolis (IN) News*, April 24, 1903; Dennis Pajot, *Baseball's Heartland War, 1902–1903: The Western League and American Association Vie for Turf, Players and Profits* (Jefferson, NC: McFarland, 2011), 137–40.

## Chapter 6

1. "Edward Payson Weston Observes the Sabbath," *Knoxville (TN) Sentinel*, March 14, 1910.
2. Thomas Hughes, *Faithful Endurance and High Aim* (London: Hamilton, Adams, 1867), 9.
3. "Big Pedestrian Event Being Planned," *New York Times*, February 28, 1909; James A. Edgerton, "Weston's Long Hike," *Florida Star* (Titusville), March 26, 1909.
4. Benjamin Orange Flower, *Progressive Men, Women, and Movements of the Past Twenty-Five Years* (Boston: New Arena, 1914), 180–81; Edgerton, "Weston's Long Hike."

5. Weston, *The Pedestrian*, 48.
6. Nick Harris, Helen Harris, and Paul Marshall, *A Man in a Hurry: The Extraordinary Life and Times of Edward Payson Weston, the World's Greatest Walker* (London: deCoubertin Books, 2012).
7. Ibid.
8. "The Great Pedestrian Feat Achieved," *Chicago Tribune*, November 30, 1867.
9. "Weston," *Weekly North Carolina Standard* (Raleigh), December 11, 1867.
10. Douglas Small, "In Victorian Britain the Crowds Approved of Sports Doping—with Cocaine," *The Conversation*, August 9, 2017, https://theconversation.com/in-victorian-britain-the-crowds-approved-of-sports-doping-with-cocaine-82225; Matthew Algeo, *Pedestrianism: When Watching People Walk Was America's Favorite Spectator Sport* (Chicago: Chicago Review Press, 2014), 66.
11. "Pedestrianism," *New Orleans (LA) Democrat*, March 21, 1879.
12. "Pedestrianism in Painesville," *North Ohio Journal* (Painesville), April 19, 1879.
13. "Walking Matches, Brutal Torture of Women," *Chicago Tribune*, reprinted from *New York Nation*, March 5, 1879.
14. "The Tramps," *The Times* (Philadelphia, PA), April 2, 1879.
15. M. Ann Hall, *Muscle on Wheels: Louise Armaindo and the High-Wheel Racers of Nineteenth-Century America* (Montreal: McGill-Queen's University Press, 2018), 37–57; "Miss Elsa von Blumen," *Highland Weekly News* (Hillsboro, OH), July 10, 1879.
16. Arch Merrill, "Rochester's Champion Lady Pedestrian," *Democrat and Chronicle* (Rochester, NY), August 6, 1961; *Bicycling World*, November 11, 1881.
17. Arthur Conan Doyle, *Memories and Adventures: An Autobiography* (1924; Ware: Wordsworth Editions, 2007), 201.
18. Simon Burnton, "Dorando Pietri's Marathon," *The Guardian*, February 29, 2012, https://www.theguardian.com/sport/2012/feb/29/50-stunning-olympic-moments.
19. "An American Won," *Checotah (OH) Enquirer*, July 31, 1908; "Cheers for Athletes," *Washington Post*, August 30, 1908.
20. Ian McGowan, "The Glory Days of Celtic Park," *Irish American*, June–July 2012; "Marathon Winner Gets Big Welcome," *New York Times*, August 24, 1908.
21. "John Hayes Tells How the Great Marathon Race Was Run and Won," *Evening World* (New York), August 20, 1908.
22. James C. Whorton, "'Athlete's Heart': The Medical Debate over Athleticism, 1870–1920," *Journal of Sports History* 9, no. 1 (Spring 1982): 30–52; "Some Stories around Town," *Paducah (KY) Evening Sun*, April 2, 1909.
23. J. P. Chalmers and Thomas Bedding, eds., *The Moving Picture World* (New York: World Photographic Publishing Co., 1909), 4:528, 769, 104.
24. "Marathon Craze Finds a Victim," *Times-Democrat* (New Orleans, LA), December 20, 1908; "'Marathon Run' Kills This Young Athlete," *Star-Gazette* (Elmira, NY) December 17, 1908; "Warning against the Marathon Craze," *Passaic (NJ) Daily Herald*, December 24, 1908.
25. Erich Goode and Nachman Ben-Yehuda, *Moral Panics: The Social Construction of Deviance* (Malden, MA: Wiley-Blackwell, 2009); "The Heart-Breaking Marathon Then and Now," *St. Louis (MO) Post-Dispatch*, April 25, 1909.
26. "Marathons Wreak Evil on Ill Trained Youth," *New Enterprise* (Madison, FL), June 10, 1909, reprinted from the *New York Herald*; "Marathon Craze Dangerous One," *Evening World* (New York), February 22, 1909.
27. "Indian Wins Marathon Race," *Times-Democrat* (New Orleans, LA), February 22, 1909; "First Marathon in the South Won by Colored Runner," *New York Age*, March 18, 1909.

## Chapter 7

1. David Irvin Craig Diary, July 4 and 5, 1910, Southern Historical Collection, University of North Carolina at Chapel Hill.
2. Baker, *Playing with God*, 85–107; "The Coming Fistic Battle," *Daily Picayune* (New Orleans, LA), July 3, 1910.
3. Joyce Carol Oates, *On Boxing* (New York: HarperCollins, 1987), 72.
4. Jeffrey T. Sammons, *Beyond the Ring: The Role of Boxing in American Society* (Urbana: University of Illinois Press, 1990), 4–7, quoted in Somers, *The Rise of Sports in New Orleans*, 166.
5. Michael T. Isenberg, *John L. Sullivan and His America* (Urbana: University of Illinois Press, 1994), 257–80; "John L. Sullivan Convicted," *Watchman and Southron* (Sumter, SC), August 21, 1889.

6. Sammons, *Beyond the Ring*, 16–19; "Will Not Drop the Pugilists' Cases," *New York Times*, January 28, 1894; Clarence Greeley, "Efforts of the International Law and Order League to Prevent Fight," *New York Times*, January 15, 1894.
7. Joseph Kitchens, "The 'Waycross War': Pugilism and Politics in the Gay Nineties," *Atlanta Historical Bulletin* 25 (Spring 1981): 41–46.
8. Quoted in Edward L. Ayers, *The Promise of the New South: Life after Reconstruction* (New York: Oxford University Press, 1992), 312.
9. Sammons, *Beyond the Ring*, 33–34.
10. Theresa Runstedtler, *Jack Johnson, Rebel Sojourner: Boxing in the Shadow of the Global Color Line* (Berkeley: University of California Press, 2012), 22.
11. "White Men Fight Blacks Tonight," *Los Angeles Times*, May 16, 1902; Dan McCaffery, *Tommy Burns: Canada's Unknown World Heavyweight Champion* (Toronto: James Lorimer, 2000), 116–17.
12. Jack London, "Jack London Describes the Fight and Jack Johnson's Golden Smile," *New York Herald*, December 27, 1908; Richard Broome, "The Australian Reaction to Jack Johnson, Black Pugilist, 1907–09," in *The Best Ever Australian Sports Writing: A 200 Year Collection*, ed. David John Headon (Melbourne: Black Inc., 2001), 536, 543, 542; "Johnson Will Fight Anyone," *New York Times*, March 10, 1909.
13. "Booker Washington Says His Victory Was Godsend to Negro Race," *Daily Picayune* (New Orleans, LA), June 7, 1909.
14. "Booker Washington and Jack Johnson," *Macon (GA) Daily Telegraph*, June 12, 1909.
15. Geoffrey C. Ward, *Unforgivable Blackness: The Rise and Fall of Jack Johnson* (New York: Alfred A. Knopf, 2004), 72; "Jeff Will Fight White Man Only," *Philadelphia Inquirer*, December 23, 1906.
16. Ward, *Unforgivable Blackness*, 166–68; Randy Roberts, *Papa Jack: Jack Johnson and the Era of White Hopes* (New York: Free Press, 1983), 89; "Jeffries Will Meet Johnson," *Los Angeles Times*, March 1, 1909.
17. "Negros Engage Church for Big Fight Details," *Atlanta Constitution*, July 1, 1910; "Negroes Will Pray for Jack Johnson," *Macon (GA) Daily Telegraph*, July 3, 1910; "Negroes Daft over Fight," *Charlotte (NC) Daily Observer*, July 4, 1910.
18. "All Richmond Fight Crazy," *Times Dispatch* (Richmond, VA), July 5, 1910; "Picayune to Post Bulletins Flashed from Scene of Battle," *Daily Picayune* (New Orleans, LA), July 4, 1910; "Two Expert Boxers Show Jeffries-Johnson Fight at Ball Park Monday," *Macon (GA) Daily Telegraph*, July 2, 1910; Jack London, "Johnson the Victor in the Fifteenth Round," *Daily Picayune* (New Orleans, LA), July 5, 1910; *Daily Picayune* (New Orleans, LA), July 5, 1910.
19. "Thousands Forswear Prize Ring When Jeffries Fails to Win," *Daily Picayune* (New Orleans, LA), July 5, 1910; "Rev. Jeffries Said 'Twas Lord's Will," *Macon (GA) Daily Telegraph*, July 11, 1910.
20. Lucian B. Watkins, "Jack Johnson," *Richmond (VA) Planet*, July 16, 1910.
21. "Great Fight in Nevada," *Richmond (VA) Planet*, July 9, 1910.
22. "His Courage as White as His Skin Is Black," *Times Dispatch* (Richmond, VA), July 5, 1910; Editorial, *Times Dispatch* (Richmond, VA), July 06, 1910.
23. Arthur Remillard, *Southern Civil Religions: Imagining the Good Society in the Post-Reconstruction Era* (Athens: University of Georgia Press, 2011), 17–26, 95–103; Charles Reagan Wilson, *Baptized in Blood: The Religion of the Lost Cause, 1865–1920* (Athens: University of Georgia Press, 1980), 1–17.Barak Y. Orbach, "The Johnson-Jeffries Fight and Censorship of Black Supremacy," *New York University Journal of Law and Liberty* 5 (2010): 300–304; "No Fight Moving Pictures," *Keowee Courier* (Pickens Court House, SC), July 13, 1910; "Fight Pictures Can't Come Here," *Times Dispatch* (Richmond, VA), July 7, 1910.
24. "Stop Moving Pictures," *Macon (GA) Daily Telegraph*, July 10, 1910; "The Moving Picture Sensation" and "Much Ado about Nothing," *Times Dispatch* (Richmond, VA), July 7 and 8, 1910.
25. Quoted in, Ward, *Unforgivable Blackness*, 283, 322; "Attacks Johnson Marriage," *New York Times*, December 12, 1912.
26. "Jack Johnson Wedding Denounced in Congress," *New York Tribune*, December 12, 1912; Proceedings of the Fifth Meeting of the Governors of the States of the Union, Richmond, Virginia, December 3–7,1912, p. 52, State Library of Virginia, Richmond; Donald G. Mathews, "Lynching Is Part of the Religion of Our People: Faith in the Christian South," in *Religion in the American South: Protestants and Others in History and Culture*, ed. Beth Barton Schweiger and Donald G. Mathews (Chapel Hill: University of North Carolina Press, 2004), 153; Remillard, *Southern Civil Religions*, 64.

27. "Governors Rebuke Mob-Law Blease for His Doctrine," *Daily Picayune* (New Orleans, LA), December 7, 1912.
28. "Willard's Victory over Johnson Is Salvation of Pugilistic Game," *Miami Herald*, April 18, 1915.
29. Quoted in, Ward, *Unforgivable Blackness*, 298.
30. "Ham Says Dance Is Just Hugging Set with Music," *Fort Worth (TX) Star-Telegram*, August 24, 1916.
31. "Judge Barker's Views on Moral Life of the Students," *Lexington (KY) Herald*, November 8, 1914.
32. "Dr. Leyburn at Davidson College," *Charlotte (NC) Daily Observer*, May 24, 1915.
33. Baker, *Playing with God*, 104–6; "Ethics of Outdoor Sports," *Miami Herald*, January 13, 1920.

## Chapter 8

1. "The Athletic Woman Reigns," *Buffalo (NY) Evening News*, February 1, 1896.
2. "The Up-to-Date Athletic Girl," *Philadelphia Times*, October 9, 1900.
3. Senda Berenson, "Significance of Basketball for Women," in *Basketball for Women*, ed. Senda Berenson (New York: Spalding, 1901), 23; Ralph Melnick, *Senda Berenson: The Unlikely Founder of Women's Basketball* (Amherst: University of Massachusetts Press, 2007).
4. Senda Berenson, "Basket Ball for Women," *Physical Education* 3, no. 7 (September 1894): 106–7; Christine Terhune Herrick, "Women in Athletics: The Athletic Girl Not Unfeminine," *Outing* 26 (1902): 721.
5. "Biking Breeds Wrinkles," *Tacoma (WA) Daily Ledger*, July 25, 1897; "Dollars Won," *Hickman (KY) Courier*, December 16, 1898; Dorothy Dix, "The Athletic Woman at Home," *Daily Picayune* (New Orleans, LA), June 24, 1900.
6. "Mrs. Belva Ann Lockwood," *Currier-Journal* (Louisville, KY), October 14, 1884; Sue Macy, *Wheels of Change: How Women Rode the Bicycle to Freedom* (New York: National Geographic Books, 2011), 22.
7. Stephen Crane, "The Bicycle Speedway," *The Tennessean* (Nashville), July 5, 1896, reprinted from S. S. McClure (New York), July 3, 1896.
8. Frances Willard, *A Wheel within a Wheel: How I Learned to Ride the Bicycle* (New York: F. H. Revell, 1895), 72–73.
9. William M. Lawrence, "The Bicycle a Moral Teacher," *Inland Wheelman* (Topeka, KS), May 29, 1896; "'Bicycle Run for Christ,'" *The World*, June 24, 1896; "Christians on Wheels," *The World*, July 4, 1896.
10. "Copying the Salvationists," *Evening Journal* (Wilmington, DE) August 21, 1896; "'The Devil's Advance Agent,'" *Daily Telegraph* (Harrisburg, PA), July 29 1896.
11. "Woman in the Saddle," *The Sun* (Baltimore, MD), July 9, 1896.
12. "Bicycle Least of Her Troubles," *Boston Daily Globe*, October 12, 1896.
13. Roger Gilles, *Women on the Move: The Forgotten Era of Women's Bicycle Racing* (Lincoln: University of Nebraska Press, 2018), 119–20.
14. Ibid.
15. Annette Kellermann, *Physical Beauty: How to Keep It* (New York: Goerge H. Doran, 1918), 11, 16–17, 88; Annette Kellermann, *How to Swim* (New York: George H. Doran, 1918), 36, 38, 46.
16. Rodger Payne, *The Self and the Sacred: Conversion and Autobiography in Early American Protestantism* (Knoxville: University of Tennessee Press, 1998); "Modern Woman Getting Nearer the Perfect Figure," *New York Times*, December 4, 1910.
17. Luke Buckmaster, "The Amazing Life of Australia's 'Million-Dollar Mermaid,'" BBC Culture, November 2, 2017, http://www.bbc.com/culture/story/20171101-the-amazing-life-of-australias-million-dollar-mermaid; "Startling Facts about 'a Daughter of the Gods,'" *Courier-Journal* (Louisville, KY), January 7, 1917; "Annette Kellermann, Diving Venus, Is 'Daughter of Gods,'" *Spokesman-Review* (Spokane, WA), May 6, 1917; "'Daughter of Gods' Charms Audience," *Washington Times*, December 19, 1916; "President Wilson and Many World Famous Men and Women Have Seen 'Daughter of Gods,'" *Courier-Journal* (Louisville, KY), January 7, 1917.
18. "Boston Arrest a Mistake," *Boston Globe*, October 11, 1953. The story of Kellermann's arrest receives mention in many accounts of the swimmer and the era. See, for example, chapter 1 of Angela Woollacott, *Race and the Modern Exotic: Three "Australian" Women on Global Display* (Clayton: Monash University Publishing, 2011) and Emily Gibson and Barbara Firth, *The Original Million Dollar Mermaid: The Annette Kellerman Story* (Crows Nest: Allen & Unwin, 2005), 1–3, 57–64. However, Peter Cox, the curator of a 2016 exhibition about Kellerman for the Museum of Applied Arts and Sciences in Sydney, argues that this story is a "myth." Primary sources from the time are lacking, and instead, he says, this was a story that Kellerman originated

in the 1930s. See Peter Cox, "Annette Kellerman Myths," Museum of Applied Arts and Sciences, November 23, 1916, https://maas.museum/inside-the-collection/2016/11/23/annette-kellerman-myths/. Indeed, in one biography of Kellerman, the authors use her unpublished memoir *My Story* in recounting the Boston episode.

19. "Science's New Sun-and-Water Cure for 'Hopeless Cripples,'" *Morning Call* (Allentown, PA), February 8, 1925, via the Newspaper Feature Service.
20. "Pretty Girl Swimmer Sets Golden Gate Record," *San Francisco Chronicle*, September 11, 1921; "Miss Curtis Sets Up New Gate Record," *San Francisco Examiner*, September 11, 1921; "Tortured to Make 'Clay Woman,'" *Oakland (CA) Tribune*, July 23, 1922; "Detroit Champion in Photo Bathing Scene," *Detroit Free Press*, December 19, 1923; *San Francisco Examiner*, November 2, 1923; Kirk Curnutt, *A Historical Guide to F. Scott Fitzgerald* (New York: Oxford University Press, 2004), 158.
21. "Marie Curtis, Coast Mermaid, Ascribes Perfect Physique to Constant Work in Water," *Brooklyn (NY) Daily Eagle*, March 1, 1922; "How Marie Curtis, Physical Weakling, Became Champion American Amateur Swimmer," *Salina (KS) Daily Union*, March 10, 1922.
22. Jack Bell, "O'er the Sports Desk," *Miami News*, August 10, 1936.
23. Alan Gould, "Helen Stephens Is Selected as Leading Feminine Athlete," *Lexington (KY) Leader*, December 15, 1936; Richard Goldstein, "Eleanor Holm Whalen, 30's Swimming Champion, Dies," *New York Times*, February 2, 2004.
24. "Helen Stephens Is a Real Girl," *Harrisburg (PA) Telegraph*, August 6, 1936.
25. "Sportswomen of Year," *New York Times*, September 27, 1983; Sharon Kinney-Hanson, *The Life of Helen Stephens: The Fulton Flash* (Carbondale: Southern Illinois University Press, 2004), 226; "Helen Stephens in Short Sprint," *Boston Globe*, July 3, 1936; "Helen Stephens Grabs Spotlight," *Windsor (Ontario) Star*, September 3, 1935.
26. Vanessa Heggie, "Testing Sex and Gender in Sports: Reinventing, Reimagining, and Reconstructing Histories," *Endeavour* 34, no. 4 (December 2010): 157–63; Clare Tebbutt, "The Spectre of the 'Man-Woman Athlete': Mark Weston, Zdenek Koubek, the 1936 Olympics, and the Uncertainty of Sex," *Women's History Review* 24, no. 5 (2015): 721–38; Sheldon Anderson, *The Forgotten Legacy of Stella Walsh: The Greatest Female Athlete of Her Time* (New York: Rowman & Littlefield, 2017), 89–112. Matt Tullis, "Who Was Stella Walsh?," SBNation, June 27, 2013, https://www.sbnation.com/longform/2013/6/27/4466724/stella-walsh-profile-intersex-olympian.
27. Ama Barker, "Can a Girl Athlete Remain Feminine?," *Daily News* (New York), January 8, 1933; Caspar Whitney, "Women in Golf," *Harper's Bazaar*, October 13, 1894; Horace G. Hutchinson, ed., *Golf*, 2nd ed. (London: Longmans, Green, 1890), 48.
28. Kevin Kenny, *Patty Berg: Pioneer Champion of Women's Golf* (Jefferson, NC: McFarland, 2019); "Curtis Cup Event Provides New Test for Patty Berg," *Evening Sun* (Baltimore, MD), March 26, 1936.
29. Don Van Natta, *Wonder Girl: The Magnificent Sporting Life of Babe Didrikson Zaharias* (New York: Little, Brown, 2011).
30. Joe Williams, "Let Her Play Golf," *Oklahoma News* (Oklahoma City), May 15, 1935, reprint from the *New York World Telegram*.
31. Grantland Rice, "The Spotlight," *Atlanta Constitution*, August 9, 1932.
32. William Oscar Johnson and Nancy Williamson, "Babe Part 2," *Sports Illustrated*, October 13, 1975, 48–57.
33. Susan K. Cahn, "From 'Muscle Moll' to the 'Butch' Ballplayer: Mannishness, Lesbianism, and Homophobia in U.S. Women's Sport," *Feminist Studies* 19, no. 2 (Summer 1993): 343–68; Van Natta, *Wonder Girl*: 139–58.
34. Mary Jo Festle, *Playing Nice: Politics and Apologies in Women's Sports* (New York: Columbia University Press, 1996), 22; Adela Rogers St. Johns, "Looking at Life," *San Francisco Examiner*, October 29, 1932; Cahn, "From 'Muscle Moll' to the 'Butch' Ballplayer."
35. Barker, "Can a Girl Athlete Remain Feminine?"
36. Mildred Didrikson, "Babe Didrikson's Life Story," *Boston Globe*, January 18, 1933. This was part 10 of a ten-segment series written by Didrikson and distributed by NANA Inc., New York City.
37. Mildred Didrikson, "I Blow My Own Horn," *American Magazine*, June 1936; Lisa J. Shaver, "Babe Didrikson Zaharias's Rhetorical Branding: When It's Not Enough to Be the World's Greatest Woman Athlete," in *Women at Work: Rhetorics of Gender and Labor*, ed. David Gold and Jessica Enoch (Pittsburgh, PA: University of Pittsburgh Press, 2019), 172–85.

38. Paul Gallico, "Golf Game Analyzed," *Daily News* (New York), April 29, 1935, reprinted from the Chicago Tribune–NY News Syndicate.
39. Van Natta, *Wonder Girl*, 242, 249–336.
40. Johnson and Williamson, "Babe Part 2"; William Oscar Johnson and Nancy Williamson, "Babe Part 3," *Sports Illustrated*, October 20, 1975, 48–64.
41. "The Babe Is Back," *Time*, August 10, 1953; Paul Gallico, "Farewell to the Babe," *Sports Illustrated*, October 7, 1956.

## Chapter 9

1. Jeremy C. Young, *The Age of Charisma: Leaders, Followers, and Emotions in American Society, 1870–1940* (New York: Cambridge University Press, 2017); "Prizefighting's Million-Dollar Gates," *Time*, March 8, 1971; Grantland Rice, *The Tumult and the Shouting: My Life in Sports* (New York: A. S. Barnes, 1954), 114.
2. Max Weber, *Max Weber on Charisma and Institution Building* (Chicago: University of Chicago Press, 1968), 48; Young, *The Age of Charisma.*
3. Mark Inabinett, *Grantland Rice and His Heroes: The Sportswriter as Mythmaker in the 1920s* (Knoxville: University of Tennessee Press, 1994), 13–24.
4. Amidon, *Something Like the Gods*, 96; Grantland Rice, "The Four Horsemen," *New York Herald Tribune*, October 18, 1924; Murray A. Sperber, *Shake Down the Thunder: The Creation of Notre Dame Football* (Bloomington: Indiana University Press, 2002), 173–82. Inabinett, *Grantland Rice and His Heroes.*
5. Robert S. Gallagher, "The Galloping Ghost: An Interview with Red Grange," *American Heritage Magazine* 26, no. 1 (December 1974): 21.
6. Michael Oriard, *King Football: Sport and Spectacle in the Golden Age of Radio and Newsreels, Movies and Magazines, the Weekly and the Daily Press* (Chapel Hill: University of North Carolina Press, 2005), 110.
7. John R. Tunis, *$port$ Heroics and Hysterics* (Rahway, NJ: John Day, 1928), 17, 19–21, 32.
8. Francis Wallace, "The Hypocrisy of Football Reform," *Scribner's Magazine*, November 1927.
9. "Knute Rockne," *Montgomery (AL) Advertiser*, April 11, 1931, reprinted from the *New York World.*
10. Sports writer Blinkey Horn used this term as early as 1922. See "Outlook for Commodore Eleven," *The Tennessean* (Nashville), October 30, 1922; "Jimmy Armistead Is Lost for Two Weeks," *The Tennessean* (Nashville, TN), September 11, 1926. Ralph McGill also used the term. See "Loss of Players Handicaps Tech Coach," *Atlanta Constitution*, November 12, 1929; "Knee Kap Klan Is Great Menace to Tech," *Atlanta Constitution*, September 19, 1937.
11. Wallace, "The Hypocrisy of Football Reform."
12. Todd Tucker, *Notre Dame vs. the Klan: How the Fighting Irish Defeated the Ku Klux Klan* (Chicago: Loyola Press, 2004), 154; "Police Unable to Handle Mob," *Luverne (AL) Journal*, May 29, 1924, reprinted from the *Klan Kourier.*
13. Sperber, *Shake Down the Thunder.*
14. Fuzzy Woodruff, *A History of Southern Football: 1890–1928*, 3 vols. (Atlanta, GA: Walter M. Brown, 1928), 2:204; Scottie McKenzie Frasier, "As We See It," *Dothan (AL) Eagle*, April 6, 1931.
15. Baker, *Playing with God*, 102.
16. Wilton Vaugh, "Detail Story of Stadium Game," *Boston Post*, October 24, 1920.
17. Melville E Webb, "Centre Wins Battle 6 to 0," *Boston Globe*, October 30, 1921; "Centre Conquers Harvard," *New York Times*, October 30, 1921; "Centre Saves South," *Atlanta Constitution*, October 30, 1921; "Center College Man Makes Talk on Faith," *Tar Heel* (Chapel Hill, NC), March 17, 1922; "Football Starts at Trinity 'Hit Trail' at Revival," *Atlanta Constitution*, December 4, 1921.
18. Woodruff, *A History of Southern Football*, 2:123, 48; Natalie Pierre, "A Look Back at 'the Game That Changed the South,'" AL.com, January 1, 2015, http://www.al.com/sports/index.ssf/2015/01/a_look_back_at_the_game_that_c.html.
19. Fuzzy Woodruff, "Golden Tornado Coach Dean of Dixie Gridiron," *Birmingham (AL) News*, October 20, 1919; "Football's Glorious Slaughter," *Sports Illustrated*, November 27, 1961.
20. John M. Heisman and Mark Schlabach, *Heisman: The Man behind the Trophy* (New York: Simon and Schuster, 2012), 166; "John Heisman Eager to Coach in North Next Fall," *Pittsburgh (PA) Press*, January 8, 1919; John W. Heisman, *Principles of Football* (St. Louis, MO: Sports Publishing Bureau, 1922), 1, 7, 336, 360.

21. Cory McCartney, *The Heisman Trophy: The Story of an American Icon and Its Winners* (New York: Sports Publishing, 2016).
22. Thea Gallo Becker, *Legendary Locals of Cleveland* (Charleston, SC: Arcadia, 2012), 82; "Baseball," *New York Times*, August 23, 1920.
23. "Thousands Attend Chapman Funeral," *New York Times*, August 21, 1920; Mike Sowell, *The Pitch That Killed: The Story of Carl Mays, Ray Chapman, and the Pennant Race of 1920* (Guilford, CT: First Lyons Press, 1989).
24. "Design for Ray Chapman Memorial," *Times Recorder* (Zanesville, OH), October 13, 1920; Larry Keller, "Remembering Baseball's Martyr," *South Florida Sentinel*, October 18, 1992; "Ray Chapman Icon," The Baseball Reliquary, n.d., https://baseballreliquary.org/ray-chapman-icon/.
25. Tyler Kepner, *K: A History of Baseball in Ten Pitches* (New York: Knopf, 2019), 52–56.
26. John B. Foster, ed., *Spalding's Base Ball Guide* (New York: American Sports Publishing Company, 1921), 9.
27. F. C. Lane, *Batting* (1925; Lincoln: University of Nebraska Press, 2001), 141.
28. Eldon L. Ham, *All the Babe's Men: Baseball's Greatest Home Run Seasons and How They Changed America* (Sterling, VA: Potomac Books, 2013).
29. Associated Press, "222 Ballots Name Ty Cobb No. 1 Immortal," *Baltimore Sun*, February 3, 1934; Rice, *The Tumult and the Shouting*, 18.
30. Steven Elliott Tripp, *Ty Cobb, Baseball, and American Manhood* (Lanham, MD: Rowman & Littlefield, 2016), 355–76; William R. Cobb, "The Georgia Peach: Stumped by the Storyteller," The National Pastime: Baseball in the Peach State, 2010, https://sabr.org/journals/baseball-in-the-peach-state/.
31. Joe S. Jackson, "On the Trail," *Detroit Free Press*, March 18, 1906; Charles Leerhsen, *Ty Cobb: A Terrible Beauty* (New York: Simon & Schuster, 2015), 119.

## Chapter 10

1. Charles W. Paddock, "The Duke Again Is King," *Billings (MT) Gazette*, June 9, 1929.
2. Ibid.
3. Patrick J. Moser, ed., *Pacific Passages: An Anthology of Surf Writings* (Honolulu: University of Hawaii Press, 2008), 117.
4. David Davis, *Waterman: The Life and Times of Duke Kahanamoku* (Lincoln: University of Nebraska Press, 2015), 17–20; Scott Laderman, *Empire in Waves: A Political History of Surfing* (Berkeley: University of California Press, 2014).
5. "Hui Nalu Luau for Returned Champ," *Pacific Commercial Advertiser* (Honolulu), October 2, 1912.
6. "Analysis of the Style of Duke P. Kahanamoku," *New York Times*, February 20, 1916.
7. Davis, *Waterman*, 17–20; Mary Ryllis Clark, "Waves of Nostalgia," *The Age* (Melbourne), January 7, 1995.
8. United Press, "Swimming Star Is Hero of Tragedy," *Visalia (CA) Daily Times*, June 15, 1925; A. B. Berry, "5 Drown in Newport Harbor," *Santa Ana (CA) Register*, June 15, 1925; Gene Hunter and Charles Turner, "Duke Kahanamoku Dead at 77," *Honolulu Advertiser*, January 23, 1968.
9. "What Duke Means to Hawaii," *Honolulu Advertiser*, October 11, 1963; "Kahanamoku Statue Sets off a Dispute," *Honolulu Advertiser*, August 19, 1990.
10. "Leslie Mayle Dies at 75," *Battle Creek (MI) Enquirer*, March 7, 1974; "Colonel Cards Ace at VA Course," *Battle Creek (MI) Enquirer*, May 2, 1964; "Christian Fellowship and Exercise Lure Businessmen to Volleyball at the 'Y,'" *Battle Creek (MI) Enquirer*, February 14, 1960.
11. "Chief Mayle Is Contender," *Harrisburg (PA) Telegraph*, March 18, 1925.
12. "Bouts Scheduled," *Evening News* (Harrisburg, PA), February 28, 1924; "Army Athletes at Harrisburg," *Lancaster (PA) New Era*, March 13, 1924; "Mayle on Way Over," *Harrisburg (PA) Telegraph*, June 18, 1924; Robert F. Berkhofer, *The White Man's Indian: Images of the American Indian, from Columbus to the Present* (New York: Vintage, 1979); Carol Spindel, *Dancing at Halftime: Sports and the Controversy over American Indian Mascots* (New York: New York University Press, 2002).
13. Matthew Lindaman, "Wrestling's Hold on the Western World before the Great War," *The Historian* 62, no. 4 (2000): 51–72; Scott M Beekman, *Ringside: A History of Professional Wrestling in America* (Westport, CT: Greenwood, 2006); "Professional Wrestling Ban," *Indianapolis (IN) Star*, April 15, 1933; George A. Barton, "Between You and Me," *Star Tribune* (Minneapolis, MN), November 10, 1935.

14. "Chief Sunoco, Graham Meet in Main Bout," *Newark (OH) Advocate*, January 21, 1937; "Chief Saunooke Dies," *Asheville (NC) Citizen-Times*, April 16, 1965.
15. "Indian Features Mat Bill Tonight," *Piqua (OH) Daily Call*, June 4, 1936; "Chief Sunoco, 318-Pound Injun Meets White," *Bluefield (WV) Daily Telegraph*, October 11, 1936; Tom Fitzgerald, "What a Toss!," *Boston Globe*, December 9, 1937.
16. "Benefit Cart Is Scheduled," *Charleston (WV) Daily Mail*, January 26, 1936.
17. "Chief Saunooke Dies"; "Arch-Enemies Wrestle Here," *Orlando (FL) Evening Star*, May 6, 1937
18. Ayele Bekerie, "African Americans and the Italo-Ethiopian War," in *Revisioning Italy: National Identity and Global Culture*, ed. Beverly Allen and Mary J. Russo (Minneapolis: University of Minnesota Press, 1997), 130.
19. Joseph McLaren, ed., *The Collected Works of Langston Hughes*, vol. 14 (Columbia: University of Missouri Press, 2003), 307; Edward Van Every, *Joe Louis, Man and Super-Fighter* (New York: Frederick A. Stokes, 1936), 23, 1–21; Harry Hansen, "The First Reader," *Wilmington (DE) Morning News*, May 21, 1936, reprinted from *New York World*.
20. Lew Freedman, *Joe Louis: The Life of a Heavyweight* (Jefferson, NC: McFarland, 2013), 193.
21. "From Our Exchanges," *Record-Democrat* (Wagoner, OK), October 3, 1935.
22. Chris Mead, *Joe Louis: Black Champion in White America* (Mineola, NY: Dover, 2011), 52–53.
23. Ibid., 54; Robert Horn, "Two Champions and Enemies," *Sports Illustrated*, May 14, 1990.
24. David Margolick, *Beyond Glory: Joe Louis vs. Max Schmeling, and a World on the Brink* (New York: Knopf, 2010), 126.
25. Patrick B. Miller, "To 'Bring the Race along Rapidly': Sport, Student Culture, and Educational Mission at Historically Black Colleges during the Interwar Years," *History of Education Quarterly* 35, no. 2 (Summer, 1995): 111, 115.
26. Dave Kindred, *Sound and Fury: Two Powerful Lives, One Fateful Friendship* (New York: Simon and Schuster, 2006), 38; Rebecca L. Davis, *Public Confessions: The Religious Conversions That Changed American Politics* (Chapel Hill: University of North Carolina Press, 2021).
27. Floyd Patterson and Gay Talese, "In Defense of Cassius Clay" (1966), in *The Muhammad Ali Reader*, ed. Gerald Early (Hopewell, NJ: Ecco Press, 1998), 64–71.
28. Floyd Patterson and Jack Mahon, "Cassius Clay Must Be Beaten," *Sports Illustrated*, October 11, 1965; Howard L. Bingham and Max Wallace, *Muhammad Ali's Greatest Fight: Cassius Clay vs. the United States of America* (Lanham, MD: Rowman & Littlefield, 2012), 109.
29. Gerald Early, "Hot Spicks versus Cool Spades: Three Notes toward a Cutural Definition of Prizefighting," *Hudson Review* 34, no. 1 (Spring 1981): 39–56; Megha Mohan, "When Muhammad Ali Took on Superman," BBC, June 7, 2016, https://www.bbc.com/news/blogs-trending-36467141.
30. Mary L. Dudziak, *Cold War Civil Rights: Race and the Image of American Democracy* (Princeton, NJ: Princeton University Press, 2000).
31. Arthur Remillard, "From Muscular Christianity to Divine Madness: Sports and/as Religion in America," in *Faith in America: Changes, Challenges, and a New Spirituality*, ed. Charles H. Lippy (Santa Barbara, CA: Praeger, 2006), 215–34; Dave Zirin, *What's My Name, Fool? Sports and Resistance in the United States* (Chicago: Haymarket Books, 2005); Kelley L. Carter, "Director Michael Mann Opens Up about Muhammad Ali," Andscape, January 17, 2017, https://andscape.com/features/director-michael-mann-opens-up-about-muhammad-ali/; "Saturday Sports: Remembering Muhammad Ali," *NPR Weekend Edition*, June 4, 2016, https://www.npr.org/2016/06/04/480731342/saturday-sports-remembering-muhammad-ali.
32. Chris Broussard, "LeBron: Muhammad Ali's Success in Ring Secondary to Work Outside It," ESPN, June 4, 2016, https://www.espn.com/nba/story/_/id/15940708/lebron-james-says-muhammad-ali-big-reason-why-african-american-athletes-enjoy-fame-opportunities.

## Chapter 11

1. Rebeccca T. Alpert, *Out of Left Field: Jews and Black Baseball* (New York: Oxford University Press, 2011), 170–71.
2. Wendell Smith, "The Sports Beat," *Pittsburgh (PA) Courier*, May 24, 1947; Ira Berkow, "Greenberg: A Kind of Beacon," *New York Times*, September 7, 1986; Wendell Smith, "What a Difference a Name Makes," *Pittsburgh (PA) Courier*, June 3, 1961; Robert C. Cottrell, *Two Pioneers: How Hank Greenberg and Jackie Robinson Transformed Baseball—and America* (Washington, DC: Potomac Books, 2012), 238.

3. A search for "sports pioneer" on Newspapers.com for the twentieth century shows the term's relative lack of use in the 1900s, slight uptick in the 1950s, and spike in the 1980s and 1990s. The results are as follows: 1900s (53), 1920s (180), 1930s (466), 1940s (599), 1950s (1,453), 1960s (2,218), 1970s (1,263), 1980s (4,873), 1990s (5,253). Rich Shea, "A Pioneer Like No Other," *Rutgers Magazine*, Spring 2019, https://ucmweb.rutgers.edu/magazine/1419archive/features/a-pioneer-like-no-other.html.
4. Paul Robeson, "The New Idealism: Rutgers College Valedictory Address, June 10, 1919," *The Targum* 50 (1918–19): 570–71; Martin Duberman, *Paul Robeson: A Biography* (New York: Knopf, 1989).
5. Barbara J. Beeching, "Paul Robeson and the Black Press: The 1950 Passport Controversy," *Journal of African American History* 87 (Summer 2002): 339–54.
6. "Paul Robeson's Antics," *Abilene (TX) Reporter-News*, June 26, 1949; Ronald A. Smith, "The Paul Robeson—Jackie Robinson Saga and a Political Collision," *Journal of Sport History* 6, no. 2 (1979): 5–27.
7. Peter Dreier, "We Are Long Overdue for a Paul Robeson Revival," *Los Angeles Review of Books*, May 8, 2014, https://lareviewofbooks.org/article/long-overdue-paul-robeson-revival-talented-person-20th-century/. I have adopted the contrast of "pioneer" and "misfit" from Marshall A. Isler, *An Unwitting Pioneer: A Journey from Jim Crow, thru Worldly Success, to Spiritual Peace* (Mustang, OK: Tate, 2011), 306.
8. "Menne's Pioneering Ball," International Bowling Museum and Hall of Fame, n.d., https://www.bowlingheritage.com/item/mennes-pioneering-ball/; Mark Miller, *Bowling: America's Greatest Indoor Pastime* (New York: Bloomsbury 2013), 26.
9. "Benefits of Bowling Are Many and Varied" (Ad), *The Sun-Advocate* (Price, UT), February 12, 1942.
10. James Surowiecki, *The Wisdom of Crowds* (New York: Knopf, 2005), 241–44; Andrew Hurley, *Diners, Bowling Alleys, and Trailer Parks: Chasing the American Dream in Postwar Consumer Culture* (New York: Basic Books, 2001), 107–94.
11. Michael Jackman, "A Lane of Their Own," *Detroit Metro Times*, May 27, 2014; Ted Page, "NBA Has Crusaded for Negro Bowlers," *Pittsburgh (PA) Courier*, April 7, 1962.
12. Louis Moore, *We Will Win the Day: The Civil Rights Movement, the Black Athlete, and the Quest for Equality* (Santa Barbara, CA: Praeger, 2017), 29; "CYO Fight on Ban against Negroes in ABC Defeated," *The Tablet* (Brooklyn, NY), April 24, 1948.
13. Moore, *We Will Win the Day*, 26–29; "Brooklyn Priest Wins 5-Year Fight to End Ban on Negroes in National Bowling Congress," *National Catholic Welfare Conference News Service*, May 15, 1950.
14. Summer Cherland, "Basement Bowlers: The National Negro Bowling Association and Its Legacy of Black Leadership, 1939–1968," in *Separate Games: African American Sport behind the Walls of Segregation*, ed. David K. Wiggins and Ryan Swanson (Fayetteville: University of Arkansas Press, 2016), 208; Bill Nunn, "Louise Fulton No Longer a Bridesmaid," *Pittsburgh (PA) Courier*, September 12, 1964; "Louise Fulton," USBC Hall of Fame, n.d., https://bowl.com/usbc-hall-of-fame/hall-of-famers/louise-fulton.
15. William C. Rhoden, "A Pioneer's Tribute Is Both a Reward and a Reminder," *New York Times*, November 25, 2014; Rhiannon Walker, "Arthur Ashe Always Had the Leadership to Change the World," *The Undefeated*, August 29, 2018, https://theundefeated.com/features/arthur-ashe-always-had-the-leadership-to-change-the-world-and-his-historic-1968-us-open-title-finally-provided-the-platform/.
16. Robert Pruter, "Tidye Pickett: The Unfulfilled Aspirations of America's Pioneering African American Female Track Star," in *Before Jackie Robinson: The Transcendent Role of Black Sporting Pioneers*, ed. Gerald R. Gems (Lincoln: University of Nebraska Press, 2017), 244; Ron Grossman, "Tidye Pickett's Legacy," *Chicago Tribune*, August 21, 2016.
17. Toni Ginnetti, "Ex-Track Star Recalls Racism at '32 Games," *Chicago Sun-Times*, August 5, 1984; Pruter, "Tidye Pickett."
18. "The Black Eagles," *Pittsburgh (PA) Courier*, July 11, 1936; Jason Cato, "The Great Race," *Tribune-Review* Pittsburgh (PA), July 29, 2021, https://triblive.com/news/uncategorized/john-woodruff-gold-medal-run-in-36-olympics/; Sherrod Brown, "Honoring the Life of Jesse Owens," *Congressional Record*, Senate, September 11, 2013, vol. 159, pt. 9, 1338.
19. A. H. Stackpole, "Lesson in Courtesy," *Harrisburg (PA) Telegraph*, August 26, 1936.
20. Florence Fisher Parry, "A Prince of Privilege," *Pittsburgh (PA) Press*, August 6, 1936.

21. "Negro Heroes Pile Up 70 of 187 U.S. Points," *New York Amsterdam News*, August 8, 1936; Mark Dyreson, "The Original Pan-American Games: The 1937 Dallas Pan-American Olympics," *International Journal of the History of Sport* 33, nos. 1–2 (2016): 6–28.
22. "Jesse Owens Dies of Cancer at 66," *New York Times*, April 1, 1980; Jacqueline Edmondson, *Jesse Owens: A Biography* (Westport, CT: Greenwood Press, 2007), 57.
23. Jennifer H. Lansbury, *A Spectacular Leap: Black Women Athletes in Twentieth-Century America* (Fayetteville: University of Arkansas Press, 2014), 71–72.
24. Ibid., 43–74; Cat M. Ariail, *Passing the Baton: Black Women Track Stars and American Identity* (Champaign: University of Illinois Press, 2020), 12–45; "Albany Pays Tribute to Alice Coachman," *Atlanta Constitution*, September 2, 1948.
25. Alan Greenblatt, "Why an African-American Sports Pioneer Remains Obscure," *NPR Code Switch*, July 19, 2014, https://www.npr.org/sections/codeswitch/2014/07/19/332665921/why-an-african-american-sports-pioneer-remains-obscure; Richard Goldstein, "Alice Coachman, 90, Dies," *New York Times*, July 14, 2014.
26. Joseph M. Turrini, "'It Was Communism versus the Free World': The USA-USSR Dual Track Meet Series and the Development of Track and Field in the United States, 1958–1985," *Journal of Sports History* 28, no. 3 (2001): 430.
27. Rita Liberti and Maureen M. Smith, *(Re)Presenting Wilma Rudolph* (Syracuse, NY: Syracuse University Press, 2015), 76.
28. Mary Snow, "Can the Soviet Girls Be Stopped," *Sports Illustrated*, August 27, 1956; Ed Corrigan, "American Men, Russian Women Lead Going into Dual Track Meet Finals," *Daily Press* (Newport News, VA), July 16, 1961; "U.S. Sprinters Doin' the Rushin'," *Press and Sun-Bulletin* (Binghamton, NY), July 16, 1961; Avery Yang, "Remembering Wilma Rudolph," *Sports Illustrated*, February 6, 2020, https://www.si.com/olympics/2020/02/06/black-history-month-wilma-rudolph-legacy.
29. Turrini, "'It Was Communism versus the Free World'"; Kenny Moore, "Life on the Run," *Sports Illustrated*, May 18, 1987.
30. Harry Missildine, "Twice Over Lightly," *The Spokesman-Review* (WA), September 22, 1965; "Spokane Greets Track Celebrity," *Spokane (WA) Chronicle*, July 27, 1964; Arthur Daley, "U.S. Rout of Russ Prompts Lesson on Temptation," *Sacramento Bee*, reprinted from the *New York Times*.
31. Timothy Noakes, *Lore of Running*, 4th ed. (Champaign, IL: Human Kinetics, 2002).
32. George Sheehan, *Running and Being* (New York: Simon and Schuster, 1978); George Sheehan, "Is Running a Religion?," GeorgeSheehan.com, n.d., http://www.georgesheehan.com/essays/essay46.html.
33. Frank Litsky, "Father of Running Boom Is Proud of His Deed," *Journal Tribune* (Biddeford, ME), October 24, 1980; William J. Bowerman and W. E. Harris, *Jogging* (New York: Grosset & Dunlap, 1967), 7; Dennis Hernet, "Jogging Improves Life," *Manitowoc (WI) Herald-Times*, February 6, 1970.
34. "A Girl in a Man's Game," *Sports Illustrated*, May 2, 1966.
35. "Lady with Desire to Run Crashed Marathon," *New York Times*, April 23, 1967; Kathrine Switzer, *Marathon Woman: Running the Race to Revolutionize Women's Sports* (Philadelphia, PA: Da Capo Press, 2017), 71.
36. Katherine Switzer, "The Girl Who Started It All," *Runner's World*, May 2007, http://www.runnersworld.com/runners-stories/girl-who-started-it-all; Myron Cope, "Angry Overseer of the Marathon," *Sports Illustrated*, April 22, 1968; Karen Given, "Arlene Pieper: The Marathon Pioneer Almost Forgotten by History," *Only a Game*, WBUR, April 21, 2017, https://www.wbur.org/onlyagame/2017/04/21/arlene-pieper-marathon; Jill Rothenberg, "Pikes Peak Marathon Legend Has Died," *Colorado Sun*, March 29, 2021, https://coloradosun.com/2021/03/29/arlene-pieper-stine-obituary-pikes-peak-marathon/.
37. Pamela Cooper, *The American Marathon* (Syracuse, NY: Syracuse University Press, 1998), 92, 101; Arthur Remillard, "Ted Corbitt: The Once-Forgotten and Now-Remembered Pioneer of American Distance Running," in *Religion and Sports in North America: Critical Essays for the Twenty-First Century*, ed. Jeffrey Scholes and Randall Balmer (New York: Routledge, 2023), 201–15.
38. Trishul Cherns, "Ted Corbitt: American Ultrarunning Pioneer," *Ultrarunning Magazine*, December 1988.
39. Gail Kislevitz, "The Ted Corbitt Legacy," *Marathon and Beyond*, May–June 2010.

40. Robert Lipsyte, "Miles to Go and Promises to Keep," *New York Times*, October 21, 1994; Robert Lipsyte, "One Runner Who Has Logged His Miles," *New York Times*, November 12, 1993.
41. Amby Burfoot, *First Ladies of Running* (New York: Rodale, 2016), 187–95; Anthony Reed, "The Pioneer: Marilyn Bevans," *Runner's World*, December 10, 2013, https://www.runnersworld.com/runners-stories/a20825589/the-pioneer-marilyn-bevans/; Chodes, *Corbitt*, 113–18; New York City Parks Department, "NYC Parks Names 6-Mile Central Park Loop for Storied Black Olympian Runner," press release, February 22, 2021, https://www.nycgovparks.org/news/press-releases?id=21816.

## Chapter 12

1. Simeon Strunsky, "The Game," *Atlantic Monthly*, August 1914.
2. Robert Ackerman, *J. G. Frazer: His Life and Work* (New York: Cambridge University Press, 1987), 95–110.
3. Strunsky, "The Game."
4. "Religion of Baseball," *Sporting Life* (Philadelphia, PA), May 28, 1910; "Religion and Baseball," *Franklin Times* (Louisburg, NC), June 28, 1889, reprinted from the *Philadelphia Enquirer*.
5. Morris R. Cohen, "Baseball as a National Religion," *The Dial* 67 (1919): 57; Morris R. Cohen, "Reflections of a Wondering Jew" (1950), in Cohen, *Reflections of a Wandering Jew* (New Brunswick, NJ: Transaction, 2010), vii–xiv.
6. Jacques Barzun, *God's Country and Mine* (New York: Knopf, 1954), 151; Joe Holley, "Jacques Barzun Dies at 104," *Washington Post*, October 26, 2012, https://www.washingtonpost.com/local/obituaries/jacques-barzun-wide-ranging-cultural-historian-dies-at-104/2012/10/26/33a202c4-c5da-11df-94e1-c5afa35a9e59_story.html?tid=ss_tw.
7. Ira Chernus, "Civil Religion," in *The Blackwell Companion to Religion in America*, ed. Philip Goff (Malden, MA: Wiley-Blackwell, 2010), 57–70.
8. Michael Novak, *The Joy of Sport: End Zones, Bases, Baskets, Balls, and the Consecration of the American Spirit* (New York: Basic Books, 1976), 18–34.
9. Ibid., 19.
10. Jeffrey Hart, "Baseball: Higher Mode of Life," *Daily Intelligencer* (Doylestown, PA), November 4, 1976, syndicated by King Features; Michael Novak, "What Winning and Losing Really Are," *New York Times*, January 30, 1977; Christopher Lehmann-Haupt, "Book of the Times," *New York Times*, May 14, 1976; John Leonard, "Serious Games, Tasty Crabs and a Natural Writer," *New York Times*, June 13, 1976; William J. Bennett, "Sports as Transcendence," *Commentary*, October 1976; Paul Newlin, "Joyless Sports," *CrossCurrents* 26, no. 4 (Winter 1977): 456–59.
11. John L. Dayries, "Review of *The Joy of Sports* by Michael Novak," *Journal of the American Academy of Religion* 45, no. 2 (1977): 245; Harold J. VanderZwaag, "Review of *The Joy of Sports* by Michael Novak," *Journal of Sports History* 5, no. 2 (1978): 89–91.
12. Allen Guttmann, *From Ritual to Record: The Nature of Modern Sports* (1978; New York: Columbia University Press, 2004), 25, 26.
13. Ibid., 108. See, for example, Craig Forney, *The Holy Trinity of American Sports: Civil Religion in Football, Baseball, and Basketball* (Macon, GA: Mercer University Press, 2012); Eric Bain-Selbo, *Game Day and God: Football, Faith, and Politics in the American South* (Macon, GA: Mercer University Press, 2009); Eric Bain-Selbo and D. Gregory Sapp, *Understanding Sport as a Religious Phenomenon: An Introduction* (New York: Bloomsbury, 2016).
14. Durkheim, *The Elementary Forms of Religious Life*, 34; Mircea Eliade, *The Sacred and the Profane: The Nature of Religion*, trans. Willard R. Trask (New York: Harcourt, Brace, 1959), 205; Robert J. Higgs and Michael Braswell, *An Unholy Alliance: The Sacred and Modern Sports* (Macon, GA: Mercer University Press, 2004).
15. Christopher H. Evans and William R. Herzog II, eds., *The Faith of 50 Million: Baseball, Religion, and American Culture* (Louisville, KY: Westminster, 2002). See also, Joseph L. Price, ed., *From Season to Season: Sports as American Religion* (Macon, GA: Mercer University Press, 2001); Joseph L. Price, *Rounding the Bases: Baseball and Religion in America* (Macon, GA: Mercer University Press, 2006); John Sexton, *Baseball as a Road to God: Seeing Beyond the Game* (New York: Penguin, 2014), 177.
16. Onaje X. O. Woodbine, *Black Gods of the Asphalt: Religion, Hip-Hop, and Street Basketball* (New York: Columbia University Press, 2016).
17. Amidon, *Something Like the Gods*, 149–52; Dave Zirin, *What's My Name, Fool? Sports and Resistance in the United States* (Chicago: Haymarket Books, 2005), 87; "The Black Power Salute," ESPN, August 2, 2012, http://www.espn.co.uk/olympic-sports/sport/story/162053.html.

18. Brent Musburger, "Bizarre Protest by Smith, Carlos Tarnishes Medals," *Chicago's American*, October 17, 1968; Joe Posnanski, "I'll Stand with You," *JoeBlogs*, October 16, 2018, https://joeposnanski.substack.com/p/ill-stand-with-you; Beth Daley, "Finally, an Apology to Peter Norman," *The Conversation*, October 12, 2012, https://theconversation.com/i-will-stand-with-you-finally-an-apology-to-peter-norman-10107.
19. Harry Edwards, *The Revolt of the Black Athlete* (New York: Free Press, 1969); Roger Bastide, "Color, Racism, and Christianity," *Daedalus* 96, no. 2 (1967): 312–27.
20. Harry Edwards, *Sociology of Sport* (Homewood, IL: Dorsey Press, 1973), 90, 260, 264–65.
21. Ibid., 341.
22. Al Copland, "Columbia Wins 2-Mile Relay Title," *Daily News* (New York, NY), April 25, 1926; Henry L. Farrell, "Columbia Wins 2-Mile Title," *Brooklyn (NY) Daily Times*, April 25, 1926; Phil Cousineau, ed., *The Hero's Journey: Joseph Campbell on His Life and Work* (Novato, CA: New World Library, 1990), 22.
23. Joseph Campbell, *The Hero with a Thousand Faces* (1968), 2nd ed. (Princeton, NJ: Princeton University Press, 2008), 23; Cousineau, *The Hero's Journey*, 21; Betty Sue Flowers, ed., *Joseph Campbell: The Power of Myth with Bill Moyers* (New York: Anchor Books, 1991), 276–77.
24. William James, "Philosophical Conceptions and Practical Results," *University Chronicle* 1, no. 4 (September 1898): 287–310; Paul Weiss, *The Making of Men* (Carbondalle: Southern Illinois University Press, 1967), 104.
25. Paul Weiss, *Sport: A Philosophical Inquiry* (Carbondale, IL: Southern Illinois University Press, 1969), 154, 17, 220–21, 238.
26. Joseph S. Ullian, "Review of *Sport: A Philosophic Inquiry* by Paul Weiss," *Journal of Philosophy* 70, no. 10 (1973): 299–301.
27. John Kaag, "Pragmatism and the Philosophy of Sport," in *Routledge Handbook of the Philosophy of Sport*, ed. Mike McNamee and William J. Morgan (New York: Routledge, 2015), 207–17; Howard Slusher, "Sports and the Religious," in *Religion and Sport: The Meeting of the Sacred and Profane*, ed. Charles S. Prebish (Westport, CT: Greenwood Press, 1993), 181. Quoations from Howard S. Slusher, *Man, Sport and Existence: A Critical Analysis* (Malvern, PA: Lea & Febiger, 1967), 124, 171.
28. George W. Cornell, "Sports, Like Religion, Described as a Way to Discover Inner Self," *Boston Globe*, October 19, 1969; Thomas M. Dicken, "Review of *Man, Sport and Existence*," *Christian Advocate*, July 24, 1969; Anthony Quinton, "Locker Room Metaphysics," *New York Review of Books*, August 21, 1969.
29. Scott Kretchmar, "Symbols, Conventions, Games, Eleanor Metheny, and the Evolution of Human Intelligence," *Research Quarterly for Exercise and Sport* 84, no. 2 (June 2013): 131–38.
30. Eleanor Metheny, *Movement and Meaning* (New York: McGraw Hill, 1968), 5, 64, 67, 77.
31. On the tendency to overlook Metheny, see Lisa Disch and Mary Jo Kane, "When a Looker Is Really a Bitch: Lisa Olson, Sport, and the Heterosexual Matrix," *Signs* 21, no. 2 (1996): 131–38; Mary Leigh and Ginny Studer, "Eleanor Metheny," *Journal of Physical Education, Recreation, and Dance* 54, no. 7 (1983): 74–77; Judith B. Carlson, "The Meaning of a Metheny," *Journal of Teaching in Physical Education* 3, no. 1 (1983): 74–77.
32. Jackie Krentzman, "In Murphy's Kingdom," *Stanford Magazine*, May 4, 2006, http://www.stanfordalumni.org/news/magazine/1998/janfeb/articles/murphy.html; Jeffrey J. Kripal, *Esalen: America and the Religion of No Religion* (Chicago: University of Chicago Press, 2007).
33. Alan Shipnuck, "Into the Mystic," *Golf Magazine*, October 23, 2019, https://golf.com/news/features/golf-in-the-kingdom-magical-power-michael-murphy/.
34. Michael Murphy, *Golf in the Kingdom* (New York: Viking Press, 1972), 28.
35. Shipnuck, "Into the Mystic"; website of the Shivas Irons Society, https://www.shivas.org/about-shivas-irons-society.
36. William James, "The Energies of Men," *Philosophical Review* 16, no. 1 (1907): 1–20; Michael Murphy and Rhea A. White, *In the Zone: Transcendent Experience in Sports* (1978; New York: Penguin, 1995), 95.
37. Kripal, *Esalen*, 274; Phil Jackson, *Sacred Hoops: Spiritual Lessons of a Hardwood Warrior* (New York: Hachette 1995), 87, 174.
38. Shane Eversfield, *Zendurance: A Spiritual Fitness Guide for Endurance Athletes* (Halcottsville, NY: Breakaway Books, 2003); Matt Fitzgerald, *Iron War: Dave Scott, Mark Allen, and the Greatest Race Ever Run* (Boulder, CO: Velo Press, 2011).
39. Michael Bamberger, *The Second Life of Tiger Woods* (New York: Simon & Schuster, 2020), 229; Gary Smith, "The Chosen One," *Sports Illustrated*, December 23, 1996.

40. Curt Sampson, *Roaring Back: The Fall and Rise of Tiger Woods* (New York: Diversion Books, 2019); Alan Shipnuck, "Golf Philosopher Michael Murphy Found a New Muse in Tiger Woods," *Golf Magazine*, June 14, 2019, https://golf.com/news/tournaments/us-open-2019-michael-murphy-new-muse-tiger-woods/.
41. Dan Kilbridge, "The Story behind the Iconic Images at Augusta," *USA Today*, April 22, 2919, https://golfweek.usatoday.com/2019/04/22/golf-tiger-woods-masters-win-story-behind-iconic-photos-augusta/.

## Chapter 13

1. Nico Hines, "Ibtihaj Muhammad: I'm Not Safe in the U.S.," *Daily Beast*, August 4, 2016, https://www.thedailybeast.com/ibtihaj-muhammad-hijab-wearing-olympic-star-im-not-safe-in-the-us; Luke Decock, "High on Spirit, Ceremonies Befit Games in Rio," *Charlotte (NC) Observer*, August 6, 2016.
2. Valeriya Safronova, "Nike Reveals the 'Pro Hijab' for Muslim Athletes," *New York Times*, March 8, 2017; "The Nike Pro Hijab Goes Global," *Nike News*, December 1, 2017, https://news.nike.com/news/nike-pro-hijab.
3. Donald G. Kyle, *Sport and Spectacle in the Ancient World* (Malden, MA: Wiley, 2014), 108; Kathryn Lofton, *Oprah: The Gospel of an Icon* (Berkeley: University of California Press, 2011), 13, 14.
4. A search of the term "sports icon" on Newspapers.com shows the term's relative lack of use until the 1990s. The results are as follows: 1960s (50); 1970s (70); 1980s (187); 1990s (4,174); 2000s (7,239); 2010s (4,753); 2020s (3,821). Dennis Hall and Susan Hall, eds., *American Icons: An Encyclopedia of the People, Places, and Things That Have Shaped Our Culture* (Westport, CT: Greenwood Press, 2006).
5. Phil Knight, *Shoe Dog: A Memoir by the Creator of Nike* (New York: Simon and Schuster, 2016).
6. Daniel Wojcik, "Pre's Rock: Pilgrimage, Ritual, and Runners' Traditions at the Roadside Shrine for Steve Prefontaine," in *Shrines and Pilgrimage in the Modern World: New Itineraries into the Sacred*, ed. Peter Jan Margry (Amsterdam: Amsterdam University Press, 2008), 201–40.
7. "40 Years of Prefontaine," *Nike News*, June 1, 2015, https://news.nike.com/news/40-years-of-prefontaine; Theresa A. Walton, "Steve Prefontaine: From Rebel with a Cause to Hero with a Swoosh," *Sociology of Sport Journal* 21, no. 1 (2004): 61–83; John Bale, *Running Cultures: Racing in Time and Space* (New York: Routledge, 2004).
8. Grant David McCracken, *Culturematic: How Reality TV, John Cheever, a Pie Lab, Julia Child, Fantasy Football, Burning Man, the Ford Fiesta Movement, Rube Goldberg, NFL Films, Wordle, Two and a Half Men, a 10,000-Year Symphony, and ROFL.con Memes Will Help You Create and Execute Breakthrough Ideas* (Boston: Harvard Business Press, 2012), 218–20.
9. Walter LaFeber, *Michael Jordan and the New Global Capitalism* (New York: Norton, 1999), 67.
10. Ibid., 15; Howard Bryant, *The Heritage: Black Athletes, a Divided America, and the Politics of Patriotism* (Boston: Beacon Press, 2019), 74; Tim Bontemps, "Michael Jordan Stands Firm on 'Republicans Buy Sneakers, Too' Quote," ESPN, May 4, 2020, https://www.espn.com/nba/story/_/id/29130478/michael-jordan-stands-firm-republicans-buy-sneakers-too-quote-says-was-made-jest.
11. O. J. Simpson, *O.J.: The Education of a Rich Rookie* (New York: Macmillan 1970).
12. Jeff Benedict and Armen Keteyian, *Tiger Woods* (New York: Simon and Schuster, 2018), 120.
13. Ibid., 119.
14. Ibid.
15. Bryant, *The Heritage*, 93.
16. Benedict and Keteyian, *Tiger Woods*, 156.
17. Ibid., 158–59.
18. Ibid., 96; Tom Liddy, "Kaepernick Kneels during National Anthem on Monday Night Football," ABC News, September 12, 2016, https://abcnews.go.com/US/colin-kaepernick-kneels-national-anthem-monday-night-football/story?id=42046111; Steve Wyche, "Colin Kaepernick Explains Why He Sat During National Anthem," *NFL.com*, August 27, 2016, https://www.nfl.com/news/colin-kaepernick-explains-why-he-sat-during-national-anthem-0ap3000000691077.
19. Matt Maiocco, "Kaepernick, Dr. Harry Edwards Talk before 49ers Practice," *NBC Sports*, August 28, 2016, https://www.nbcsports.com/bayarea/49ers/kaepernick-dr-harry-edwards-talk-49ers-practice; Carlos Ballesteros, "Kaepernick Is This Generation's Civil Rights Leader," *Newsweek*, November 12, 2017, https://www.newsweek.com/colin-kaepernick-black-lives-matter-john-carlos-ali-709026.

20. Liddy, "Colin Kaepernick Kneels during National Anthem on Monday Night Football"; Harry Berrien, "Kaepernick Ready to Sit Out National Anthem . . . on Military Night," *DailyWire*, September 1, 2016, https://www.dailywire.com/news/kaepernick-ready-sit-out-national-anthem%E2%80%A6-military-hank-berrien; Bill Hoffmann, "Sarah Palin to Flag-Mocking Quarterback: 'Get the Hell Out,'" Newsmax, August 29, 2016, https://www.newsmax.com/Newsfront/sarah-pain-nfl-football-colin-kaepernick/2016/08/29/id/745728/; Ian Schwartz, "Trump: Kaepernick 'Should Find a Country That Works Better for Him,'" *RealClear Politics*, August 30, 2016, https://www.realclearpolitics.com/video/2016/08/30/trump_kaepernick_should_find_a_country_that_works_better_for_him.html; Connor Hughes, "Boomer Esiason 'Disgusted' by Colin Kaepernick, Calls QB a 'Disgrace,'" NJ.com, August 30, 2016, https://www.nj.com/jets/2016/08/boomer_esiason_disgusted_by_colin_kaepernick_calls.html.
21. Jai Lennard, "Harry Edwards Is Not Who You Think He Is," *Victory Journal*, n.d., https://victoryjournal.com/stories/harry-edwards/; Harry Edwards, "Statement on the New Nike Ad Campaign Featuring Colin Kaepernick," Institute for the Study of Sport, Society and Social Change, San Jose State University, n.d.,https://www.sjsuwordstoaction.com/statement-from-dr-harry-edwards-on-the-new-nike-ad-campaign-featuring-colin-kaepernick/.
22. Samer Kalaf, "The NFL All but Admits That Colin Kaepernick Was Right All Along," *Slate*, June 3, 2020, https://slate.com/culture/2020/06/nfl-george-floyd-colin-kaepernick-roger-goodell-peaceful-protest.html; Brakkton Booker, "Roger Goodell on Colin Kaepernick's Possible Return to the NFL," NPR, June 16, 2020, https://www.npr.org/sections/live-updates-protests-for-racial-justice/2020/06/16/878810674/roger-goodell-on-colin-kaepernicks-possible-return-to-nfl-i-welcome-that; "Harry Edwards: Goodell Should Hire Kaepernick as an Assistant," ESPN (video), June 22, 2020, http://www.espn.com/video/clip/clip?id=29347674; Siobhan McAndrew, "Growing Grassroots Campaigns Aim to Erect Kaepernick Statue on UNR Campus," *Reno (NV) Gazette Journal*, June 17, 2020, https://www.rgj.com/story/news/2020/06/17/collin-kaepernick-statue-unr-campus-pushed-students-alumni-campaign/3207527001/.
23. Nardos Haile, "Colin Kaepernick Is Still Seemingly Shut Out," *Slate*, September 27, 2023, https://www.salon.com/2023/09/27/nfl-colin-kaepernick-ny-jets-letter/; Alysia Montaño, "Nike Told Me to Dream Crazy, Until I Wanted a Baby," *New York Times*, May 12, 2019; Allyson Felix, "My Own Pregnancy Story," *New York Times*, May 22, 2019.
24. Nicole Lyn Pesce, "Serena Williams Says Nike Is 'Learning from Mistakes,'" *Market Watch*, May 28, 2019, https://www.marketwatch.com/story/serena-williams-says-nike-is-learning-from-mistakes-and-doing-better-in-paying-female-athletes-2019-05-28.
25. Nicole R. Fleetwood, *On Racial Icons: Blackness and the Public Imagination* (New Brunswick, NJ: Rutgers University Press, 2015); Ramona Coleman-Bell, "'Droppin' It Like It's Hot': The Sporting Body of Serena Williams," in *Framing Celebrity: New Directions in Celebrity Culture*, ed. Su Holmes and Sean Redmond (New York: Routledge, 2006), 198; Laurel Wamsley, "French Open Bans Serena Williams' Catsuit," NPR, August 24, 2018, https://www.npr.org/2018/08/24/641549735/one-must-respect-the-game-french-open-bans-serena-williams-catsuit.
26. Krystin Arneson, "Nike Has the Perfect Response to That Serena Williams Catsuit Ban," *Glamour*, August 25, 2018, https://www.glamour.com/story/nike-response-to-serena-williams-catsuit-ban.
27. Benedict and Keteyian, *Tiger Woods*, 305–19.
28. Ibid., 320–30.
29. Ben Rosenbaum, "Hey Tiger! Did You Really Learn Anything?," *Bleacher Report*, April 8, 2010, https://bleacherreport.com/articles/375420-hey-tiger-did-you-really-learn-anything; Adam B. Vary, "Tiger Woods' New Nike Ad," *Entertainment*, April 7, 2010, https://ew.com/article/2010/04/07/tiger-woods-new-nike-ad-earl-woods/.
30. Chris Isidore, "Tiger Woods' Masters Victory Made Nike a Winner," CNN, April 15, 2019, https://www.cnn.com/2019/04/15/media/tiger-woods-nike-ad/index.html.
31. Brett Regan, "Chicks Dig the Long Ball," *Fanbuzz*, February 16, 2021, https://fanbuzz.com/mlb/chicks-dig-the-long-ball/.
32. Michael A. Katovich and Ronald Burns, "The Home Run: A Dramaturgical Moment in Time," *Studies in Symbolic Interaction* 30 (2008): 337–59. Marc Fisher and Jon Jeter, "The Home Run Chace in Black and White, *Washington Post*, September 5, 1998,https://www.washingtonpost.com/wp-srv/sports/baseball/longterm/chase/articles/chase0905.htm; Rob Mason, "1998 Home Run Chase," *Pro Look Sports*, June 17, 2020, https://prosportsoutlook.com/the-best-in-sports-1998-home-run-chase/; Eldon L. Ham, *All the Babe's Men: Baseball's Greatest Home Run Seasons and How They Changed America* (Sterling, VA: Potomac Books, 2013), 85.

33. Neil Paine, "Sammy Sosa and Mark McGwire, Welcome to Our Hall of Pretty Damn Good Players," *FiveThrityEight*, June 19, 2020, https://fivethirtyeight.com/features/sammy-sosa-and-mark-mcgwire-gave-baseball-a-show-it-will-never-forget/; Greg Johnson, "McGwire Will Be Batting Millions in Endorsements," *Los Angeles Times*, September 10, 1998, https://www.latimes.com/archives/la-xpm-1998-sep-10-fi-21250-story.html.
34. Michael Bausch, "McGwire Is Picture of Focused Athlete," *The Reporter*, October 2, 1998; Chris Landers, "The 10 Most Iconic Home Runs in MLB History," MLB, May 19, 2017, https://www.mlb.com/cut4/what-are-the-most-iconic-home-runs-in-mlb-history-c230593090; Gary Smith, "Big Swingers," *Sports Illustrated*, December 21, 1998.
35. Michael Bamberger, "Athletes to Rely More Than Ever on Banned Performance Enhancers," *Sports Illustrated*, April 14, 1997; Tom Verducci, "Totally Juiced," *Sports Illustrated*, June 3, 2002.
36. Mary Douglas, *Purity and Danger: An Analysis of the Concept of Pollution and Taboo* (1966; New York: Routledge, 2002), 2; Mark Kiszla, "Clean Up Baseball?," *Denver Post*, January 14, 2008, https://www.denverpost.com/2008/01/14/clean-up-baseball-ship-out-selig-first/.
37. Nathan Vinton, "U.S. Track and Field's Dirty Dozen Affected by BALCO," *New York Daily News*, April 12, 2008, https://www.nydailynews.com/sports/more-sports/u-s-track-field-dirty-dozen-affected-balco-article-1.283753/.
38. Jeff Bradley, "Still the Natural," *ESPN the Magazine*, March 20, 2002; "About Ken Griffey Jr.," Baseball Hall of Fame, https://baseballhall.org/hall-of-famers/griffey-jr-ken; Zac Wassink, "Seattle Mariners Unveil Ken Griffey Jr Statue," *Bleacher Report*, April 13, 2017, https://bleacherreport.com/articles/2703605-seattle-mariners-unveil-ken-griffey-jr-statue-outside-safeco-field.
39. Rick Reilly, "Lance Armstrong: Sportsman of the Year," *Sports Illustrated*, December 16, 2002; Reed Albergotti and Vanessa O'Connell, *Wheelmen: Lance Armstrong, the Tour de France, and the Greatest Sports Conspiracy Ever* (New York: Gotham Books, 2013).
40. Albergotti and O'Connell, *Wheelmen*, 157.
41. Ibid., 129–30, 181; Paul Springer, *Ads to Icons: How Advertising Succeeds in a Multimedia Age*, 2nd ed. (Philadelphia, PA: Kogan Page, 2009), 121.
42. Robert Lipsyte, "He Went the Distance before This Race Began," *New York Times*, August 1, 1999; Berry Tramel, "Lance Armstrong's Seven Tour de France Titles," *Pittsburgh (PA) Post-Gazette*, July 26, 2005.
43. Albergotti and O'Connell, *Wheelmen*, 319.
44. Andrew Clausen, "The Rise and Fall of Lance Armstrong: An Oral Timeline," *The Cauldron*, February 9, 2015, https://the-cauldron.com/the-rise-and-fall-of-lance-armstrong-an-oral-timeline-deba42fc5a3; Alexander Abad-Santos, "A Recent History of Lance Armstrong Apologists," *The Atlantic*, January 13, 2013.
45. James Barragan, "Why Is Livestrong Throwing Out Thousands of Its Yellow Wristbands?," *Austin (TX) American-Statesman*, October 15, 2016, https://www.statesman.com/story/news/2016/10/15/why-is-livestrong-throwing-out-thousands-of-its-yellow-wristbands/10091144007/.
46. Jason Cappell, "The Livewrong Foundation," *Bleacher Report*, January 21, 2013, https://bleacherreport.com/articles/1495507-lance-armstrong-the-livewrong-foundation.
47. Huizinga, *Homo Ludens*, 11–12.

## Afterword

1. Arthur Remillard, "Steelers Nation and the Seriously Religious Side of Football," *Marginalia Review of Books*, August 28, 2013, https://themarginaliareview.com/steelers-nation-and-the-seriously-religious-side-of-football/.
2. Ted Miller, "Fan's Heart Aches for Beloved Steelers," *Seattle Post-Intelligencer Reporter*, January 27, 2006, https://www.seattlepi.com/sports/seahawks/article/fan-s-heart-aches-for-beloved-steelers-1194184.php.
3. Warren St. John, *Rammer Jammer Yellow Hammer: A Road Trip into the Heart of Fan Mania* (New York: Three Rivers Press, 2004).
4. See, for example, Eric Simons, *The Secret Lives of Sports Fans: The Science of Sports Obsession* (New York: Abrams Press, 2013); David Epstein, *The Sports Gene: Inside the Science of Extraordinary Athletic Performance* (Shelton, CT: Current, 2013).
5. Douglas, *How Institutions Think*, 97.
6. Bill Sheets, "Lake Stevens Runner Just Feet from Blast in Boston," *Herald*, April 15, 2013, https://www.heraldnet.com/news/lake-stevens-runner-just-feet-from-blast-in-boston/.

7. "SI Selects Tlumacki Photo for Cover," Boston, April 16, 2013, https://www.boston.com/uncategorized/noprimarytagmatch/2013/04/16/si-selects-tlumacki-photo-for-cover; Edward T. Linenthal, *The Unfinished Bombing: Oklahoma City in American Memory* (New York: Oxford University Press, 2003), 145.
8. Daniel Burke, "Boston Marathon's Holy Ground and Sacred Bonds," Religion News Service, April 16, 2013, https://religionnews.com/2013/04/16/boston-marathon-holds-a-religious-allure-for-runners/.
9. "The Rise of the Boston Marathon, a Runner's 'Holy Grail,'" NPR, April 13, 2013, https://www.npr.org/2013/04/13/177120282/the-rise-of-the-boston-marathon-a-runners-holy-grail; Sheets, "Lake Stevens Runner Just Feet from Blast in Boston."
10. Rebecca Carballo, "Bill Iffrig, Runner in Iconic Boston Marathon Bombing Photo, Dies at 89," *New York Times*, January 20, 2024, https://www.nytimes.com/2024/01/20/us/bill-iffrig-dead.html.

# Index

*For the benefit of digital users, indexed terms that span two pages (e.g., 52–53) may, on occasion, appear on only one of those pages.*